AMAZING ANIMALS!

80 Ready-to-Use Stories & Activity Sheets for Building Reading Comprehension Skills

READING LEVELS 3-6

STANTON L. BARNES

THE CENTER FOR APPLIED RESEARCH IN EDUCATION
West Nyack, New York 10994

Library of Congress Cataloging-in-Publication Data

Barnes, Stanton L.
    Amazing Animals: 80 ready-to-use stories and activity sheets for building reading comprehension
    skills/Stanton L. Barnes.
        p. cm.
    ISBN 0-13-089816-3 (spiral wire)   ISBN 0-13-060042-3 (paper)
    1. Reading comprehension--Study and teaching (Elementary) 2. Anuimals. I. Title.
    LB1573.7.B27 2000
    372.47--dc21
                                                                          00-031557

Printed in the United States of America

10 9 8 7 6 5 4 3 2 1   10 9 8 7 6 5 4 3 2 1

ISBN 0-13-089816-3 (spiral wire)   ISBN 0-13-060042-3 (paper)

ATTENTION: CORPORATIONS AND SCHOOLS

The Center for Applied Research in Education books are available at quantity
discounts with bulk purchase for educational, business, or sales promotional use. For
information, please write to: Prentice Hall Direct Special Sales, 240 Frisch Court,
Paramus, NJ 07652. Please supply: title of book, ISBN number, quantity, how the book
will be used, date needed.

**THE CENTER FOR APPLIED
RESEARCH IN EDUCATION**

West Nyack, New York 10994

www.phdirect.com/education

About the Author

Stanton L Barnes received his B.S. in Education from Otterbein College in Ohio and his M.Ed. from Western Washington University in Washington State. He has been teaching elementary students in the state of Washington for the past 30 years. He has specialized in teaching reading skills at all elementary reading levels, and is well known for emphasizing scientific thinking and reasoning skills with students. He has also organized science clubs for students who want to learn more about the animals and plants of their region. This book is affectionately dedicated to all those students whose deep love for animals inspired its writing.

About This Book

Amazing Animals! is written to help reading and elementary teachers get students excited about a subject that they really like, *animals*, while steadily improving their reading and comprehension skills. All of the stories and accompanying activity sheets found in this unique reading program are designed to meet the following four objectives:

1. To pique children's natural interest in animals and science,

2. To improve reading vocabulary and comprehension,

3. To help children understand basic fact or opinion concepts,

4. To improve the independent thinking skills of all students.

Included are 80 ready-to-use, fully illustrated stories and activity sheets that are designed to build reading vocabulary, comprehension, and thinking skills. The stories are arranged in four sections from grade levels 3 through 6, with each reading level containing 20 two-page stories and 20 accompanying two-page activity sheets. A handy contents page begins each section so you can easily locate the stories that will interest your students. Before reading the stories, you are provided with "New Vocabulary" and "Questions to Ask" in order to prepare students for each reading selection. In addition, each section contains ten reproducible enrichment activities as well as complete answer keys for all activity sheets.

The reading content and illustrations on each animal are created to develop reading comprehension by covering the most fascinating and pertinent information on that creature. For example, *"Despite its amazing strength, the largest members of the primate family are gentle giants"* (gorillas), *"They dig so fast they can out-dig moles and gophers. They eat those two as well as ground squirrels, mice, snakes, and other small animals"* (badgers), and *"While many insects are considered pests, this one gets love and respect. There are over 150 different kinds found in the United States"* (ladybugs). Students learn new vocabulary by hearing the words used in context, often with accompanying clues to the meaning built into the story. Vocabulary is repeated in successive lessons to reinforce its learning and to make it part of the child's growing capital of words. Reading comprehension skills—such as using facts to answer specific questions, recognizing the main concepts, distinguishing fact from opinion, understanding cause and effect, and making evaluative judgments—are all stressed in each story and related activity sheets.

The thinking questions typically require the students to use deductive reasoning and to draw inferences and reach conclusions. Students should discover processes that are essential to reading and science, and will realize how important their reading skills are in drawing inferences, predicting outcomes, and solving problems.

I have successfully used these stories with students of varying ability levels for the past 30 years. I suggest that you use them as a tool to stimulate reading growth, curiosity, and original thinking. It will give you the opportunity to set up a reading program that invites all students to participate and to be successful.

Stan Barnes

Contents

Reading Level 5

Before Reading the Story: New Vocabulary

Reading Level 6 .309

Before Reading the Story: New Vocabulary and Questions to Ask 310

How to Use This Book

Before beginning any of the stories in each section, introduce the "New Vocabulary" to ensure that students know the pronunciation and meaning of words like *aphids, nectar, hibernate, extinct,* and *species.* There are also four to six questions for each story designed to arouse interest as well as to activate prior knowledge in the selection. Discuss with your class or small groups how they should approach the reading, writing, and thinking aspects of each story and accompanying activity sheets. Depending upon your students' abilities, some possibilities include:

- The whole class or large group reads and discusses the story.

- Smaller groups of three to five students read and discuss the story and write answers.

- A pair of students works together to read, discuss, and solve questions.

- Individual students read and answer questions independently.

- You could use any combination of the above or try all of these techniques. For example, you may prefer having students read in any type of group you choose, but prefer them to write independently or in a different group.

The activity sheets completed by an individual or group need to be evaluated and discussed. You may want to evaluate individual or group responses differently in order to plan for successive lessons. For example, those working in a group may do extremely well on the written responses. However, when these same students work on their own or in pairs, the written responses fall below expectations. You need to determine which areas they are experiencing difficulty with (fact or opinion, predictions, cause and effect, etc.) and review them so students will be better prepared for the next lesson.

The stories may inspire students to want to learn more about an animal or endangered species. Additional resources from the library should be made available for those who want to read more or perhaps report on other characteristics of a species. Art, writing, language, social studies, and other experiences could be integrated into this research.

As with any group of students, some will find the stories and activities difficult while others may find them relatively easy. Following are some techniques that should help you with these situations:

For students who find these lessons difficult, you can—

- Place students whose reading or vocabulary skills are weak with those whose skills are strong. (Perhaps they can reciprocate in the thinking section of the activity sheets.)

- Try to reach those students before they get confused and help them with the harder words and concepts.

- Teach them strategies like crossing off terms used, or skipping to vocabulary words they already know to narrow the list and make the work easier.

- Have students read the comprehension/thinking questions before reading the story. It has been my experience that many students benefit from this technique.

For students who find these lesson relatively easy, you can—

- Have them use all or most of the new vocabulary in writing their own story or short summary of the story on that animal.

- Add new terms to the vocabulary list provided, and have them search out the meanings and write sentences/stories using the new terms.

- Present opportunities for students to do further research on the animals, finding interesting information that wasn't presented in the story and sharing it with the class.

- Use these students as peer tutors after they have been taught how to help others with word skills, comprehension, or thinking processes. Such experiences often benefit the tutor as much as the tutee.

Reading Level 3

Before Reading the Story:
New Vocabulary and Questions to Ask

1. A Friendly Spring Bird

New Vocabulary:

benefit	grubs
blend	migrate
brood	orchard
caption	twigs

Questions to Ask:

What bird is often called a sign of spring?
Why are male robins easier to find?
Where have you seen robins nesting?
Are robins harmful birds in any way?

2. The Shy American Bear

New Vocabulary:

burrow	insects
den	pesky
diet	ruin
doze	shy
glimpse	

Questions to Ask:

What is the most common bear in the United States?
Do bears eat mostly meat or plants?
Can you outrun a bear?
How big do you think a newborn cub is?
Do bears really sleep all winter?

3. The Beautiful Ladybug

New Vocabulary:

aphids	larva
beetle	poison
cozy	popular
hibernate	respect

Questions to Ask:

Are ladybugs always red and black?
Why are ladybugs so popular?
Can they ever be harmful insects?
Do ladybugs hibernate in winter?

4. Is Jack a Rabbit?

New Vocabulary:

cactus	litter
danger	moisture
enemies	plains
form	tortoise

Questions to Ask:

Is the jack rabbit really a rabbit?
How can jack rabbits live in the desert?
How do jack rabbits escape enemies?
Are baby rabbits and hares different?

5. Monarch Butterflies Flutter By

New Vocabulary:

antennae	pupa
caterpillar	pollen
cocoon	roost
migrate	scales
nectar	veins

Questions to Ask:

What colors are monarch butterflies?
Why don't they get eaten by birds?
How are new baby monarchs born?
What happens to monarchs in winter?
Why are monarchs good to have?

6. A Cute and Friendly Furball

New Vocabulary:

arid	miniature
colonies	prey
entrance	rodents
grain	safety
hind	species

Questions to Ask:

Where do wild gerbils live?
What do gerbils like to eat best?
What do gerbil babies look like?
What kind of gerbils are good pets?
Are gerbils ever a problem animal?

7. Can Squirrels Really Fly?

New Vocabulary:

abandoned	haunches
creatures	insulate
creep	soar
fungi	spy
glide	unique

Questions to Ask:

Can flying squirrels really fly?
Why do few people ever see them?
How can they see to fly at night?
Do they only like to eat nuts and seeds?
What enemies do they have?

8. Saving Siberian Tigers

New Vocabulary:

boars	nape
captivity	pounce
carnivores	range
extinct	sheathed
endangered	stalk

Questions to Ask:

Where do tigers live in the wild?
How big are Siberian tigers?
How much and what do tigers eat?
Why are so few tigers left on Earth?
Why are tigers so feared and admired?

9. What Big Teeth You Have!

New Vocabulary:

Arctic	pressure
blubber	shallow
bristles	survive
ivory	tusks

Questions to Ask:

How do you easily know the walrus?
How can walruses live in freezing water?
What do walruses eat mostly?
Why is the walrus an endangered species?

10. The Biggest Land Mammal

New Vocabulary:

bulls	sensitive
cousins	texture
funeral	vegetation
habitat	wrinkled

Questions to Ask:

What is the biggest land mammal?
What can the trunk be used for?
What do elephants like to eat?
Why are elephants endangered?

11. American Marsupials

New Vocabulary:

abdomen	nocturnal
hisses	odor
limp	pouch
marsupial	temperature

Questions to Ask:

What is a marsupial?
Where might you see an opossum?
What do opossums like to eat?
What do we know about their babies?

12. The Great Desert Taxi

New Vocabulary:

brow   muzzle
cattle   nurse
cud   stomach
digest   transportation

Questions to Ask:

Where do most of the camels live?
How can camels survive desert life?
Are camels' humps really full of water?
What uses do humans have for camels?

13. Friendly Chips

New Vocabulary:

bold   habits
bushy   nature
exit   omnivore
identified   scamper

Questions to Ask:

How are chipmunks like other squirrels?
What do they like to eat?
Where do they live and raise babies?
Why do their cheeks look so fat?

14. Clever as a Fox

New Vocabulary:

canine   poultry
communicate   rabies
fables   rustle
intelligent   snout
kennel   vixen

Questions to Ask:

Why do people think the fox is so clever?
How is the fox like a dog in many ways?
What do you think the fox eats?
Where do you think foxes have young?
How and why is the fox used in a sport?

15. Reptiles with Shells

New Vocabulary:

algae   lungs
cold-blooded reptile
flesh   rookery
flippers   surface

Questions to Ask:

What are reptiles?
Why are turtles in the reptile family?
How do turtles raise their babies?
Why are sea turtles endangered now?

16. A Big, Beautiful, Black Bird

New Vocabulary:

carcass   incubate
chick   mate
clutch   somersault
glossy   wingspan

Questions to Ask:

What is the largest bird of the crow family?
Why don't we see ravens around cities?
What is the raven's favorite food to eat?
Why are ravens famous in stories?

17. Patient Prairie Wolves

New Vocabulary:

adapt   relative
erect   reputation
lair   vary
prairie   wily

Questions to Ask:

Have you heard wild howls at night?
Do coyotes live around here?
What do coyotes like to eat the most?
Why do people think coyotes are wily?

18. Short-horned Grasshoppers

New Vocabulary:

chemicals	molt
compound	swarms
concentrate	thigh
diagram	tropical
manure	

Questions to Ask:

Where do grasshoppers live in the world?
What have you noticed about 'hoppers?
Who thinks locusts and 'hoppers are related?
Where do grasshoppers go in the winter?

19. The Most Famous Deer of All

New Vocabulary:

antlers	lichen
coarse	severe
dense	sleigh
fawn	stag
hooves	tundra

Questions to Ask:

What deer are tamed for humans' use?
Where do most reindeer live?
Do you know anything unusual about them?
How are reindeer like camels?

20. Our Worst Friend

New Vocabulary:

ancient	produce
attacked	scent
disease	spoil
harvest	urine
items	weird

Questions to Ask:

How many of you like/hate mice?
Are mice more harmful or beneficial?
Have you ever seen a baby mouse?
Do you know any other kinds of mice?
How can mice be helpful to people?

1. A Friendly Spring Bird

The North American robin is very friendly and popular. It is a member of the thrush family. People who came to America from Europe called the pretty, red-breasted birds robins because they looked like small birds called by that name back in Europe. The American robin has been so popular that three states call it their state bird. Robins migrate south from some of our northern states when winter gets cold. The robin has been a sign that spring has come for those states. People love to see robins showing that winter is over.

The male robin is about 10 inches long when he's fully grown. He is the bird most people can recognize due to his reddish-orange breast. Many people wouldn't recognize the female robin so easily. The females are smaller and much duller in color. Scientists think bright colors would make the female too easy to see when she is still on the nest to hatch her eggs. The baby robins will also look duller and have a speckled breast to help them blend with the plants until they can fly better to escape.

Robins used to live mostly in the forest, but now they like to live near people and are often found in cities. They build nests in trees, but they also build nests on a ledge of a porch, a windowsill, or some other part of a building. The female does most of the work building the nest. She will use mostly grass and twigs. She may also use any little bits of paper or string she finds. A nest will be lined with mud, which

This speckled baby looks hungry enough to eat a worm!

© 2000 by The Center for Applied Research in Education

the female smoothes out with her breast. She probably looks forward to a bath later.

The female lays three to six light blue eggs in the nest. People sometimes call a light blue color "robin-egg blue." The mother robin will sit on her eggs for two weeks before they hatch. The male will now help to feed the babies. Both mother and father robin will make many trips to the nest to feed their brood. A baby robin will eat more than its own weight in a single day. The parents will raise two or three broods like this each summer.

People are happy to learn that robins eat many harmful grubs and insects. The robin eats several earthworms a day, too. That is not good since earthworms are needed in the soil. Robins also love fruit, and some farmers are not happy when they see the damage done to their berry crop or fruit trees. Many farmers make sure that robins have a good supply of wild berries so they will leave their fields and orchards alone. People will have to decide whether the robin is more of a benefit or a harm in their life.

Caption: (Please write one here.)

_____

_____

_____

A Friendly Spring Bird

Vocabulary Checkup Write the words from the box on the correct blanks.

benefit	blend	brood	caption
grubs	migrate	orchard	twigs

1. A _____ is a number of young hatched at one time.

2. Pieces of limbs from trees and shrubs are called _____.

3. To _____ means to move from one area to another.

4. Something that is good or an advantage is a _____.

5. The _____ are worm-like larva of some beetles and insects.

6. To mix or fit it so you can't see each part is to _____.

7. A _____ is an explanation for a picture.

8. A group of fruit or nut trees is called an _____.

Comprehension You may need to look back at the story to answer the questions correctly.

1. Where did the robin get its name? _____
   _____

2. Why do scientists think the female robin doesn't have the reddish-orange breast?
   _____
   _____

3. What are at least four of the nesting materials robins use to build their nest?
   _____
   _____

4. What are some of the foods that robins eat? _____
   _____
   _____

Name _____ Date _____

A Friendly Spring Bird

Fact or Opinion Print **F** beside statements that can be proven true as a fact. Print **O** beside statements that are just a belief or an opinion.

_____ 1. The robin is the most popular bird in the whole United States.

_____ 2. Three states have named the robin as their state bird.

_____ 3. Female robins are smaller and duller in color than male robins.

_____ 4. People love to see robins hopping along looking for spring worms.

_____ 5. The father robin is not very helpful around the nest.

_____ 6. A baby robin will eat more than its own weight in food in a day.

_____ 7. It is very difficult to keep a brood of baby robins fed.

_____ 8. Robins are often found in cities.

_____ 9. People have named a color "robin-egg blue."

_____ 10. The robin is the easiest bird for people to recognize worldwide.

Thinking About Robins Please think carefully before giving your opinion.

1. Why do you think the robin is so well liked by so many people?

   _____

   _____

2. Why do you think the female does nearly all of the work in building the nest?

   _____

   _____

3. Do you think the robin is more of a benefit to people or more of a harmful bird?

   _____

   Please explain why you think this way.

   _____

   _____

   _____

Name _____ Date _____

2. The Shy American Bear

The Teddy Bear that many young children love was first made in the early 1900s. President Teddy Roosevelt had caught a black bear cub for a pet while hunting, and it was so cute that toy companies began making stuffed "teddies" to sell.

Strange as it may seem, black bears can be brown, gray, or even have some white on them. Most American black bears are dark colored, and they may look all black when a person only gets a glimpse of a fast-moving bear. Even a 5-foot-long, 300-pound male black bear can run 25 miles per hour. That is faster than humans can run!

Visitors to Yellowstone National Park are likely to see a few black bears. Those pesky bears are always looking for a free meal. Campers have to keep the food out of the bears' reach. Black bears in most forests are really very shy and are not seen very often unless people leave food where bears can get it easily. Scientists place black bears with the meat-eaters. Black bears do eat insects, grubs, fish, and small animals they can catch. However, most of the bear's diet is made up of leaves, buds, berries, roots, nuts, and even tree bark. You can tell if a bear is feeding in the area because it tears logs apart, moves stones, and will ruin young plants.

Black bears feed mostly at night. When winter is coming and they need to put on extra weight, they will feed during the day as well. In the winter they will make a den in a cave, hollow log, or a burrow they dig in a bank. The bear will doze in its den all winter unless the weather warms up. Bears don't really sleep all winter like some animals. They will be much thinner and very hungry by the time spring comes.

The females give birth to two or three cubs during January or February in their dens. The cubs weigh less than 1 pound, have no hair, and are blind at birth. They must be kept warm and fed by the mother until spring. By then they are ready to play

"We are great tree climbers! I want those bird eggs for breakfast."

(The Shy American Bear, *continued*)

and follow their mother as she searches for food. Cubs will still get milk from the mother for about six more months. They will spend the next winter with her in the den before they are ready to set off looking for food on their own the next spring. You can see that the female won't be able to have cubs every winter. She has to feed, protect, and raise these cubs first. If you ever see young cubs with or without the mother, you should stay far away from them. The mother can get angry fast if she thinks there is a danger for her cubs.

Black bears were hunted too much several years ago. In the 1950s there were nearly 700 black bears killed to make hats for British guards when a new queen was crowned. Laws now protect bears from being overhunted. Scientists have learned the age of some bears by cutting one of the bear's teeth in half and counting the growth rings in it. Most bears will live to be about twenty-five years old in the wild. You may be lucky enough to see some black bears since there are more of them now. Just remember to watch from a safe distance, please.

Caption: (Make one up, please.)

_____

_____

_____

The Shy American Bear

Vocabulary Checkup Write the words from the box on the correct blanks.

burrow	den	diet	doze	glimpse
insects	pesky	ruin	shy	

1. To sleep very lightly off and on is to _____.

2. A hole that is dug in the ground is a _____.

3. A very short or quick look at something is a _____.

4. The food you choose to eat is called your _____.

5. Anything troublesome or annoying is called _____.

6. To injure or destroy permanently is to _____.

7. An animal's cave-like home is called a _____.

8. An animal that is very timid or bashful is said to be _____.

9. The tiny animal group of bugs with six legs are _____.

Comprehension You may need to look back at the story to answer the questions correctly.

1. What is the strange thing about the color of black bears? _____
_____
_____

2. Why are you not very likely to outrun a black bear? _____
_____
_____

3. What main foods are included in the black bear's diet? _____
_____
_____

Name _____   Date _____

The Shy American Bear

4. Why do mother black bears only have cubs every two or three years?

_____

_____

5. What is the unusual way scientists have found out the age of some black bears?

_____

_____

Thinking About Black Bears Think carefully before anwering the questions.

1. Why do you think most stuffed toy bears are called teddy bears?

_____

_____

_____

2. Why do you think bears are so much thinner when they come out in the spring?

_____

_____

_____

3. What do you think you will do if you spot some cute bear cubs along the road?

_____

_____

_____

4. What signs do you think you could recognize to tell if bears are in the area where you are?

_____

_____

_____

Name _____ Date _____

3. The Beautiful Ladybug

The ladybug is a small red or yellow beetle that often has black spots on its back. While many insects are considered pests, the ladybug gets love and respect. Pictures of ladybugs appear on shirts, artwork, student folders, and other places. How could a little beetle become so popular?

These small, flying beetles are found on every continent on Earth where the temperature is warm and plants grow. There are over 150 different kinds of ladybugs found in the United States. There are some you might not even recognize since they have stripes instead of spots. Some ladybugs are all black. You won't see ladybugs in the winter unless you live in an area that is warm all year long. When cold weather comes, ladybugs crawl under some bark or into other protected places to hibernate. Whole groups of ladybugs will sleep in that cozy spot all winter. When it warms up in the spring, the female lays as many as 300 eggs, which will hatch in about one week.

The larvae (newly hatched babies) are the thing that makes ladybugs popular and respected insects. Each larva will eat up to 400 aphids in the first two weeks of its life in order to grow into an adult ladybug. Those aphids are tiny insects the size of a pinhead. Aphids suck the juices out of plants and can ruin a farmer's crops. Farmers love to have ladybugs eat all of the aphids, of course. Sometimes the farmers buy gallons of ladybugs to get rid of pests like aphids, scale bugs, and spider mites. The ladybugs can be much safer and do a better job than using poison sprays to get rid of those pests. Fruit growers in California brought some ladybugs over from Australia to save their crops from scale bugs almost 100 years ago.

The bright colors on a ladybug help to warn birds and other animals that this is a bad-tasting bug. If that warning doesn't work, then ladybugs send some blood out through their leg joints. The blood has a smell that keeps anything from wanting to eat the ladybugs.

(The Beautiful Ladybug, *continued*)

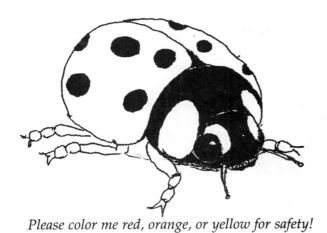

Please color me red, orange, or yellow for safety!

Ladybugs have to watch out for three main enemies. Sometimes people don't see the little ladybugs and step on them or hurt them with machines. People spray poisons to kill the harmful bugs, but they also wind up poisoning good ones like our ladybugs. There is a tiny wasp that lays its eggs on ladybugs. When the wasp eggs hatch, they eat the ladybugs.

Ladybugs like to live in weedy areas or vegetable gardens that have not been sprayed. The best way to find ladybugs is to check flower gardens. Ladybugs look for aphids on rose bushes and some fruit

trees. You should not take the ladybugs away from their feeding spots. They won't hurt you, but you might hurt them. You may enjoy watching them eat aphids. If you look carefully on the underside of leaves, you should be able to find some orange clumps of the tiny ladybug eggs. The ladybugs don't fly away, so maybe they don't mind people watching them.

Caption: (Please write one here.) _____

The Beautiful Ladybug

Vocabulary Checkup Write the words from the box on the correct blanks.

aphids	beetle	cozy	hibernate
larva	poison	popular	respect

1. _____ means to sleep all through the winter.

2. _____ are tiny insects that suck juices from plants.

3. _____ means it is well liked by many people.

4. _____ is to honor, look up to, and hold in high regard.

5. A _____ is anything that can injure or kill life.

6. A _____ is an insect with a shell covering its flight wings.

7. The _____ is the newborn, feeding stage of an insect.

8. _____ means snugly warm and comfortable.

Comprehension You may need to look back at the story to answer the questions correctly.

1. The story says that ladybugs can be several different colors. Name at least three.

    1 _____ 2 _____ 3 _____

2. How do people sometimes show their love and respect for ladybugs?

    _____

    _____

3. Name the three things that ladybugs like to eat.

    1 _____ 2 _____ 3 _____

4. Why don't birds and other animals eat ladybugs very often?

    _____

    _____

Name _____ Date _____

The Beautiful Ladybug

Fact or Opinion Print **F** for **facts**, and print **O** for **opinions**.

_____ 1. The ladybug is the best bug of any bug in the United States.

_____ 2. Ladybugs can be black, orange, yellow, or red.

_____ 3. Some ladybugs have stripes instead of spots.

_____ 4. Everybody likes ladybugs because they eat harmful bugs.

_____ 5. Ladybugs hibernate in areas where winters are colder.

_____ 6. Some farmers buy ladybugs by the gallons.

_____ 7. Ladybugs have the prettiest colors of any insects.

_____ 8. The ladybug's bright colors warn birds that ladybugs don't taste good.

_____ 9. Ladybugs are a lot safer to use than poison sprays.

Thinking About Ladybugs Think carefully before answering the questions.

1. Which one of the seven continents do you think would not have ladybugs? (Circle one.)

   North America   South America   Europe   Asia   Australia   Antarctica   Africa

2. Why do you think many farmers would choose ladybugs rather than using sprays?

   _____

   _____

3. Why do you think children like ladybugs so much?

   _____

   _____

4. Let's see — 300 larvae hatch, and each larva eats 400 aphids in two weeks, so 300 x 400 = 120,000 aphids gobbled up. Wow! What do you think of that?

   _____

   _____

Name _____   Date _____

4. Is Jack a Rabbit?

Jack rabbits with black tails are found mostly on the southwestern plains and deserts of the United States. White-tailed jack rabbits are found on many northern plains of the United States and in Canada, too. Jack rabbits and snowshoe rabbits are really members of the hare family. Hares are larger than rabbits. The jack rabbit and other hares have longer legs and ears than rabbits. Rabbits live in burrows and their babies are blind and have no hair when they are born. Hares don't live in burrows, and their babies are born with fur and their eyes wide open. So Jack Rabbit is really a hare. Jack may even be the famous hare that lost the race with the tortoise. Instead of "The Tortoise and the Hare," it could have been called "The Tortoise and the Jack Rabbit."

The jack rabbit's body has some important differences to help jack rabbits live in dry, desert-like places. Their very long ears allow them to hear danger from far away. Their ears also have many blood vessels close to the surface to help get rid of body heat to keep them cool. Their large eyes are on the sides of the head to help them see in all directions. Their long legs help them reach speeds up to 50 miles per hour and jump over bushes or rocks 5 feet tall to escape their main enemy, the coyote. Their brown and gray colors help them hide well as they doze motionless during the day.

People got rid of some of the old enemies of the jack rabbits. Wolves and cougars (pumas or mountain lions) were killed off. Then there were so many jack rabbits in those areas that they became real pests to

A hare lies in its hollowed-out form if it's hot out.

farmers, whose crops were being gobbled up. The pests were then hunted until there were fewer again.

Jack rabbits feed mostly at night when it is cooler. They eat grasses, leaves, and even some twigs. They don't have much water near where they live, so they have to get water from the plants they eat. Sometimes they will get moisture from tree bark or from eating desert cactus. Jack rabbits return to their shady, hollowed-out spots called forms, when the sun comes up.

The mother jack rabbit will begin having babies in early spring and may have three or four litters in a year. A litter often has five or six babies in it. The mother will soon place each baby in a different spot to hide from enemies. If all the babies were kept in one nest, the way rabbits are, then the whole litter might

get caught by a coyote or mountain lion. Of course, this makes it more difficult for the mother to feed her litter since she has to hop all around to

the different spots to feed each baby one at a time. The babies will begin to eat some plants before long. They are out on their own before they are one month old. The new hares may have babies of their own in another six months.

Is Jack a Rabbit?

Vocabulary Checkup Write the words from the box on the correct blanks.

cactus	litter	danger	moisture
enemies	plains	form	tortoise

1. The hollowed-out resting spot for a hare is called a _____.

2. A _____ is a group of babies born to an animal in a day.

3. Things that are harmful or a danger to another are _____.

4. _____ is another word for water or wetness.

5. One kind of land turtle is called a _____.

6. The _____ is a desert plant that often has sharp needles.

7. A mostly flat area of land that often has grass is called a _____.

8. A _____ is anything risky, unsafe, or threatening.

Comprehension You may need to look back at the story to answer the questions correctly.

1. How can we tell the difference between a rabbit and a hare by looking at them?

_____

_____

2. What three body parts help a jack rabbit live in desert and plains regions?

_____

_____

3. How are rabbit babies and hare babies different from the moment of their birth?

Baby rabbits _____

_____

Baby hares _____

_____

Name _____   Date _____

Is Jack a Rabbit?

4. How do jack rabbits know when a coyote is near, and how do they escape if its close?

_____

_____

_____

Thinking About Jack Rabbits Think carefully before answering the questions.

1. Why do you think these hares were named jack rabbits instead of jack hares?

_____

_____

_____

2. Do you think the famous tale should be called "The Tortoise and the Jack Rabbit?" (Circle one.) Yes   No

Why? _____

_____

_____

3. How do you think the number of jack rabbits in one area should be controlled?

_____

_____

_____

4. What do you think is the most interesting thing you learned about jack rabbits?

_____

_____

_____

Name _____   Date _____

5. Monarch Butterflies Flutter By

The monarch butterfly is the most beautiful insect. It has the six legs, three body parts, and feelers in common with other insects. But the wings of the monarch butterfly are works of art. The bright orange and gold on the wings are outlined in black. These colors make monarchs very easy to see. Birds know the colors mean a bad-tasting insect and will not bother monarchs. A viceroy butterfly has almost the same colors, and birds leave them alone, too, thinking they might have a bad flavor.

Monarch butterflies migrate north in spring. They lay their eggs on milkweed plants. The larvae that hatch out in three or four days are the ugliest looking caterpillars you've ever seen. They eat and drink from the milkweed for a couple of weeks. The milkweed juices make a poison in the caterpillar. Any bird that eats the caterpillar will get sick. The caterpillar's skin is like a shell that has to be shed several times for that caterpillar to grow to its full size.

The caterpillar sheds its skin for the last time and closes itself into a cocoon or shell-like case. This is the pupa stage in which a strange change will take place. The pupa inside the cocoon begins to swell and the head, body, and the wings of a beautiful butterfly burst out. In about half an hour the new monarch butterfly is ready to fly.

The monarch butterfly has two pairs of wings—a front pair and a rear pair. These wings have tube-like veins to hold them in shape.

The wings are also covered with thousands of scales that overlap each other. The scales have the colors of the butterfly. Those scales can be rubbed off the wing if it's touched by your fingers.

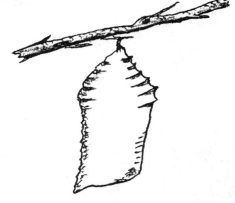

The butterfly now flies around looking for food. Scientists think it can use its feelers, called antennae, to smell and perhaps even to hear with the bulb on the end of each antenna. The butterfly lands on a flower and pushes a tube coiled under its mouth into the nectar or sweet juices of the flower. Nectar is the only food it will eat. The butterfly will carry some pollen on its feet away to another flower. This helps flowers to make seeds and fruit.

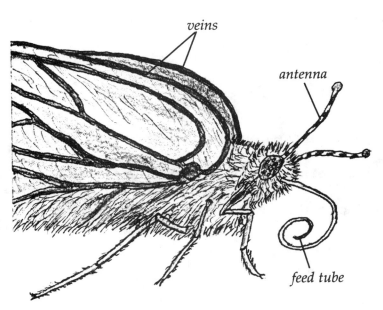

veins

antenna

feed tube

Huge flocks of monarchs will gather at the end of summer. When the flock gets large enough, the monarchs will begin to migrate south to warmer regions in southern California or central Mexico. They can fly about 80 miles in one day, traveling at speeds of 10 to 11 miles per hour. Some monarch butterflies have flown over 3,000 miles in such a migration. When they reach their southern "camp," they will roost until it is time to go north the following spring. It must be an amazing sight to see 10 to 15 million monarch butterflies roosting in a small pine forest in central Mexico. Can you imagine the huge cloud of monarchs taking off for their spring journey?

Monarch Butterflies Flutter By

Vocabulary Checkup Write the words from the box on the correct blanks.

antennae	caterpillar	cocoon	migrate	nectar
pollen	pupa	roost	scales	veins

1. _____ is the fine grains of powder that make seeds and fruit.

2. A _____ is the worm-like larva of a butterfly or moth.

3. The _____ are the tube-like framework of an insect's wings.

4. The _____ are the feelers a monarch uses to smell.

5. _____ is the sweet juice the monarch eats from a flower.

6. _____ are the thin, flat plates that cover butterfly wings.

7. A _____ is a shell-like covering for the pupa to grow in.

8. The _____ is the stage where the larva caterpillar changes into an adult butterfly.

9. _____ means to move from one place or climate to another.

10. A _____ is a spot where animals sit or lie to rest for a while.

Comprehension You may need to look back at the story to answer the questions correctly.

1. Monarch butterflies are insects since they have _____
   _____.

2. Birds don't eat monarch butterflies because _____
   _____.

3. Monarch butterflies migrate south in the fall because _____
   _____.

4. Monarch butterflies are helpful to humans since they _____
   _____.

Name _____ Date _____

Monarch Butterflies Flutter By

5. Draw the next three stages of the life of a monarch butterfly under the names:

eggs   larva   pupa   adult

Thinking About Monarchs Think carefully before answering the questions.

1. Why do you think monarchs only lay their eggs on milkweeds?

_____

_____

_____

2. What is a statement in the story that you think is really just the author's opinion?

_____

_____

_____

3. Why do you think you should not touch a monarch's wings?

_____

_____

_____

4. Why do you think monarchs are valuable to people?

_____

_____

_____

5. What was the most amazing thing you learned about monarch butterflies?

_____

_____

_____

Name _____ Date _____

6. A Cute and Friendly Furball

Gerbils are small rodents with soft fur. Many people like these little creatures for pets because they are so friendly, clean, playful, and easy to care for. They are shaped like a rat or mouse. They use their long tail for balance as they sit up and hop along on their hind legs like a miniature kangaroo. Their soft fur is often some shade of brown with white patches. The colors usually match the Earth colors where they live in the wild. If the sand and rocks are darker blacks and browns, the gerbils are, too. If the ground has tan and lighter colors, then the gerbils will match those colors.

There are more than 100 different species (kinds) of gerbils. The wild gerbils live in arid (dry, nearly barren) parts of Africa and Southwest Asia. A few interesting species in those arid lands are North African jirds; Indian gerbils; great gerbils, with a body as big as your two fists; Wagner's gerbils, which eat snails; fat-tailed gerbils, with a short, thick tail; and Mongolian gerbils, which have become the popular pets sold in pet stores in America.

Gerbils in the wild live in groups called colonies, which dig burrows in the ground. They dig tunnels to connect these burrows. They use one burrow for storing food, another for sleeping, and another for a nest to raise their babies. They plug the entrances during the day for safety from snakes. That also helps it stay cooler in their underground home.

Gerbils come out of the ground to eat when it's cooler at night. Their favorite food is seeds, but they will eat any other parts of plants, too. Gerbils will get nearly all the moisture they need from plants eaten. They like to take the seeds, stems, bulbs, etc., back to their burrow to eat. They prefer to eat at home to save moisture. Eating out is

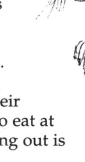

also dangerous because birds of prey (like eagles, owls, and hawks) are out looking for small animals to eat. Sometimes gerbils can be a problem to humans by stealing grain crops and digging in bad places. California won't let people have gerbils as pets because they are afraid some will get away and have lots of babies. A colony could live in warm areas of California and eat large amounts of farmers' crops.

Gerbils will have many babies in one year if the weather is warm enough and there is plenty of food. A female can begin having babies when she is three months old, and she can have an average of four in a litter each month. Soon her children will be having babies, and by the end of the year her grandchildren can be having babies. Gerbils are born blind, have no hair, and are pretty helpless. They feed on the mother's milk for less than three weeks before they go off to take care of themselves.

You might like to have a gerbil for a pet. A wire cage with a good lid (or a fish aquarium), a water bottle, and a feed dish are all you really need. You may want some wood shavings or sawdust for bedding. You can get plastic tunnels with rooms like burrows at a pet store, or you can use tubes from paper rolls for the gerbil to play in. Gerbils are fun to watch as they run around a wheel. They are interesting animals to watch, and they don't cost much to feed or take care of. If you decide you want a pair of gerbils, just remember what you have learned about how many gerbils you may have in a very short time.

A Cute and Friendly Furball

Vocabulary Checkup Write the words from the box on the correct blanks.

arid	colonies	entrance	grain	hind
miniature	prey	rodents	safety	species

1. Nibbling animals whose front teeth keep growing are _____.

2. Legs located toward the back end of an animal are _____ legs.

3. Anything that is smaller than normal is called _____.

4. Very dry and barren pieces of land are said to be _____.

5. In plants or animals, different kinds or types are _____.

6. The seed of plants like corn, wheat, rye, etc., is _____.

7. Groups of animals living in a place are called _____.

8. Any animal hunted as food for another is its _____.

9. The place to go in or enter is called the _____.

10. Acts done to make safe or protect are for _____.

Comprehension You may need to look back at the story to answer the questions correctly.

1. Why are wild gerbils so many different colors? _____
   _____

2. What are the two reasons wild gerbils plug entrances to their burrows every day?
   _____
   _____

3. What are two reasons why gerbils would rather eat in their burrows than outside?
   _____
   _____

Name _____ Date _____

A Cute and Friendly Furball

4. Why does California have a law against people there having pet gerbils?

_____

_____

5. What equipment would you want to have to keep your own pet gerbils?

_____

_____

Thinking About Gerbils Think carefully before answering the questions.

1. Why do you think so many people love gerbils for pets? _____

_____

_____

2. Which species of gerbil did you think was strange? _____

_____

Why? _____

_____

3. Why do you think pet gerbils like to play in tubes or on wheels?

_____

_____

4. Please explain why you would (or would not) like to have pet gerbils.

_____

_____

Name _____ Date _____

7. Can Squirrels Really Fly?

The forests of Canada and the northern states in the United States have a beautiful, big-eyed rodent that soars through the night sky. Flying squirrels are hard to study because they only come out at night. Can they really fly? They are mammals, but scientists tell us that they do not really fly. The only mammals that fly are the bats. The flying squirrel glides through the air on wing-like skin flaps stretched between its front legs and hind legs. Flattened out and acting more like a parachute, flying squirrels can float from one tree over and down to another. It helps that the 8- to 10-inch-long gliders weigh half as much as other tree squirrels.

Flying squirrels are not seen by very many people. Flying squirrels only come out at night unless something forces them to leave their den in the daytime. They are so quiet and shy in the darkness of night that it is hard to see them. Their soft brown and gray fur helps them blend in with the trees, also. Their large eyes are specially made so they can see well in all directions in the dark. They can spy nuts, seeds, and fungi (mushrooms) to eat in total darkness. The flyers are different from other squirrels since flyers like meat and will eat many insects, eggs, and even a bird or two. Flyers are like other squirrels, that often hide some of the food they gather. All squirrels have to do this because they do not hibernate and need food all winter long. Some scientists think squirrels can smell where they hid that food even under snow. Others believe squirrels simply remember their food hiding spots very well.

Flying squirrels build their winter nests in hollows of trees or abandoned woodpecker holes. Summer nests are often built from twigs and leaves in the fork of a tree branch. The winter nest is lined with moss or tree bark that is chewed up by the adults. These materials help insulate them from the winter cold. The insulation also helps the mother keep her babies warm since they are often born in very early spring. A litter of three to five pink baby flyers will keep the mother busy. She will feed them every three hours for the next ten weeks. It may seem strange, but the father is chased away by the mother before the litter is born and is not allowed to help raise them. By the time babies are one month old, they will get their first gliding lessons. They will not be good at flying until they are four or five months old. By then they will have learned to sit up on their haunches and hold seeds and nuts in their front paws using their thumb-like claw.

Flying squirrels will stay in trees most of the time to avoid being caught by their enemies. It is safer for them way up in the air. The owl, which hunts mainly at night, is their biggest enemy. The owl can swoop in and pick a flying squirrel out of the air as it's gliding. A flying squirrel can use its feet and tail to steer it away from an owl and get to the landing spot it wants. Those amazing little flyers can glide 160 feet or even loop in a circle!

If you wanted to see these shy creatures in action, you would need to creep quietly into the forest. You would have to sit or lie down and be very still and silent for at least an hour. You should listen for sounds of rustling leaves or scritch-scratching of claws on bark. If you keep looking up through the open spaces between trees, you may get lucky and spy a furball flattened out and gliding through that open space. You would then be one of the very few people who have ever seen a wild flying squirrel. You should take some notes if you see anything unusual. Scientists are always looking for any new information on these unique creatures.

Can Squirrels Really Fly?

Vocabulary Checkup Write the words from the box on the correct blanks.

abandoned	creatures	creep	fungi	glide
haunches	insulate	soar	spy	unique

1. _____ means to catch sight of or see quickly.

2. _____ are animals.

3. _____ means to fly or glide high in the air.

4. _____ is to move slowly low to the ground.

5. _____ means to move smoothly and easily along a path.

6. _____ is left behind or given up.

7. _____ is to cover with material to keep in heat.

8. _____ means unusual or one of a kind.

9. _____ are plants like mushrooms and molds.

10. _____ are the hips and hind legs animals sit on.

Comprehension You may need to look back at the story to answer the questions correctly.

1. How is the flying squirrel able to "fly" as much as 160 feet from tree to tree?

   _____

   _____

2. Why don't people know much about or even see flying squirrels very much?

   _____

   _____

3. How are flying squirrels like the other squirrels? _____

   _____

Name _____ Date _____

Can Squirrels Really Fly?

4. How are flying squirrels different from other squirrels?

   _____

5. What is the flying squirrel's main enemy, and how can it often escape this enemy?

   _____

   _____

Thinking About Flying Squirrels Think carefully before answering the questions.

1. Why do you think flying squirrels have different summer and winter nests?

   _____

   _____

2. How do you think flying squirrels catch birds? _____

   _____

   _____

3. Explain why you believe squirrels know where their winter foods are hidden.

   _____

   _____

4. Why do you think the females chase the father away and won't let him help raise the babies?

   _____

   _____

5. What plan would you use to watch wild flying squirrels and learn more about them?

   _____

   _____

Check It Out Find out about the giant flyers of Asia (Ratufu) that are up to 36 inches long.

Name _____ Date _____

8. Saving Siberian Tigers

The largest cats in the world are the Siberian tigers. We could make a good case for them to be called king of the beasts. A lion is not quite so large or so strong as these tiger cats. The Siberian tiger stands about 42 inches tall at the shoulder, and it would look straight across into the eyes of the average third grader. It would weigh from 400 to 650 pounds (the record holder weighed 850 pounds). The tiger's roar can be heard over 2 miles away!

Wild Siberian tigers live in Northeast Asia in the corner of China, North Korea, and Siberia. These tigers have a coat of fur that is longer and more shaggy than the fur of the Bengal tigers of India. A Siberian tiger needs the heavy fur coat to live in its very cold climate, where temperatures can get down to 50 degrees below zero. Their fur will also be lighter colored in the winter to help them blend in with the snow. Fur will darken and be thinner in the summer heat. If it is too hot, the tiger will lie in the water to cool off and get rid of pesky flies.

Siberian tigers often have a range of 30 miles in every direction. They need to claim a large territory for their hunting grounds. They are carnivores (meat-eaters) and hunt mostly for deer and wild boar (a pig). A tiger hiding in the brush and shadows is hard to see or hear. It stalks its prey, staying downwind and creeping closer. The tiger stalks on silent, padded paws. As it leaps through the air, those sheathed claws spring out

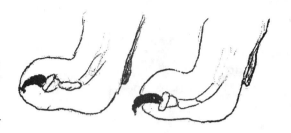

to dig into the back of its prey. A pounce can be 30 feet (clear across your classroom) and will knock a deer flat. The tiger will grab the throat of its prey to cut off the air supply. When tigers catch animals as small as a snowshoe hare, they grab the nape of the neck and snap it.

The tiger needs to eat an average of 20 pounds of meat per day, but it may catch nothing for a whole week. In nine out of ten pounces the tiger will miss its meal. When it catches larger mammals, however, it may eat 80 to 100 pounds of meat in a feast. The tiger is so strong that it can drag a 1,000-pound animal to a stream, where it will eat, drink, sleep, and eat some more until it has eaten the whole thing.

Female tigers usually only have cubs every two years. They will have three or four cubs, each weighing about 3.5 pounds. The cubs are born blind and helpless. They will drink their mother's milk for five or six months even though she brings them some meat to eat as soon as they

have teeth at three months. She will teach them to hunt as they stay with her for two years. By then she may have a new litter coming and force the older cubs to go find their own range.

All tigers are on the endangered species list. Scientists think Siberian tigers are most endangered since there are less than 400 of them left in the wild. Hunters killed many of them for sport or for their skins. Now it is illegal to kill them, but thieves are still trying to make big money from tigers. A bigger threat to the tigers is the loss of their hunting range and prey as humans take forest and food the tiger needs to survive. People used to capture wild tigers to place in zoos and the circus. Now there are enough cubs born in captivity to supply the zoos. Amazingly, there are now more Siberian tigers in zoos and on game farms than in the wild. Perhaps the captured tigers will be the best chance to save the Siberian tigers from becoming extinct like the saber-toothed cats.

Saving Siberian Tigers

Vocabulary Checkup Write the words from the box on the correct blanks.

Hind

Front

| boar | captivity | carnivore | endangered | extinct |
| nape | pounce | range | sheathed | stalk |

1. Covered or enclosed in a protective layer is _____.

2. A wild pig is sometimes called a _____.

3. An animal that is no longer active or living is _____.

4. The very back part of the neck is called the _____.

5. An animal that eats meat is called a _____.

6. To go after a prey with slow, sneaky moves is to _____.

7. Anything held and forced to be a prisoner is in _____.

8. The area of land where an animal lives is its _____.

9. Anything threatened or at risk of extinction is _____.

10. To jump or spring upon suddenly is to _____.

Comprehension You may need to look back at the story to answer the questions correctly.

1. Color red that area on the world map where wild Siberian tigers live.

2. What are the two ways a Siberian tiger's fur differs from summer to winter?

_____

_____

3. Why don't Siberian tigers have a litter of cubs every year? _____

_____

Name _____ Date _____

Saving Siberian Tigers

4. What are the two biggest causes of making Siberian tigers an endangered species?

_____

_____

_____

Thinking About Tigers Think carefully before answering the questions.

1. How do think you could convince some people that the tiger is king of the beasts?

_____

_____

_____

2. What do you think makes the Siberian tiger such a good hunter?

_____

_____

_____

3. What did you think was the most awesome thing about the Siberian tiger?

_____

_____

_____

4. How do you think humans can help more tigers to be endangered no longer?

_____

_____

_____

Check It Out Find out about

Saber-toothed tigers

Bengal tigers

Sumatran tigers

Caspian tigers

Tigons or ligers

Name _____ Date _____

9. What Big Teeth You Have!

Most people know what a walrus looks like even though these creatures live way up in the icy Arctic region. Maybe they are well known because of their great size. They can get 12 feet long and weigh 3,000 pounds. But these largest members of the seal family are probably best known because of their tusks. When twenty-eight third- and fourth-grade students were asked what a walrus was, they all said something about those tusks right away.

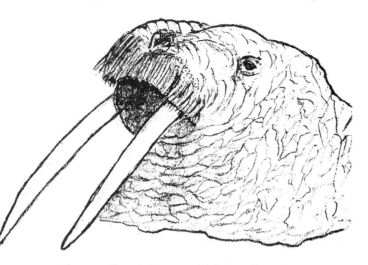

The walrus has special features that will help it survive in the icy waters of the far north. It has thick skin and a layer of blubber (fat) up to 6 inches thick to keep it warm. The male or bull can have skin 3 inches thick on its neck. The walrus has flippers that make it a great swimmer, but it is hard for it to move on land. It also has bristles on its upper lip that help it feel food as it digs with those tusks in the cold mud. Those tusks also

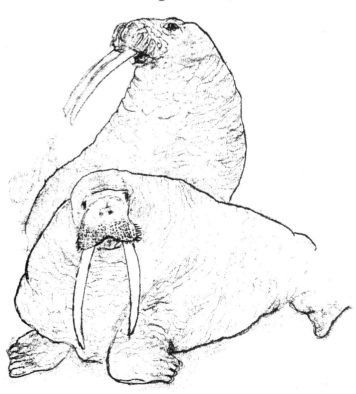

work like an ice pick or hook to help the walrus pull itself out of the water onto the ice. The walrus is also able to dive nearly 300 feet under water to look for food. Scientists are not sure how the walrus can stand the pressure of all that water pushing on it. Maybe its thick skin or blubber helps.

The walrus can dive very deep and stay under water for 10 minutes, but they prefer to dig in shallow water. The main food they like to eat is clams. They use their tusks to dig in the mud and sand until their bristly whiskers feel a clam. They swallow clams without chewing them up. Scientists

© 2000 by The Center for Applied Research in Education

think that stones in the walrus's stomach then grind the clams up. The walrus also eats shrimp, sea cucumbers, worms, and a fish or even an octopus once in a while.

The walrus lives in a herd or colony with several hundred friends and family. At times the whole herd may pull themselves up on a rocky beach or island to doze in the sun. They may look red rather than brown when they sun themselves. Blood will rush to the surface of their skin to help get rid of the heat. They are better suited to live in cold weather than in the heat.

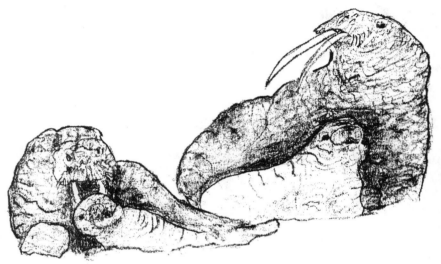

Baby walruses are born during these times on land or ice. The baby calf is carried inside the cow (female) for more than a year before it is born. The calf can be over 4 feet long and weigh about 150 pounds at birth. It will hold on to the cow's neck for about two weeks until it can swim on its own. The cow usually only has one calf every other year because she will be giving her rich milk to that calf for a year and a half. When it is two years old, the calf will leave to join a young herd of walruses.

Humans have hunted walruses for hundreds of years. Many walruses were killed just to get their ivory tusks. Now walruses are protected from extinction by laws that keep most people from killing them. Eskimos still hunt a few walruses for meat to eat, blubber to burn for heat and light, and skins for making tents and covering boats. Some Eskimos carve walrus tusk into beautiful figures, but they never kill the walrus just to get the tusks. The walrus is still considered somewhat of an endangered species because of the low number of new babies being born.

What Big Teeth You Have!

Vocabulary Checkup Write the words from the box on the correct blanks.

arctic	blubber	bristles	ivory
pressure	shallow	survive	tusks

1. The fat of large, ocean animals is called _____.

2. Hard, white material on elephant and walrus tusks is _____.

3. The very cold area near the North Pole is called the _____.

4. Water or anything not very deep is called _____.

5. Very long teeth of a walrus, elephant, or boar are _____.

6. The short, stiff hairs of some animals are called _____.

7. To continue to live through something is to _____.

8. To push or place force on the top of a thing is _____.

Comprehension You may need to look back at the story to answer the questions correctly.

1. What are two things a walrus has to help it survive in the Arctic, and how do they help?

   _____

   _____

   _____

2. Why does the walrus look red when it stays out in the sun too long?

   _____

   _____

3. What are some of the things you learned about the baby walrus?

   _____

   _____

Name _____ Date _____

What Big Teeth You Have!

4. What are the two main reasons that walruses have become an endangered species?

_____

_____

Thinking About Walruses Think carefully before answering the question.

1. What do you think makes the walrus able to dive so deep, and how does it work?

_____

_____

_____

2. What do you think is an important thing about the walrus, and why is it important?

_____

_____

_____

3. Why do you think the walrus chooses to live in a large colony?

_____

_____

_____

4. Should Eskimos be allowed to kill walruses? (Circle one.) Yes   No

   Why? _____

_____

_____

Check It Out Find out about

Seals

Sea lions

Uses of ivory

Eskimo life

Arctic animals

Blubber uses

Record walrus tusk = 3 feet long and 11 inches thick!

Name _____   Date _____

© 2000 by The Center for Applied Research in Education

10. The Biggest Land Mammal

The African elephant is bigger and stronger than any other land mammal. In fact, they would be the biggest living animal in the world if there were no whales. African elephants weigh 8,000 to 12,000 pounds, with the males (bulls) being heaviest. A male can be 25 feet long, with its tail at one side of your classroom and its trunk reaching to touch the other side. Of course, it would have pushed the ceiling out since it is over 10 feet tall at the shoulder. The bulls and cows both have tusks that grow all sixty to seventy years of their life. An old bull's tusks have been measured at more than 10 feet long, weighing more than 200 pounds each. The African elephants' cousins are the Asian elephants, which are smaller and have smaller ears, trunks, and tusks. Asian species are a lighter gray, and they are easier to tame than their big African cousins.

The dark gray African elephant's skin is about 1 inch thick and wrinkled. You may think it looks baggy and doesn't fit. You are aware that their nose is called a trunk; but did you know it can be used to pick up tree trunks and is also capable of picking up a peanut? The trunk has two fingers on its tip to pick up small things. That same trunk is used to put

food in the mouth, to breathe, and to smell, the elephant's most important sense. Even though they can hear well, elephants depend on smelling danger. The trunk can suck up as much as 6 quarts of water to drink or spray over the elephant's back. The trunk is sensitive enough to feel heat and texture (how hard or soft something is).

African elephants eat as much as 500 pounds of vegetation in a day. They eat grass, leaves, twigs, and some fruits. They can do a lot of damage to trees since they sometimes knock down 30-foot trees to get the leaves and twigs at the top. Elephants always stay near some water. They drink about 40 gallons a day and like to bathe in the evening. Strange as it may seem, they always throw dirt and dust all over their wet body after their bath. Scientists believe they do this to keep insects from biting.

An African cow elephant will begin having calves when she is about fourteen or fifteen years old. She will carry the baby inside her for almost two years; longer than any other animal. She will go into thick brush to give birth to a 200-pound, 3-foot-tall calf that has lots of hair. It follows the herd when it's a day old and will drink its mother's milk for about two years. When the calf is a year old it begins eating vegetation. It also will lose much of that hair in its second year. It quickly learns to obey all of its aunts and grandmothers as well as its mother. It is better protected than most mammal babies, but one out of four calves will die or be killed by a lion or other carnivore.

Elephants have a closer family than most animals. The cows and their calves stay with other cows and calves, which are usually aunts, grandmothers, and even great-grandmothers who are often the leaders of herds. If one of the family members dies, the others are sad and even have a funeral, where they pile limbs on the body. The bulls wander alone and will visit the herd only when invited. When young bull calves mature, they are chased from the mostly female herd to wander with the other bulls. All elephants seem to talk in a grunting or rumbling voice. They only use the trumpeting sound you may know about in anger or as a warning to enemies. Most of the time the elephants get along very well, with hardly any family fights.

African elephants have not been captured and tamed so often as Asian ones. A bigger threat to African elephants is the loss of habitat to farms and villages. Water is needed for humans, so there isn't enough to support so many elephants. People are still killing many African elephants for their tusks even though there are laws against selling the ivory. Game parks may be the only way to save these great mammals.

The Biggest Land Mammal

Vocabulary Checkup Write the words from the box on the correct blanks.

bulls	cousins	funeral	habitat
sensitive	texture	vegetation	wrinkled

1. To have ridges and creases in the skin is to be _____.

2. A ceremony held before the dead are buried is a _____.

3. The males of some large animals like elephants are called _____.

4. Plants or plant life growing in an area is _____.

5. The natural place where animals or plants live is the _____.

6. The rough or smooth look or feel of material is its _____.

7. The children of aunts and uncles are called _____.

8. Having sensation or feeling easily means something is _____.

Comprehension You may need to look back at the story to answer the questions correctly.

1. African elephants can weigh as much as _____ pounds and can be as long as _____ feet and as tall as _____ feet at the shoulders.

2. The elephant's _____ is called a trunk, and it is used for _____ _____ _____.

3. The African elephant is different from the Asian elephant. The African elephant has _____ _____ _____.

4. Mother elephants carry the baby inside for almost _____ years. That is longer than _____.

Name _____ Date _____

The Biggest Land Mammal

5. Baby elephants weigh about _____ pounds and are about _____ feet tall at the time of birth. They have lots of _____ and drink their mother's milk for about _____ years. At age one they lose most of the _____ and begin eating some _____.

Thinking About Elephants Think carefully before answering the questions.

1. Why do you think very few animals ever bother an adult elephant?

   _____

   _____

2. Why do you think African elephants get along so well with so few family fights?

   _____

   _____

3. What do you think is the most unusual thing African elephants do, and why is that so strange?

   _____

   _____

4. Why do you think baby elephants obey all adults so well?

   _____

   _____

5. What do you think could be done to stop thieves from killing elephants for tusks?

   _____

   _____

Check It Out Find out about

    Mastodons or mammoths   Rogue elephants

    Elephant training   Work elephants

    Capturing elephants

Name _____   Date _____

11. American Marsupials

You may have seen an unusual animal about the size of a house cat beside the road while you were riding in a car at night. You may have thought it was a large rat, but what you saw was probably the only marsupial (or pouched mammal) that lives in the fields and woods of North America. It is the common opossum, often named Virginia opossum, and usually just called 'possum. It is very nocturnal, which means active at night, so you are not likely to see one in the daytime. The 'possum spends daylight hours sleeping in its den, which may be in a hollow tree, a pile of rocks, another animal's abandoned burrow, or under a building. The den or nest is lined with leaves and grass to help insulate the 'possum in the winter. Opossums don't really hibernate, but when it gets very cold they lower their body temperature and sleep a lot while living off their stored-up fat.

The opossum has grayish-colored fur covering most of its body. The head is usually white, and the ears and feet are black with white tips. The pointed nose, ears, and tail have very little hair on them. Their feet have five toes that look more like fingers. One toe on each hind foot works more like a thumb to help the 'possum hold onto limbs. Even though it spends most of its time on the ground, the 'possum is a good climber, and is famous for being able to hold on and even hang by its tail. A full-grown 'possum will be holding on with a hind foot also since it falls too often if it just uses its tail.

Opossums will eat just about anything. The reason you may see them along a road is because they even eat dead animals they find killed there. They also eat a lot of insects, worms, fruit, grain, and small mammals they can catch. They catch roosting birds at night and raid their nests to eat the eggs, too. Farmers are aware of this and protect their chickens and eggs from 'possums as much as they can. If it is in danger, the 'possum hisses and gives off a bad odor, but its favorite trick is to go limp, fall over, and play dead. Have you heard a saying about someone "playing 'possum"? In the southern part of the United States many people hunt 'possum and consider it a good meat to eat. I wonder if it tastes like chicken?

Opossum females have large litters as often as three times a year. They can have as many as twenty-four babies in one litter, but ten to twelve is more common. They only carry the babies inside them for less than two weeks. The babies are no bigger than a honeybee when they are born and are hairless. The whole litter can fit into a teaspoon! Their front legs are strong enough to crawl up through their mother's hair to a pouch, where they will live for the first couple of months. They will drink milk constantly during this time in the pouch. When the babies are about ten weeks old, they will leave the pouch and sleep in the nest. They will travel with the mother when she goes out looking for food by holding onto the fur on her back. The eight or nine babies that survive will be able to go away to hunt and live on their own in about two or three weeks.

The 'possum is the only American animal to carry the young in a pouch. The kangaroos and koala bears of Australia are the other two famous marsupials (or pouched animals) in the world. The opossum is not so famous, but it is American.

American Marsupials

Vocabulary Checkup Write the words from the box on the correct blanks.

abdomen	hisses	limp	marsupial
nocturnal	odor	pouch	temperature

1. A scent or smell is an _____.

2. A mammal that carries its young in a pouch is a _____.

3. Between the chest and hips on the body is the _____.

4. Animals active only at night are _____.

5. Anything that lacks stiffness and is floppy is called _____.

6. A small bag-like pocket for marsupial babies is a _____.

7. The degree of heat in a living body is the _____.

8. Whistles through the teeth using the "s" sound are _____.

Comprehension You may need to look back at the story to answer the questions correctly.

1. What are some of the names used to identify the opossum in North America?

   _____

   _____

2. Describe what an opossum looks like in detail. _____

   _____

   _____

   _____

3. What are some of the reasons you are likely to see 'possums at night along a road?

   _____

   _____

   _____

Name _____ Date _____

American Marsupials

4. What are four of the foods opossums could eat if they live in your area?

_____

_____

Thinking About Opossums Think carefully before answering the questions.

1. Why do you think opossums are mainly nocturnal?

_____

_____

_____

2. What plan can you think of to watch opossums eating and raising their babies?

_____

_____

_____

3. What did you think was the strangest thing about opossums, and why?

_____

_____

_____

4. Why do you think the kangaroo and koala bear are famous and the 'possum isn't?

_____

_____

_____

Check It Out Find out about

Murine opossums

Wooly opossums

Yapoks

Prehensile tails

Opossum fur uses

Name _____ Date _____

12. The Great Desert Taxi

One of the strangest but most useful creatures in the world is the camel. There are two kinds of camels: Arabian camels, with one hump, and Bactrian camels, with two humps. A Bactrian camel has longer hair. There are a few wild herds of them living in the very cold Gobi (gō-bē) Desert north of China.

Full-grown camels are 6 to 7 feet tall at the shoulders and weigh 1,000 to 1,600 pounds. Their hair is usually brown, but some have grayer fur. Camels have a long neck and long legs with knobby knees and built-in knee pads. They have more unique body features that help them survive in the desert. The first ones you probably notice are the humps. Humps are made of stored fat that help the camel go without food or water for a long time. Humps are not full of water, as some people have said. Camels' humps shrink as they go without food and will even sag and hang down on the camel's side if the fat is mostly used up. The hump will build back up again when the camel eats. Camels' eyes have three eyelids and long eyelashes to keep blowing sand out. There are bushy brows of hair above the eyes to help keep the sun and sand out also. Camels' nose slits can be closed off, and their ears are full of hair so sand can't blow in during a storm. The feet have two toes with a tough pad between them that lets the toes spread out so a camel does not sink into the sand. All of these features show you how unique camels are.

Camels can eat just about any part of most plants. They eat grass, leaves, twigs, seeds, and even cactus. The inside of their mouth is so tough that the thorns of the cactus don't hurt. Camels get most of the water they need from the foods they eat. Camels living in the Sahara Desert often go all winter without drinking any water! In very dry conditions a camel can go ten times as long without water as a person can.

Camels have a split upper lip like a rabbit or hare. They grab their food with the lips and swallow it with very little chewing. Their stomach has three sections in it, and the unchewed food goes into the first section. Later the camel will bring the glob of food back up and chew it like our farm cattle do. This is called chewing the cud. After the camel is done chewing the cud, the food goes to the other sections of the stomach, where the animal will digest it to use for energy or to store as fat in the hump.

A baby camel is carried inside its mother for eleven to thirteen months. The baby will be born with its fur coat on and its eyes wide open. It can run beside her in a few hours, making a sheep-like "baaa" sound. The baby will nurse on the mother for nearly five years. By then its color has turned from the light brown of a baby to the darker brown of its parents. The mother is likely to have another calf by the time she is done nursing the first one.

Camels have been trained for use by people for thousands of years. Millions of people living in the desert use camels for just about everything. The camel is often their only transportation. They ride them, use them to pull plows, and have them carry large packs. The camels do not work without complaining, however. They are hard to train since they have a nasty temper. They will kick, bite, and spit at people. Camels wear a muzzle to prevent biting. In spite of their bad habits, people have learned to use camels for many of their daily needs. They milk them and use the rich milk to drink and make cheese. They also eat some of the meat and even melt the hump down to make it into butter. They use the skin for making things like tents, bags for water, and shoes or sandals. The hair is used for making cloth for clothing. They even use the bones to make spoons and other tools. Believe it or not, they dry camel droppings and use them to burn for heat. You are more likely to see camels in a zoo. They are such unique creatures that crowds come to see them, but they better not get too close!

The Great Desert Taxi

Vocabulary Checkup Write the words from the box on the correct blanks.

brow	cattle	cud	digest
muzzle	nurse	stomach	transportation

1. The sac-like organ in the abdomen for food is the _____.

2. The ridge of hair above the eye is called the _____.

3. A way of moving people or goods is _____.

4. The food some animals spit back up to chew is called the _____.

5. A thing put over an animal's mouth so it can't bite is a _____.

6. To change food into a form the body can use is to _____.

7. Dairy and beef animals raised for milk or meat are _____.

8. Mother mammals give milk to a baby or _____ them.

Comprehension You may need to look back at the story to answer the questions correctly.

1. How can you tell Arabian camels from Bactrian camels?

   _____

   _____

2. What are three features of the camel's body that help it survive in the desert?

   _____

   _____

3. How can a camel go so long without food or water? _____

   _____

4. What are some of the uses desert people have for camels?

   _____

   _____

Name _____ Date _____

The Great Desert Taxi

Thinking About Camels Think carefully before answering the questions.

1. Why do you think there aren't more wild camels? _____

_____

_____

_____

2. Why do you think camels seem to look down their nose at people or other things?

_____

_____

_____

3. What did you think was the strangest use for camels? _____

_____

Why do you think that is strange? _____

_____

_____

4. Why do you think the author told you not to get too close when looking at a camel?

_____

_____

_____

5. What surprised you the most about the camel's unusual body and habits?

_____

_____

_____

Check It Out Find out about

Dromedary

Alpaca

Camel's-hair cloth

Vicuna

Gobi Desert

Split Hoof

Name _____   Date _____

13. Friendly Chips

When you hear the call of chip-chip-chip, you may recognize it as one of nature's cutest, friendliest creatures: the chipmunk. Chipmunks are so popular that they have been used as cartoon figures and even sing on tapes and compact disks (CDs). Perhaps you have been to a park or wooded area where you have seen them. If so, you know they are easy to make friends with by offering them bread, nuts, or other bits of food. Some chipmunks live right next door to humans. Many of them are so bold they will eat out of your hand.

There are twenty-two species of chipmunks scientists know about in the world. Some of them are called ground squirrels. All of the species belong to the squirrel family, as you might have guessed. Chipmunks are different from other squirrels in several ways. Chipmunks spend most of their time on the ground even though they can climb well. They dig tunnels and burrows underground for safety. They even build their nests underground. A few of the chipmunk species share the same burrow, with as many as three or four families living in it. The tail of a chipmunk is not so long and bushy as the tree squirrel's tail. Chipmunks are identified by most people because of the black and white stripes down their back. The other squirrels don't have such fancy racing stripes.

Chipmunks also have many of the same body features and habits of the other squirrels. Even though the chipmunk is much smaller than most any other squirrel, its body is very similar to the squirrels. It has four toes on the front foot and five toes on the hind foot like all squirrels. The eyes,

(Friendly Chips, *continued*)

ears, nose, and other body parts are a miniature look of other squirrels, too. The chipmunk eats seeds, nuts, berries, and other plant parts like all squirrels do. The chipmunk is an omnivore (plant- and meat-eater), so it eats a few slugs, beetles, bird eggs, and a mouse or baby snake once in a while, too. Other squirrels don't eat bugs, snakes, or slugs, but they'll eat a few bird eggs. All squirrels have the same habit of burying some food to eat in the winter. Chipmunks carry as many as seven or eight nuts in their cheek pouches at one time to hide them. All squirrels sit on their haunches and eat food held in the front paws in that cute way.

   The burrows of chipmunks are very interesting. They dig a tunnel under a tree root or rock so it is harder to find the entrance. Tunnels can go several feet below ground level and can be as long as your classroom (30 feet) or more. Some species spend their whole life making their tunnels and burrows longer. There is usually a nesting room as well as a food storage room or two. The chipmunk may have several entrances and exits. Some of them may be blocked with a little dirt to keep enemies out. The nesting room is where the two litters of four to eight babies will be born and nursed for a month. They will live in the same burrow with the mother for another month. She will teach them where to look for food so they will be ready to leave and start their own burrows. The next time you are around chipmunks, watch them scamper about and see if you can find the entrance to their home.

Friendly Chips

Vocabulary Checkup Write the words from the box on the correct blanks.

bold	bushy	exit	identified
habits	nature	omnivore	scamper

1. An animal that eats both plants and meat is an _____.

2. Showing courage and bravery is being very _____.

3. Regular practices or acts that are repeated are _____.

4. To run in a hurry or in a playful way is to _____.

5. The way out or a passage away from is an _____.

6. The natural world of plants and animals is _____.

7. To be recognized as a certain person or thing is to be _____.

8. To spread like a bush or shaggy head of hair is to be _____.

Comprehension You may need to look back at the story to answer the questions correctly.

1. You can tell a chipmunk is different from other squirrels by looking for a chipmunk's
_____ and
_____.

2. The things we can see that help us know chipmunks are in the squirrel family are
_____
_____.

3. The home of the chipmunk has several interesting features, like the _____
_____ and
_____.

4. The things that a chipmunk eats that make it different from the larger squirrels are
_____
_____.

Name _____ Date _____

Friendly Chips

5. The chipmunk's cheeks look very fat when _____

_____

_____ .

Thinking About Chipmunks Think carefully before you answer the questions.

1. Why do you think chipmunks are so friendly, bold, and easy to tame?

_____

_____

_____

2. How do you think scientists can tell apart twenty-two different species of chipmunks?

_____

_____

_____

3. What habits can you think of that show that chipmunks don't truly hibernate?

_____

_____

_____

4. What things can you think of that help to keep from having too many chipmunks?

_____

_____

_____

Check It Out Find out about

Eastern chipmunks

Yellow pine chipmunks

Gray squirrels

Fox squirrels

Ground squirrels

Name _____ Date _____

14. Clever as a Fox

Fables and folk tales have been told about clever tricks played by the fox for hundreds of years. Native Americans as well as people from other lands around the world have respected the fox as one of nature's most intelligent creatures. There is some species of fox or fox-like animal nearly everywhere in the world. Those foxes all belong to the canine family, which we usually call the dog family.

We will look at the red fox and gray fox since they are the two most common species in North America. The red fox is found all across the northern part of the United States and into Canada. Their back is a rusty, red-orange color with white under the chin clear down the chest and belly. There is even a white tip on their rusty red tail. The gray fox is found all over the United States and is more common in the southern states than the red fox. Gray foxes have a black and white mix of fur on their back, giving them a gray look. Their underside is also white, but their tail has a black tip. Both red and gray foxes have some black hair on their legs. They are both about two feet long and weigh 8 to 11 pounds. Their beautiful, 15-inch-long, bushy tails are often called a brush. They both have four toes on the hind foot and five toes on the front. One of the front toes (called the dewclaw) doesn't touch the ground. They both have fairly large ears and a long, pointed snout for their nose.

Foxes don't form packs the way wolves do. They do live as a family quite often, hunting as a pair as they work together to raise a litter and teach the young. Foxes communicate with growls, barks, and yelps just like many other dog species. A gray fox is the only one in the canine family to climb trees. They are sometimes called tree foxes, but scientists aren't sure why they climb trees.

The fox is a very skilled hunter that can run down a zigzagging rabbit or creep up on a bird and pounce on it like a cat. Foxes can hear the sound of mice rustling in the grass or worms squirming in their holes. They are quick enough to catch frogs, snakes, and lizards, too. They will wait for chipmunks, groundhogs, and other animals to come out of their burrows. They even eat insects when they are hungry. They are true carnivores even though they eat a little fruit and grass. They like to hunt at night since their eyes see well in near darkness. Their eyes look green if light hits them at night.

The fox sleeps right out in the woods by a tree or shrub with its bushy tail curled up over its nose and front paws. The female (vixen) will move into an abandoned burrow or cave when it is time to have her babies. The red fox will dig a den or make a burrow deeper and wider. Gray foxes like to use a cave, rock pile, or hollow log for a den (kennel) to have their pups or cubs. Gray foxes have three to five pups, but red foxes have from four to nine pups. These pups will look like puppies of other dogs and will be born with their eyes closed for a week or more. The vixen will stay right with them to nurse and protect them for a month. The male fox (called a dog) will bring the vixen food to eat. The dog and vixen will start bringing pups live mice to catch and eat. Those pups will leave the kennel to play and learn to hunt at about five weeks of age. Pups will be out on their own by the end of the summer.

People have hunted the fox for hundreds of years. It is a sport in some places to use foxhounds to chase down foxes. The fox is so clever. It will backtrack, run through water, and use other tricks to escape. The fox usually is not killed in this strange game. Some people do kill the fox for its pretty fur. Red fox fur is liked best, and some people raise red foxes on a fur farm. Farmers raising chickens and turkeys used to kill foxes because they were eating their poultry. The farmers soon found that they needed the fox to control the number of mice and rats. It was smarter to fence in the poultry. Since foxes can carry the rabies virus, you should leave cute fox pups alone if you ever find any. Wild creatures are better off in the wild.

Clever as a Fox

Vocabulary Checkup Write the words from the box on the correct blanks.

canine	communicate	fables	intelligent	kennel
poultry	rabies	rustle	snout	vixen

1. Short tales using animals to teach a lesson are called _____.

2. A female or mother fox is also called a _____.

3. A dog or a member of the dog family is called a _____.

4. A disease often transferred by the bite of animals is _____.

5. Birds like chickens, ducks, and turkeys are raised as _____.

6. To exchange ideas or thoughts is to _____.

7. The forward part of an animal's head with jaw and nose is a _____.

8. To make a soft, gentle sound like leaves rubbing is to _____.

9. Another name for a den where dogs are kept is _____.

10. Having good mental ability or "smarts" is _____.

Comprehension You may need to look back at the story to answer the questions correctly.

1. The fox belongs in the _____ or _____ family.

2. Red and gray foxes weigh about _____ pounds and are _____ feet long with a bushy tail another _____ inches long.

3. Some of the ways the gray fox differs from the red fox are in _____

_____

_____.

4. Some of the things foxes do as a family are _____

_____.

Name _____ Date _____

Clever as a Fox

5. Five things the fox eats are _____, _____, _____, _____, and _____.

Thinking About Foxes Think carefully before answering the questions.

1. I think the fox is seen as clever and intelligent because _____
_____
_____
_____.

2. I think the gray fox sometimes climbs trees because _____
_____
_____
_____.

3. I think the fox chooses to move into a den or kennel to raise its pups because
_____
_____
_____.

4. I think the fox is a benefit to people because _____
_____
_____.

5. I think the fox is bad for people to have around because _____
_____
_____.

Check It Out Find out about

Kit foxes

Arctic foxes

Fennecs

Bat-eared foxes

Fox hunts

Name _____ Date _____

15. Reptiles with Shells

Reptiles are animals like snakes, lizards, crocodiles, alligators, and tortoises and turtles. They all are cold-blooded, which means that their body temperature will be about the same temperature as the air, water, or dirt around them. Tortoises and turtles are the only reptiles with shells covering their bodies. They have some bones inside, but that tough shell instead of skin is great protection. Many turtles can pull their head and legs inside their shell for safety. Sea turtles can't pull inside their shells, however, and they have flippers instead of legs like the land turtles.

The green turtle lives in all of the warm waters of the world including the waters along the coast of the United States. These sea turtles grow as long as 5 feet and weigh up to 400 pounds. Green turtles are brown or green with yellow spots. They get their name from their greenish-colored flesh. They have lungs to breathe air like mammals, but the green sea turtle can stay underwater for five hours before coming to the surface for air. Green turtles can't draw back into their shell for safety, but they can swim as fast as 20 miles per hour. You probably can't run that fast on land, and of course nobody can swim that fast.

The green turtle stays in shallow waters most of the time. Young turtles will eat small crabs and shrimp. Adults like to eat sea grasses and algae. They reach up and nibble leaves off tropical trees that hang over the water. But their favorite food is eel grass, which grows in the muddy waters along North and South America. Turtles don't have teeth, so they depend on the sharp jaws of their beak to cut the grass and mash it. They have very strong jaws, so don't stick your finger in there.

Female green turtles will sometimes be seen far out at sea as they migrate to a nesting beach called a rookery. Some of them will migrate thousands of miles to a warm spot on their favorite rookery to lay their eggs. Ascension Island in the middle of the Atlantic Ocean has thousands of green turtles nesting there each year. The female will pull herself up the beach and use her flippers to dig a hole in the warm sand. She will lay as many as 100 golf-ball-sized eggs in it and pull some sand over the nest. She can do the same thing several times for a month before leaving to migrate back home. She will let the heat of the sun hatch her eggs in two or three months. If the temperature in the nest is close to 80 degrees, all males will hatch. If it is close to 90 degrees, only females will be hatched. The newly hatched babies will dig out of their nest at night and try to make it to the water before being eaten by seabirds. They swim slowly until they are a little older, so they are easy prey for many creatures as they float around eating on shrimp, baby crabs, and algae. Their parents won't stay to protect them. Scientists think only two out of every 100 baby green turtles will live to see their first birthday.

The green turtle has very little defense against its main enemy—humans. People have hunted green turtles for food and for their shells for thousands of years. Green turtles are a very popular food in many parts of the world. In some places the turtles' eggs are dug up for food, too. Most countries have passed laws against killing them, but many people have ignored the laws and still depend on the turtles for food. All seven sea turtle species are listed on the endangered list. About thirty other kinds of turtles and tortoises are also endangered. Scientists are trying to find out more about how turtles live in the wild to save them. They are also trying to discover better ways to raise them on turtle farms and in aquariums.

Reptiles with Shells

Vocabulary Checkup Write the words from the box on the correct blanks.

| algae | cold-blooded | flesh | flippers |
| lungs | reptiles | rookery | surface |

1. Air-breathing, cold-blooded animals with scales are _____.

2. Broad, flat feet or legs to help in swimming are _____.

3. A group of tiny plants that grow in wet places are called _____.

4. The top or outermost layer of something is the _____.

5. The soft, meaty part of an animal's body is called _____.

6. Animals with backbones breathe by using sacs called _____.

7. Animals whose blood temperature fits the surrounding materials are said to be

_____.

8. A nesting area for large numbers of a species is called a _____.

Comprehension You may need to look back at the story to answer the questions correctly.

1. Turtles are like snakes and other reptiles because their _____

_____

_____.

2. Even though they are brown, green, and yellow, some sea turtles are named "green turtles" because

_____

_____.

3. Green sea turtles show they are great swimmers by _____

_____

_____.

Name _____   Date _____

Reptiles with Shells

4. The two greatest dangers to green sea turtles are _____
_____
_____.

Thinking About Green Turtles Think carefully before answering the questions.

1. I think green turtle mothers don't stay to protect their hatchlings because they
_____
_____
_____.

2. I think adult sea turtles are in greater danger than other turtles because they
_____
_____
_____.

3. I think the main reasons so few baby sea turtles live to be a year old is that
_____
_____
_____.

4. What do you think is the easiest way to save green sea turtles from extinction?
_____
_____
_____.

Check It Out Find out about

Snapping turtles

Terrapins

Mud turtles

Box turtles

Leatherbacks

Soft-shelled turtles

Name _____ Date _____

16. A Big, Beautiful, Black Bird

Hundreds of years ago there were many large, black birds called ravens living near people in lands north of the equator. Northwestern Native Americans admired them and made ravens one of their story heroes. Other people killed many of them because they thought the birds were a sign of evil and had strange powers. So those birds named ravens moved up into the forests, mountains, and sea cliffs to get away from people. The raven still lives all across North America in quiet areas. The northern ravens live from Alaska across Canada to Greenland and in northern and eastern parts of the United States. American ravens live in the western states, and white-necked ravens live in the southwestern states.

All of the ravens are larger than hawks and ducks. They are about two feet long, weigh up to 3 pounds, and have a wingspan of 4 feet. Their feathers are glossy black with a purple sparkle on the back and a green shine on the abdomen. The shaggy feathers at the throat may have a gray look or even be white in the southwest. Their beak or bill is very large and strong. Their tail is broad, and the wing feathers look like long fingers as they fly overhead making a sound like *crock* or *corruk*.

Many people never get to see ravens unless they drive up to their habitat in the mountains or forests. If you find their home range, be sure to watch long enough to see these large, black birds do their acrobatic flying. They can dive straight toward Earth and pull up at the last second. They also do rolls, somersaults, and other fancy moves you wouldn't expect from such a large bird.

Ravens eat a lot of dead animal carcasses they find. They look for animals that have died in accidents or bad weather. They can use their large beak to kill small mammals if they can't find any dead ones. They also eat small birds, frogs, eggs, and seeds and fruit. They eat enough plants, seeds, and buds to be omnivores even if they are more famous for picking clean the carcass of a dead animal.

    In their mountain or cliff habitat, ravens make a large nest on the edge
of a rock ledge. However, forest ravens nest in trees. Nests are made of
sticks and twigs held together with mud and moss. A pair of ravens will
work together to build the nest. The pair mates for life, which can be
fifteen to twenty years. The female will lay a clutch of four to six speckled
eggs in the early spring. The male will bring her food for three weeks
while she incubates the eggs to hatch them. Both parents will bring food
to the chicks for about five or six weeks after they are hatched. The
parents will also bring fur, wool, or grass to insulate the nest for the
chicks. They will remove some insulation as the temperature warms up.
The chicks' feathers are a dark brown and are not shiny until they can fly.
Some people think ravens aren't good parents because they roost at night
in some spot away from their chicks.

    Ravens in captivity have lived to be sixty-nine years old, but the wild
ravens only live fifteen years. People trying to get rid of coyotes and
wolves near their stock used poisoned meat or steel traps baited with
meat. Many ravens died in traps or from the poison. Scientists did
experiments to prove the raven is one of the most intelligent of all
animals, so you would think ravens would be smart enough to stay away
from poison meat and steel traps. We have laws now that prevent these
practices, so wild ravens may now live longer.

A Big, Beautiful, Black Bird

Vocabulary Checkup Write the words from the box on the correct blanks.

carcass	chick	clutch	glossy
incubate	mate	somersault	wingspan

1. One of a pair, as a husband or wife, is a _____.

2. A hatch of eggs in a nest is called a _____.

3. The dead body of an animal is the _____.

4. A young bird is called a _____.

5. A move where the body rolls end over end is a _____.

6. To sit on or heat to hatch is to _____.

7. The distance between the wing tips is the _____.

8. Shiny or glowing with light is _____.

Comprehension You may need to look back at the story to answer the questions correctly.

1. Ravens belong to the same family as the black _____, but ravens are much bigger at _____ feet long and weighing up to _____ pounds.

2. Some flying tricks ravens can do are _____

_____

_____

3. Ravens eat many things, including _____

_____

_____

4. Ravens build nests out of these materials: _____

_____

_____

Name _____ Date _____

A Big, Beautiful, Black Bird

5. Wild ravens only live about _____ years, but ravens in captivity have lived as long as _____ years.

Thinking About Ravens Think carefully before answering the questions.

1. I think ravens have moved far away from people because _____
   _____
   _____
   _____.

2. I believe ravens are very valuable birds because _____
   _____
   _____
   _____.

3. I think it is a good thing raven chicks are a dull brown because _____
   _____
   _____
   _____.

4. I believe ravens really are good parents because _____
   _____
   _____
   _____.

5. I think it is great that ravens mate for life because _____
   _____
   _____
   _____.

Check It Out Find out about

American crows

Fish crows

Rooks

"The Raven" by Edgar Allan Poe

Name _____ Date _____

17. Patient Prairie Wolves

A relative of the dog and wolf family that is famous for its nightly *yip-yip-yip-yowlll* is the prairie wolf. They are also called coyotes. Some people say kī o' tē and others say kī' ōt, and both are correct. They are a wily (meaning sly or clever) creature no matter how you say their name. The range of many animals has been cut back, but the coyote has spread its range all over North America. If you haven't heard those howls in your area yet, it won't be long before you do. Coyotes were only in the West a few hundred years ago. While people moved to settle the West, coyotes moved to settle the North and East. They spread to anyplace that had food as the number of coyotes grew rapidly. They seemed to adapt to differences in deserts, prairies, mountains, or near cities quite easily.

The coyote, at nearly 40 pounds and 4 feet long, is bigger than the fox. Coyotes do have a bushy "brush" of a tail about 14 inches long, as does the fox. The coyotes' colors vary from a yellowish-brown or yellowish-gray to a buff-gray. Coyotes' fur often has black tips on it. Their ears are fairly large and usually stand erect. They use their keen hearing as well as their sense of smell to catch their prey. The coyote is one of the fastest mammals in North America, running as fast as 38 miles per hour. It can chase its prey for a long distance until the prey is worn out and easy to catch. The coyote also is so patient it can hear or smell a mouse in the grass and wait and wait until the best time to pounce on it like a cat. Wily coyote, with all that skill, still can't catch the roadrunner.

Coyotes are carnivores and eat just about any kind of meat in their territory. Rabbits and squirrels are its favorite prey. Coyotes are such expert hunters that they can catch a gopher, mouse, rat, bird, prairie dog, opossum, raccoon, or snake. They will join with other coyotes to chase down a larger animal like a young deer, goat, sheep, or antelope. Coyotes seldom form a pack like wolves do. Coyotes often hunt as a pair or as a

(Patient Prairie Wolves, *continued*)

family, however. They even catch house cats, chickens, and other animals people are raising. You may need to protect pets if there are hungry coyotes in your area, especially in the winter months.

Coyotes are very good parents. They often mate for life and work together to raise their litter of pups. The female will usually make her lair, or den, in a burrow that has been abandoned or in a hollow tree. After carrying her young inside her for about two months, she will give birth in the spring to five or six pups. The pups won't open their eyes for the first two weeks. The mother will nurse them for six or seven weeks, but both of the parents will spit up some partly digested meat for the pups when they are a month old. Then pups begin to risk trips outside of the lair to explore the night world and play, too. There is lots of food in the spring, and it is the best time for parents to teach the pups all of the different hunting methods. By summer's end, the pups go out on their own.

There are more coyotes than ever despite their bad reputation around farms and their howling at night near cities. Many people don't like coyotes because they think they kill too many of the animals they love. Other people believe they are quite helpful in controlling the number of rodents. Some states have trapped, hunted, and killed many coyotes. Other states protect them from hunters. The patient, intelligent coyote will have to keep hiding and howling until it is better understood.

Patient Prairie Wolves

Vocabulary Checkup Write the words from the box on the correct blanks.

adapt	erect	lair	prairie
relative	reputation	vary	wily

1. An extensive, grassy, fairly level piece of land is a _____.

2. To be very sly and clever is to be _____.

3. To adjust to new conditions is to _____.

4. To change or differ in some way is to _____.

5. Standing up in an upright position is _____.

6. Related by blood or in the same family is a _____.

7. A den or home for an animal is often called a _____.

8. The respect a person or thing gets is its _____.

Comprehension You may need to look back at the story to answer the questions correctly.

1. Coyotes belong to the _____ family and are also called _____ in some parts of the United States.

2. Coyotes can weigh up to _____ pounds and be about _____ long. This is much larger than the _____ that also is a canine and has a bushy tail.

3. Coyotes use their senses of _____ and _____ to find prey. They can run as fast as _____ miles per hour to catch their prey.

4. Coyotes' favorite prey are _____ and _____ but they also eat _____, _____, and _____.

5. Spring is a good time for coyotes to raise their pups because _____ _____ _____.

Name _____ Date _____

Patient Prairie Wolves

Thinking About Coyotes Think carefully before answering the questions.

1. I think coyotes spread all over North America because _____
   _____
   _____.

2. I feel the coyotes' most amazing skill is _____
   _____
   _____.

3. I think coyotes are good and helpful animals because they _____
   _____
   _____.

4. I think coyotes are bad and harmful animals because they _____
   _____
   _____.

5. The most interesting thing I learned about coyotes was _____
   _____
   _____.

6. I feel we may need to be more careful to protect our pets from coyotes in the winter
   months because
   _____
   _____
   _____.

Check It Out Find out about

Coyote pelts

Legends of the coyote

Coyotes' lifespan

Coydogs

Name _____ Date _____

18. Short-horned Grasshoppers

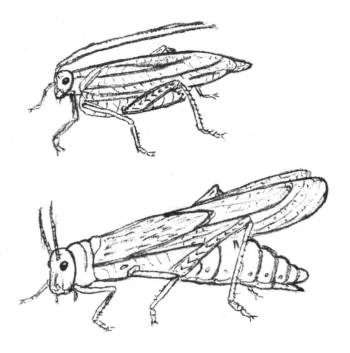

There are more than 10,000 different kinds of grasshoppers jumping and flying in every part of the world where there are any plants growing. Look at the length of feelers or antennae (horns) to divide them into two large groups: (1) Long-horned grasshoppers, which include the Mormon crickets and katydids, and (2) short-horned grasshoppers, which have heavier, shorter antennae and are also called locusts. The bodies and habits of long- and short-horned 'hoppers are a lot alike, so we will concentrate on the locusts or shorter-horned 'hoppers.

Grasshoppers (or locusts) don't always live in grassy areas. Some kinds live in deserts and others live in tropical forests. "Hoppers" may not be the best way to name them. A hop is a short jump. These insects can use their powerful hind legs to leap more than twenty times their own body length! To equal that jump, you would need to jump a length of a gymnasium or a full basketball court. Even if you could do that, can you guess what the landing would be like? Maybe we should call them grassleapers instead of grasshoppers.

Many of the grasshoppers or locusts do have two pairs of wings, but they didn't even use them to make that huge leap. Sometimes when they hop they do spread their wings and fly if they want to travel farther. They have front wings that are strong and cover their larger, thinner flying wings. Many 'hoppers' flying wings have bright red, yellow, blue, or green colors that show only when they fly. Locusts sometimes get together in large bunches called swarms and migrate to other areas. Swarms eat so much that they destroy farmers' crops. Scientists aren't sure why some locusts swarm.

You can use the diagram shown on the next page to understand the body of the locust or grasshopper better. They actually have five eyes. They have a compound eye on each side of their head with over 1,000 lenses that helps them see in every direction. There is a tiny eye at the base of each antenna and one in between them, but nobody knows what grasshoppers use these eyes for. Their mouth has two strong jaws for biting off leaves and teeth to grind them up. They eat just about any kind of plants, not just grass like their name hints. The antennae are used for smelling food, but some species even eat manure! They have claws on their front legs, which they can use to hold food. They have an ear just above each of the middle legs. The long rear legs have big thigh muscles to help grasshoppers leap far. The abdomen has holes for breathing.

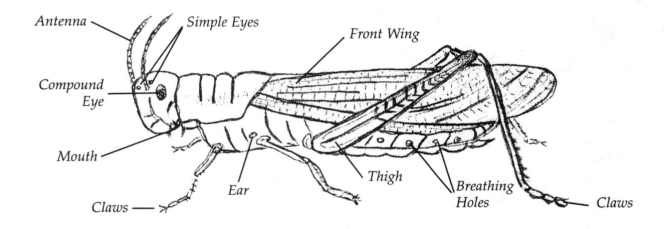

The back of the female's abdomen can grow longer and has a point to dig into the ground or cut a leaf or stem to hide her eggs. She will lay anywhere from two to 120 eggs at a time. She has to hide her eggs from some flies that will lay their own eggs with her eggs. The newborn flies hatch and eat the grasshopper's eggs. Most grasshopper eggs won't hatch until next spring. They look a lot like the adults, but they won't get their wings for two months. They hop around and eat lots of leaves and molt (shed their skin) to get larger. After they molt for the fifth time, the wings are strong enough for the grasshoppers to fly to new feeding grounds. Their color may change during this molting from brown or gray to red, green, or yellow.

Grasshoppers' main enemies are birds, snakes, rodents, spiders, and humans. If you've ever caught a grasshopper, you know they spit out a brown juice that scientists think helps make ants and beetles leave them alone. Our farmers sometimes spray chemicals on swarms of locusts to keep them from eating their crops. However, people in several countries catch and eat cooked locusts. Grasshoppers or locusts don't seem to be in any danger of becoming extinct, however.

Short-horned Grasshoppers

Vocabulary Checkup Write the words from the box on the correct blanks.

chemicals	compounds	concentrate	diagram
manure	molt	swarm	thigh	tropical

1. To shed skin or feathers in a growing process is to _____.

2. Having to do with the warm area near the tropics is _____.

3. Substances used or produced in chemistry are _____.

4. A drawing, chart, or plan that explains a thing is a _____.

5. The big part of the leg above the knee is called the _____.

6. A waste product from animals used to fertilize soil is _____.

7. Things made of many parts working together are _____.

8. A large number of flying insects together is a _____.

Comprehension You may need to look back at the story to answer the questions correctly.

1. What are the names of the two groups all grasshoppers are divided into?
   _____ and
   _____.

2. Why are swarms of locusts such a bad thing for people living in the area?
   _____

3. Grasshoppers that have just hatched from eggs need to molt because _____
   _____.

4. Two ways that humans get rid of grasshoppers are _____ and
   _____

Name _____   Date _____

Short-horned Grasshoppers

Thinking About Grasshoppers Think carefully before answering the questions.

1. Where in the world do you think there are no grasshoppers living, and why?

   _____

   _____

2. Why do you think the author wanted to change their name to "grassleapers"?

   _____

   _____

3. Why do you think locusts get together in large groups and swarm to a new area?

   _____

   _____

4. What did you feel was the most interesting or unusual thing about a grasshopper's body?

   _____

   _____

5. Do you think you would like to try eating grasshoppers? _____

   Please explain why you would or would not try it. _____

   _____

6. What else can you think of that farmers could do besides spraying chemicals?

   _____

   _____

   _____

Check It Out Find out about

    Cicadas

    Crickets

    Katydids

    Walking sticks

    How grasshoppers sing

Name _____ Date _____

19. The Most Famous Deer of All

The reindeer is an easily tamed deer famous in stories around the world. Songs and stories tell how a jolly, white-bearded man uses a team of reindeer to pull his sleigh full of gifts. Reindeer live near the North Pole, so they have to be able to stand freezing temperatures. I can't tell you where that man really lives, but I can tell you that reindeer live in the Arctic and are used by many people to pull sleds. You will learn how they have gone down in history as the most useful deer of all.

Most reindeer weigh close to 300 pounds and are about 3 to 4 feet tall at the shoulder. Females are shorter and weigh less than males. Reindeer can stand the severe cold because they have a dense (thick) layer of hair to insulate their body. The dense hair traps air to help insulate, but this also makes the reindeer a terrific swimmer. They can swim across large rivers when they migrate. There is coarse, waterproof hair on top of that dense layer. Even the nose is covered by hair! These deer also have split hooves that can spread out to help support their weight on top of snow and still give them a good hold on ice and frozen snow.

The reindeer is the only member of the deer family where both the males (stags) and females have horns called antlers. You may have thought about that when you looked at the names of the famous team of reindeer pulling that sleigh. They all have antlers! Females usually have shorter antlers than stags. The stags shed their antlers in December. (Hmmm, I wonder if it's before December 25?) However, the females don't shed their antlers until spring, when their calves are born.

Reindeer live on the tundra, which is a large plain with few trees in the northern Arctic regions of North America, Europe, and Asia. They live in herds of 20 to 1,500 animals all summer. They wander across the tundra eating the coarse grass, twigs, and leaves there in summer. They join together in huge herds of more than 200,000 reindeer every fall to migrate to southern tundra. They can live on lichen (lī' ken) and moss that grows on the tundra by using their hooves to dig through several feet of snow to get it.

Spring is the time of new plant growth and the calving season. The female will try to go to her same private calving spot each spring. The newborn calf (fawn) weighs about 15 or 16 pounds, but it can run faster than you can by the time it is one day old. Many baby deer have spots when they are young, but reindeer fawns don't have any spots. Fawns nurse until it is time for the fall migration, so their mothers are glad they don't get antlers until the next spring when they are a year old.

Many people in northern Europe and Asia depend on the reindeer much like desert people depend on camels. They tame reindeer for carrying heavy loads and pulling sleds and sleighs. They also eat the meat, drink the milk, make cloth from the hair, make tents and shoes from the hide, and carve tools and other things from the antlers and bones. The reindeer is their horse, sheep, and cow.

The United States brought about 1,000 reindeer from Siberia nearly 100 years ago. These reindeer were for the Eskimo in Alaska to raise and use for food. There are now over a million reindeer living in Alaska! Large herds of reindeer are raised on ranches in some parts of Alaska and Canada. Their meat and hides are sold in many markets. Reindeer are not in any danger of becoming extinct because of these people raising them for so many human uses.

One of the strangest things about reindeer is the sound they make when they run or walk. They have bones in their feet that click together with every step. Perhaps we don't hear that clicking very often because of the jingling of the sleigh bells.

The Most Famous Deer of All

Vocabulary Checkup Write the words from the box on the correct blanks.

antlers	coarse	dense	fawn	hooves
lichen	severe	sleigh	stag	tundra

1. A young baby deer is often called a _____.

2. The horns of animals in the deer family are _____.

3. An adult male deer is called a buck or a _____.

4. The hard feet of some animals are called _____.

5. Thick and close together is what _____ means.

6. A big sled on runners pulled by animals is a _____.

7. Very rough, shaggy, or uneven is _____.

8. A large frozen plain with few trees is called a _____.

9. Very harsh, serious, or difficult is what _____ means.

10. One plant that grows on the tundra is called _____.

Comprehension You may need to look back at the story to answer the questions correctly.

1. How can reindeer stand the freezing Arctic temperatures? _____

   _____

   _____

2. What are some of the uses people have found for reindeer? _____

   _____

   _____

3. How do reindeer find food in the winter, and what do they eat then? _____

   _____

   _____

Name _____ Date _____

The Most Famous Deer of All

4. What are some ways reindeer fawns are different from other fawns?

_____

_____

_____

5. What are two ways that adult reindeer are different from other deer?

_____

_____

_____

Thinking About Reindeer Think carefully before answering the questions.

1. A reindeer's most important body feature is its _____

_____

because _____

_____

2. I believe reindeer are the most useful deer because _____

_____

3. I think the strangest thing I learned about reindeer was _____

_____

_____ .

4. (Circle a choice and explain.) I (would) (would not) want to eat reindeer meat

because _____

_____ .

Check It Out Find out about

   Red deer

   Lapland's people

   Caribou

   Antlers in velvet

   Life on the frozen tundra

Dewclaw

Name _____ Date _____

20. Our Worst Friend

Everywhere humans live in the world, the house mouse also lives. Hundreds of kinds of mice live in all parts of the world. They can stand the heat of the desert or the freezing cold of the Arctic. They adapt by eating whatever humans and nature give them, and they can be a real pest. The tiny rodents don't eat much, but they sure can spoil lots of food meant for people. We are lucky that many animals also eat the mice or they could be a severe problem. Some people think these little grayish-brown critters with big ears and large sparkling black eyes are cute. Many people shiver or even scream at the glimpse of a mouse.

The mouse got its name from an ancient word in Asia that meant "thief." The little thieves steal our food, but they spoil more food and can also carry diseases. Scientists think the first mice spread from Asia to Europe. Then they came to America on ships almost 500 years ago. They may live in the fields during warmer months and move into our buildings when it gets colder, and that is when they become our worst friend. They chew up many of our things since they are gnawing rodents whose front teeth keep growing their whole life. They use some of the paper, cloth, and things they chew up to build their nests.

People often find that the worst thing about mice is the terrible odor they make. This odor comes from their habit of spreading their urine, or yellow liquid, and little black droppings over territory they claim. Mice live in small colonies, which they try to keep uncrowded. They spread the scent of their colony around, and any mouse that doesn't smell like it belongs will get attacked.

Mice can't see things more than a few inches away very well. They depend on their big ears and their sharp nose to tell them where food is or when danger is near. They can hear sounds people can't begin to hear, but mice searching for food may run right out in front of you if you are very quiet and don't move. They don't need much food, but they are always looking for more. They will eat just about anything, but their favorite foods are seeds and anything made of grains. They have eaten some strange household items, like soap, glue, candles, and cork. They must smell something good in those items. They can squeeze through spaces no wider than your thumb. They're very light and can climb right up inside the walls of your house in their search for food.

Baby mice are born with their eyes shut and have no hair. So the pinkish newborns look weird. They nurse for eighteen days until they can begin finding their own food. Females begin having babies when they are only nine weeks old, and they can have litters of four to eight babies as often as once a month. One female can produce as many as eighty to ninety young in a year. Each of her female babies will be having babies in nine weeks. Wow!

Humans are probably the mouse's worst enemy. People trap them, poison them, and do everything they can to get the mouse out of their house. We know how much odor, damage, and disease they can cause. We also know how fast they produce babies. It is a good thing mice are food for several other animals. We need all of their help, too.

We have learned a lot about the house mouse. There are several other kinds of mice you may be interested to know more about. For instance, American harvest mice are smaller and have more hair on their tails than house mice. They live in fields, making nests of grass and harvesting seeds to eat. Grasshopper mice like meat and eat lots of desert locusts and grasshoppers in our southwest (I'll bet you guessed that). Deer mice are sometimes called white-footed mice, and they can be nearly twice as big as our house mice. Their colors are similar to many deer, but they also will stomp their front feet like some deer when danger is near. White mice are really just a type of house mouse that has been raised to be used as a pet or as a science project to test new drugs, learn about sickness, and find out more about how animals act. You may not like mice very well, but you can see that some are also a benefit to people.

Our Worst Friend

Vocabulary Checkup Write the words from the box on the correct blanks.

ancient	attacked	disease	harvest	items
produce	scent	spoil	urine	weird

1. To ruin, damage, or make unfit for use is to _____.

2. A yellow liquid animals make in the kidney is _____.

3. _____ means acted on in a forceful or violent way.

4. _____ are separate articles or pieces.

5. A special odor or smell of something is called its _____.

6. To gather or reap crops is to _____.

7. _____ means very old or from times long ago.

8. _____ means odd, strange, or very unusual.

9. An illness or weak condition of a body is a _____.

10. To bear offspring or bring to life is to _____.

Comprehension You may need to look back at the story to answer the questions correctly.

1. What are three bad things the house mouse can do in a house? _____
   _____
   _____

2. What are some of the strange foods mice sometimes eat? _____
   _____
   _____

3. Why do mice gnaw or chew on wood and other nonfood items? _____
   _____
   _____

Name _____ Date _____

Our Worst Friend

4. What are two signs that mice are in the house even if you haven't seen them?

_____

_____

Thinking About Mice Think carefully before answering the questions.

1. How do scientists think mice probably got spread all over the world? _____

_____

_____

_____

2. Do you think mice are (A) cute or (B) scary? (Circle A or B as a choice.)
   Why? _____

_____

_____

3. Think of enemies other than humans that mice have and list them below:

_____

_____

_____

4. Why do you think it is so hard to keep a pet mouse's cage from smelling bad?

_____

_____

_____

5. Do you agree with the author that baby mice look weird? _____
   Why? _____

_____

_____

Check It Out Find out about

Jumping mice   Pack rats

Lemmings   Rodents

Albino mice

Name _____ Date _____

Answer Key for Activity Sheets

Robins *(A Friendly Spring Bird)*

Vocabulary—1) brood 2) twigs 3) migrate 4) benefit 5) grubs 6) blend 7) caption 8) orchard.

Comprehension—1) People from Europe named it for similar European birds. 2) They think it would make her too easy to see while nesting. 3) Grass, twigs, paper, string, and mud. 4) They eat grubs, insects, worms, and fruit.

Fact or Opinion—1) O 2) F 3) F 4) O 5) O 6) F 7) O 8) F 9) F 10) O.

Thinking—1) Students may say it's due to friendliness or color or close nests. 2) Answers will vary. 3) Benefit because it eats insects and grubs, and sings. Harmful because it eats worms and fruit crops.

Black Bear *(The Shy American Bear)*

Vocabulary—1) doze 2) burrow 3) glimpse 4) diet 5) pesky 6) ruin 7) den 8) shy 9) insects.

Comprehension—1) They're not just black; also brown, gray, and have white. 2) They can run 25 mph and we can't. 3) Leaves, buds, berries, roots, nuts, and bark. 4) She has to care for cubs for two years. 5) They cut a tooth and counted the rings.

Thinking—1) The first ones were modeled after the cub Teddy Roosevelt had. 2) They haven't eaten much all winter and used up most of their stored fat. 3) Hopefully, they will keep a safe distance and observe quietly. 4) The ground may be all torn up, rocks and logs moved, or bark and twigs torn off trees.

Ladybugs *(The Beautiful Ladybug)*

Vocabulary—1) hibernate 2) aphids 3) popular 4) respect 5) poison 6) beetle 7) larva 8) cozy.

Comprehension—1) Red, orange, yellow, black. 2) Copy pictures of them on clothing or on other items and not harm them. 3) Aphids, scale, and spider mite. 4) They know the colors mean it's bad tasting, and it can send a bad smell also.

Fact or Opinion—1) O 2) F 3) F 4) O 5) F 6) F 7) O 8) F 9) F.

Thinking—1) Antarctica. 2) They are safer and last longer. 3) Answers vary. 4) Answers vary, but hopefully they're astonished.

Jack Rabbits *(Is Jack a Rabbit?)*

Vocabulary—1) form 2) litter 3) enemies 4) moisture 5) tortoise 6) cactus 7) plains 8) danger.

Comprehension—1) Hares are bigger and have longer ears than rabbits. 2) Big ears, long hind legs, large eyes, and fur colors blend. 3) Rabbits are born without hair and blind, but hares are born with fur and can see. 4) They can hear and see very well. They run 50 mph and jump 5 feet over obstacles.

Thinking—1) Answers will vary, but they may say that some people (Jack?) did not notice the differences when they named them. 2) Probably will say no, because the story is famous as "The Tortoise and the Hare." 3) They may mention trapping and moving them, introduction of predators, or letting nature take its course. 4) Answers will vary as to most interesting, but may mention their 50-mph speed, 5-foot leaps, "cool" ears, or their babies.

Monarchs *(Monarch Butterflies Flutter By)*

Vocabulary—1) pollen 2) caterpillar 3) veins 4) antennae 5) nectar 6) scales 7) cocoon 8) pupa 9) migrate 10) roost

Comprehension—1) 6 legs, 3 body parts, feelers. 2) They have a poison that makes birds sick. 3) Winters are too cold up north. 4) Pollinate flowers (beauty). 5) They should have drawn a caterpillar, cocoon, and butterfly.

Thinking—1) They learned the juice makes them poison, so it's a defense. 2) May mention "most beautiful insect," or "wings are a work of art." 3) Scales come off, they may die. 4) Pollination and a beauty to see. 5) Answers will vary. May say 3,000-mile migration, or change from ugly to beautiful.

Gerbils *(A Cute and Friendly Furball)*

Vocabulary—1) rodents 2) hind legs 3) miniature 4) arid 5) species 6) grain 7) colonies 8) prey 9) entrance 10) safety.

Comprehension—1) Colors match the different soils where they live. 2) To stay cooler and to keep snakes out. 3) It is safer and it saves moisture. 4) It's warm and gerbils could escape and eat crops. 5) Cage, food and water containers.

Thinking—1) May mention costs, clean, cute, or small space. 2) Answers will vary. 3) May mention exercise, or how a tube is like tunnels dug by them. 4) Answers will vary.

Flying Squirrels *(Can Squirrels Really Fly?)*

Vocabulary—1) spy 2) creatures 3) soar 4) creep 5) glide 6) abandoned 7) insulate 8) unique 9) fungi 10) haunches.

Comprehension—1) It flattens out its folds of skin and floats or glides down. 2) They only come out at night and are quiet and shy. 3) They eat some same foods and hide some, don't hibernate, live in trees, and bodies are similar. 4) Flyers have folds to glide with, are strictly nocturnal, and have bigger eyes. 5) Owl is avoided by turning in air or changing flight path.

Thinking—1) May say summer nest is cooler or winter nest is warmer. 2) May think of birds that roost at night or invading nests. 3) Discuss remembering or smelling. 4) May mention they like meat. 5) Camp, lie down, sit quietly, build a blind, etc.

Tigers *(Saving Siberian Tigers)*

Vocabulary—1) sheathed 2) boar 3) extinct 4) nape 5) carnivore 6) stalk 7) captivity 8) range 9) endangered 10) pounce.

Comprehension—1) They should color the upper right-hand part of the map. 2) It is darker in summer and lighter color in winter; winter coats are heavier too. 3) Each litter takes two years to raise. 4) Hunted for money; loss of food and habitat.

Thinking—1) May say its biggest, loudest, strongest, etc. 2) May say stealth, claws, teeth, long pounce. 3) Answers will vary. 4) Raise in zoos, save habitat, etc.

Walruses *(What Big Teeth You Have!)*

Vocabulary—1) blubber 2) ivory 3) arctic 4) shallow 5) tusks 6) bristles 7) survive 8) pressure.

Comprehension—1) Blubber insulates it and so does skin; flippers help it swim; tusks help it dig food and haul itself out of water; bristles sense food in cold mud. 2) Blood is near the surface to cool it off. 3) Newborns weigh 150 lb., 4 ft. long, only one calf, clings to mom's neck and stays with her for two years. 4) Hunted lots and so few calves born.

Thinking—1) May say blubber or thick skin 2) Answers vary. 3) Friendly, protection, breeding. 4) Should since some Eskimos need survival. Shouldn't because they are endangered. You may want to discuss this.

Elephants *(The Biggest Land Mammal)*

Vocabulary—1) wrinkled 2) funeral 3) bulls 4) vegetation 5) habitat 6) texture 7) cousins 8) sensitive.

Comprehension—1) 12,000 lb.; 25 ft.; 10 ft. 2) Nose, breathing, smelling, feeling, picking things up, and drinking or spraying. 3) Bigger body, ears, tusks, and trunk, darker gray skin, and a wilder nature. 4) 2 years; any other animal. 5) 200 lb.; 3 ft.; hair; 2 years; hair; vegetation.

Thinking—1) May mention their size. 2) Answers will vary. 3) Answers will vary. 4) May say size difference. 5) May say punish or guarding better.

Opossum *(American Marsupials)*

Vocabulary—1) odor 2) marsupial 3) abdomen 4) nocturnal 5) limp 6) pouch 7) temperature 8) hisses.

Comprehension—1) 'possum, Virginia possum, or common opossum. 2) It's house-cat size, grayish fur but no fur on tail, ears, or nose, five finger-like toes per foot, and long pointed nose. 3) They hunt at night and look for roadkill and move slowly. 4) Dead animals, bugs, worms, small mammals, birds, and any fruit or grain growing in the area.

Thinking—1) May say because they're slow and defenseless. 2) Answers will vary. 3) Answers will vary. 4) May mention zoos or cuteness.

Camels *(The Great Desert Taxi)*

Vocabulary—1) stomach 2) brow 3) transportation 4) cud 5) muzzle 6) digest 7) cattle 8) nurse.

Comprehension—1) Arabians have one hump and shorter hair. 2) Humps of fat to live on, eyes and noses keep sand out, and feet that support them in sand. 3) It uses its great store of fat in the hump. 4) Transport people and goods; eating meat and drinking milk; hair and skin for shoes, clothes, tents, and bags; pulling plows.

Thinking—1) May say most have been captured. 2) May say it's looking down through lashes, lids, and under brows. 3) Answers will vary. 4) It spits, bites, and kicks! 5) Answers will vary, but may mention hump sagging, eyelids, nose closes, or nastiness.

Chipmunks *(Friendly Chips)*

Vocabulary—1) omnivore 2) bold 3) habits 4) scamper 5) exit 6) nature 7) identified 8) bushy.

Comprehension—1) Stripes; and burrows or less bushy tail. 2) Its feet, nose, ears, and body similarities. 3) Hidden entrances, nesting room, food storage area, and long tunnels. 4) Slugs, beetles, mammals, and snakes. 5) Stuffed with food.

Thinking—1) May say they have learned to trust us. 2) May mention difference in stripes, size, habits, or homes. 3) They bury food to eat in winter and come out. 4) The predators and lack of food may be mentioned.

Foxes *(Clever as a Fox)*

Vocabulary—1) fables 2) vixen 3) canine 4) rabies 5) poultry 6) communicate 7) snout 8) rustle 9) kennel 10) intelligent.

Comprehension—1) Dog or canine. 2) 8–11 lb.; 2 ft.; 15 in. 3) Color of back is gray, not red, and a black tip on gray tail, and gray more common in South, and gray fox climbs, and gray not in burrow and only have three to five pups. 4) Hunt together, teach pups together, play and work. 5) Mice, rats, worms, rabbits, squirrels, frogs, snakes, lizards, birds, fruit, grass.

Thinking—1) May say fables or tricks done. 2) Answers may include seeing better, escape, etc. 3) May say it's too cold out, or safety. 4) Should mention rodent control. 5) May say poultry eaten or rabbits and other nice mammals, or carriers of rabies.

Turtles *(Reptiles with Shells)*

Vocabulary—1) reptiles 2) flippers 3) algae 4) surface 5) flesh 6) lungs 7) cold-blooded 8) rookery.

Comprehension—1) Body temperature adjusts to the surroundings, and they have skeletons. 2) Their flesh is actually greenish colored. 3) Swimming as fast as 20 mph and holding breath for five hours and swimming across oceans. 4) People eating them or their eggs and birds and other predators eating their young.

Thinking—1) May mention they don't have enough food at rookeries or the long two- to three-month wait, or lack of defense. 2) May say they can't pull back into shell, or their meat is liked for food. 3) They swim poorly, float on the surface, and are defenseless. 4) Answers may include sanctuary or enforcing laws.

Ravens *(A Big, Beautiful, Black Bird)*

Vocabulary—1) mate 2) clutch 3) carcass 4) chick 5) somersault 6) incubate 7) wingspan 8) glossy.

Completion—1) Crows; 2 feet; 3 lb. 2) Dive and swoop, roll, somersault, etc. 3) Eat dead animals, small mammals, birds, frogs, eggs, seeds, fruit. 4) Nests of sticks, mud, moss, grass, fur, wool, and hair. 5) 12–15 years; 69 years.

Thinking—1) May mention safety, fear, quieter, food, etc. 2) Answers will vary. 3) They're harder for predators to see. 4) They feed chicks and keep warm. 5) Answers will vary, but may mention faithful companions or family ties.

Coyotes *(Patient Prairie Wolves)*

Vocabulary—1) prairie 2) wily 3) adapt 4) vary 5) erect 6) relative 7) lair 8) reputation.

Comprehension—1) Dog or canine; prairie wolves. 2) 40 lb.; 4 ft.; fox. 3) Hearing and smell; 38 mph. 4) Rabbits or hares and squirrels; any rodents or any other meat animal on land. 5) Because there is lots of food for pups to hunt.

Thinking—1) May mention food supply or people's intrusion. 2) Answers will vary. 3) Eat rodents and snakes. 4) Harmful to pets and stock. Noisy too. 5) Answers will vary. 6) They may say that food is more scarce or that coyotes are hungrier.

Grasshoppers *(Short-horned Grasshoppers)*

Vocabulary—1) molt 2) tropical 3) chemicals 4) diagram 5) thigh 6) manure 7) compounds 8) swarm.

Comprehension—1) Long-horned; short-horned. 2) They eat vegetation and destroy food for people and animals. 3) They need more room to grow larger. 4) By spraying chemicals or by catching and eating them.

Thinking—1) Arctic and Antarctic regions because they're too cold and no plants. 2) He thought their jumps were huge leaps instead of hops. 3) Answers will vary. 4) Anwers will vary but may include legs, eyes; breathe through holes in abdomen called spiracles; ears. 5) Answers will vary. 6) May think of using flies to eat eggs or some other natural control. Some may even think of traps or other devices to reduce their numbers.

Reindeer *(The Most Famous Deer of All)*

Vocabulary—1) fawn 2) antlers 3) stag 4) hooves 5) dense 6) sleigh 7) coarse 8) tundra 9) severe 10) lichen.

Comprehension—1) They have a thick fur undercoat with waterproof outer fur that traps air and insulates them. 2) Eating, transportation, clothing, tools, etc. 3) They dig through deep snow and uncover lichen, moss, and grass. 4) They are faster, don't have spots, and can be easily tamed. 5) Females have antlers, can be tamed, and have clicking bones in their feet.

Thinking—1) Answers will vary, but should show thought about value of features. 2) May say they can be tamed, pull sleighs, people depend on them, etc. 3) Anwers will vary but may include clicking hooves, hairy nose, female antlers, ranches. 4) Answers will vary.

Mice *(Our Worst Friend)*

Vocabulary—1) spoil 2) urine 3) attacked 4) items 5) scent 6) harvest 7) ancient 8) weird 9) disease 10) produce.

Comprehension—1) They chew stuff up, leave droppings and urine scent, and spoil food or cause disease. 2) Eat soap, glue, candles, cork. 3) Because their teeth keep growing too long. 4) Droppings found, odor, items chewed up.

Thinking—1) Carried by travelers from Asia to Europe and then crossed the oceans on ships to the Americas. 2) Cute due to looks or as a pet. Scary due to the diseases or odors and food spoiled. 3) Fox, coyote, squirrel, opossum, owls, hawks, eagles, raccoon, snakes, cats, dogs, cougar, etc. 4) Mice mark area with urine as a habit, so they will mark their cage as soon as you clean it up. 5) Answers will vary.

Enrichment Activities:
Teaching Ideas and Answer Key

1. **Mammal Word Search:** You may want to review the concept of mammals as outlined in the first paragraph with many of your students. It may also be helpful for those students who struggle with thinking of themselves as animals to help them classify things on Earth as animals, plants, or minerals. In addition to those two learning objectives, it's a goal of this activity to enhance their self-image as an intelligent animal capable of a difficult task. You may want to hint that ten animal names go up and down while only seven go across. *Bear* and *Raven* are end to end horizontally at the top and *Fox* is also horizontal. It is totally up to you whether you make this word search a contest individually or with partners, an assignment to do when time permits, or an accomplishment you want to reward.

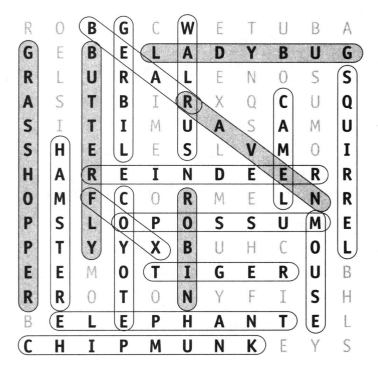

Mammals that should be circled: ⬭

Non-mammels that should be circled and colored pink:

2. **Best Friends Puzzle:** Many straight lines were used to design this puzzle to enable students with poorly developed motor skills to cut pieces more easily. One of the objectives in this lesson is for students to think about people as animals, too, even their best friends. You may want students to glue/paste pieces on a piece of paper to take home rather than keeping it as a puzzle. They could always turn it back into a puzzle again by cutting it out after it was glued down. It should be a fun activity.

Puzzle reads: **"MY BEST FRIENDS ARE ANIMALS."**

3. **What Animal Do I Admire?:** This is a language arts writing activity designed to guide students in thinking about animals they admire and why. You might choose to talk about characteristics of some species in a class discussion beforehand. You also may suggest what type of descriptive writing you're looking for (colorful adjectives or adverbs, action verbs, etc.). Students should be able to convince others that this animal deserves respect and illustrate why they are in awe of it.

4. **Scrambled Animals:** This is a language arts (spelling) activity intended to help students organize letters to correctly spell animal names. There are many ways you may want students to accomplish this task. They can do it independently, with a partner or two, or as a whole class using the overhead projector. You could make it a contest for individuals or groups, or you might choose to reward those completing the scramble. You might challenge students finishing early to make a scramble of animal names they can spell very well or utilize the list of twenty extra names at the bottom of the page. Some students may want to add animal names to their spelling list for the week or month, too.

   The names are as follows:

   1. gerbils
   2. foxes
   3. coyote
   4. tigers
   5. raven
   6. walrus
   7. grasshopper
   8. reindeer
   9. elephant
   10. mouse
   11. turtles
   12. bears
   13. opossum
   14. robins
   15. camels
   16. ladybug
   17. chipmunk
   18. rabbits
   19. squirrel
   20. butterfly

5. **You Be the Artist:** This is intended as an art activity where students get to develop their creativity. It also is presented in a game format for students to share their creation with others. You can add any additional requirements you want (color, shading, cut and paste, other shapes, etc.).

6. **Plan Ahead!:** This lesson is designed to help students develop better study/organizational skills. It may be a procedure you want them to often use before embarking on the research steps of a report. Many of the suggestions made are up to you to decide. Do you want them to work alone, in pairs, or groups? Do you want reports to be on different animals, or can more than one person report on a certain animal? Are they going to do a report or just learn resources for doing one?

7. **Animal Concentration:** How you use this lesson is going to depend on what choice of grouping you or students make. You need to make copies as per that grouping decision. Guide students as they discuss how they will play the game (if it's used as a game), how to time, score, cooperate, etc. Closure or follow-up activity may include a discussion of the relative speeds of various animals. How many of the animals listed are slower than people? Can we outswim any water animals? (Some humans can swim 5 mph.) Which animals shown are mammals? (Bats are!)

8. **Check Your Memory Bank:** You may want to use this activity as a pretest and use it again as a posttest. You may want to encourage students to discuss why they say yes or no first before citing evidence. Some qualifying answers are as follows:

   1. Yes, stones may chew them up.
   2. Yes, that's why they gnaw lots.
   3. Yes, across the classroom.
   4. No, they have flaps and glide.
   5. Yes, the longest gestation.
   6. Yes, some over 3,000 miles.
   7. No, name comes from Europe.
   8. No, many have brown or white.
   9. Yes, to hear in open and cool off.
   10. Yes, they eat harmful aphids.
   11. Yes, both have pouches for babies.
   12. No, it is full of fat (myth says water).
   13. Yes, extensive burrows under roots.
   14. Yes, each lays several clutches.
   15. No, they are large and intelligent.
   16. No, they raid ranches and catch pets.
   17. Yes, locusts is another name used.
   18. Yes, they may get loose and eat crops.
   19. No, reindeer females do (vixen).
   20. No, gray foxes do climb up to 20 ft.

9. **Animal Puzzle Pieces:** The puzzle pieces will fit together correctly only if they are cut out carefully. Even though the tiger, opossum, and camel are upside down in the puzzle, the words on them are upright. For students who are struggling, you could give these hints: The bear has the elephant's trunk on top of his head in the upper left-hand corner. Walrus is in the upper right-hand corner and is sitting on tiger's belly. Camel is at the bottom with fox on his belly. Raven's beak fits behind reindeer's horn. The assembled puzzle is intended to be a resource list of books about those animals. Students may enjoy making a similar puzzle using their own animal pictures, or they may want to use old magazines to make a collage of animals to list books or interesting facts.

10. **Crazy Captions:** This is a good opportunity for students to use their imagination and have fun writing. Guide students to ensure that the captions are fun and not negative in tone. A good example is "We have something in common—we both can fly!"

1. Mammal Word Search

Where do you think you fit into the whole picture of life on our planet, Earth? You are an animal. You are a **mammal.** Mammals are warm-blooded, have backbones, have some hair on their body. Female mammals feed their babies with milk from their body.

Of course, you are a very special mammal, with more brainpower than any bird, insect, reptile, fish, or other mammal. You can create and build things and solve problems far better than other animals.

Please use some of that great brainpower to spot and circle the animal names in the Word Search. (Use the list in the Word Box.) Then lightly color pink those circled animals' names that are *not* mammals. (Use light pink for non-mammals.)

Word Box

ROBIN	OPOSSUM
BEAR	LADYBUG
HARE	BUTTERFLY
GERBIL	SQUIRREL
TIGER	WALRUS
CAMEL	ELEPHANT
FOX	CHIPMUNK
HAMSTER	COYOTE
RAVEN	GRASSHOPPER
MOUSE	REINDEER

Word Search

R	O	B	G	C	W	E	T	U	B	A
G	E	B	E	L	A	D	Y	B	U	G
R	L	U	R	A	L	E	N	O	S	S
A	S	T	B	I	R	X	Q	C	U	Q
S	I	T	I	M	U	A	S	A	M	U
S	H	E	L	E	S	L	V	M	O	I
H	A	R	E	I	N	D	E	E	R	R
O	M	F	C	O	R	M	E	L	N	R
P	S	L	O	P	O	S	S	U	M	E
P	T	Y	Y	X	B	U	H	C	O	L
E	E	M	O	T	I	G	E	R	U	B
R	R	O	T	O	N	Y	F	I	S	H
B	E	L	E	P	H	A	N	T	E	L
C	H	I	P	M	U	N	K	E	Y	S

Name _____   Date _____

2. Best Friends Puzzle

Do you know who your best friends are? This jigsaw puzzle activity will help you find out who your friends really are. Follow these steps to make the puzzle:

1. Glue or paste this page onto a piece of construction paper to make it last.

2. Cut out all puzzle pieces very carefully so you can put the puzzle together.

3. Think about the saying on the puzzle and explain it to your friends nicely.

3. What Animal Do I Admire?

This is the name of an animal that I admire or think is great.

_____

Here are two things that I admire the most about this animal:

_____

_____

_____

I will now tell you what this animal is like and what makes me feel so proud of it. I'll explain why I respect it so much and then you will understand.

_____

_____

_____

_____

_____

_____

_____

_____

_____

_____

_____

_____

Name _____ Date _____

4. Scrambled Animals

The names of twenty animals are shown below. We don't know how their names got all scrambled up, but we are sure you can fix the problem. We sure would like the correct list as soon as possible. (Oh, in case you get stuck, there is a small helping list at the bottom of the page.)

1. sliberg _____

2. sofex _____

3. yootec _____

4. sigter _____

5. venar _____

6. sluwar _____

7. sharpgropes _____

8. dreenire _____

9. pelthane _____

10. osume_____

11. rustlet _____

12. arebs _____

13. sopsumo _____

14. sinorb _____

15. maslec _____

16. yabglud _____

17. punchmik _____

18. bartibs _____

19. quelrirs _____

20. trybutfel _____

bears, foxes, owls, seahorse, ostrich, tigers, mouse, skunk, walrus, raccoon, camels, wart hog, raven, ladybug, lion, coyote, groundhog, gerbils, elephant, roadrunner, chipmunk, cardinals, kangaroo, robins, panda, zebra, opossum, porcupine, rabbits, sea cucumber, koala bear, squirrel, jellyfish, butterfly, grasshopper, giraffe, hummingbird, reindeer, carp, turtles

Name _____ Date _____

5. You Be the Artist

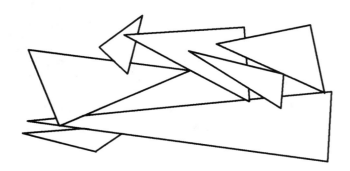

Triangles come in all kinds of shapes. Use only triangles to draw a mammal with four legs. Don't tell anyone what it is. Be sure you draw details like toes, eyes, ears, nose, tail, and body covering.

Now see if a friend can figure out what mammal you drew just by looking at your art work. If they can't figure it out, then you should give them clues. The following ideas would be good clues:

1. The best place to see my mammal is in _____.

2. This mammal loves to eat _____.

3. You are bigger/smaller than the adults in this mammal's family. (Choose one.)

4. The name of this mammal begins with the letter _____.

Name _____   Date _____

6. Plan Ahead!
Don't wait until the last minute!

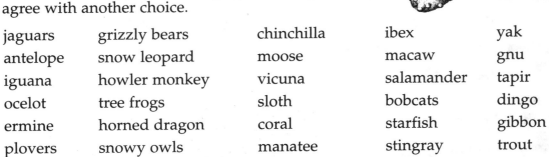

(A) You are getting ready to make an animal report for your class. If you work with a partner, all choices should be made together. The first step is to choose an animal from this list, or to get your teacher to agree with another choice.

jaguars	grizzly bears	chinchilla	ibex	yak
antelope	snow leopard	moose	macaw	gnu
iguana	howler monkey	vicuna	salamander	tapir
ocelot	tree frogs	sloth	bobcats	dingo
ermine	horned dragon	coral	starfish	gibbon
plovers	snowy owls	manatee	stingray	trout

(B) The second step is to choose which of the following ways will help you the most in gathering information to make the report a great one. Read all of the choices first, then write a #1 by the one you think is the best place to gather information, #2 by the second best, #3 for third best, etc.

_____ asking others   _____ watching TV   _____ magazines

_____ library books   _____ newspapers   _____ textbooks

_____ encyclopedias   _____ video   _____ computer

_____ at the zoo   _____ other (_____)

(C) Your third move is to write a four-step plan now for gathering the information.

1. _____

2. _____

3. _____

4. _____

Name _____ Date _____

7. Animal Concentration

You could work with one or two friends to see who can remember the most animals shown below. Follow these steps carefully:

1. Discuss the following rules and decide how you will play the game.

2. Each person needs a clean sheet of paper to write on after step #4.

3. Just look at the pictures of the animals on this page for one or two minutes.

4. Turn this paper over face down so nobody can see the pictures.

5. Secretly write the names of all the animals each of you remember seeing.

6. Turn this paper back over after everyone is done writing. You could give one point for each right answer and take away one point for any wrong ones.

7. You may want to play again adding the speed of animals for bonus points.

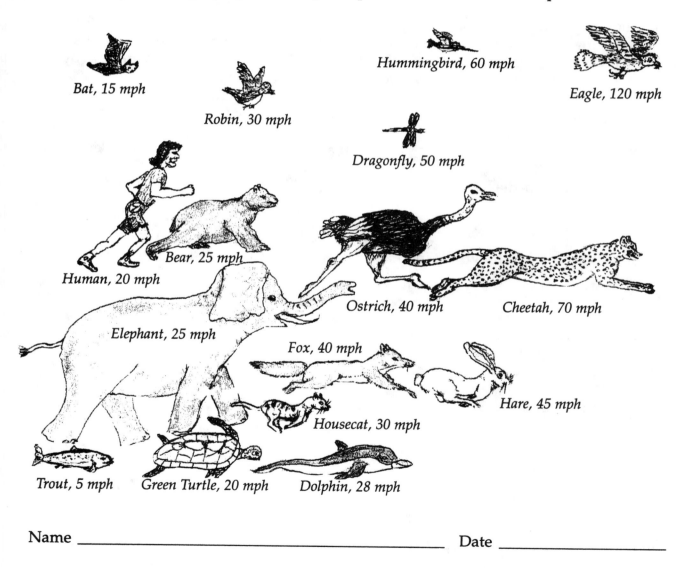

Bat, 15 mph

Robin, 30 mph

Hummingbird, 60 mph

Eagle, 120 mph

Dragonfly, 50 mph

Human, 20 mph

Bear, 25 mph

Ostrich, 40 mph

Cheetah, 70 mph

Elephant, 25 mph

Fox, 40 mph

Hare, 45 mph

Housecat, 30 mph

Trout, 5 mph   Green Turtle, 20 mph   Dolphin, 28 mph

© 2000 by The Center for Applied Research in Education

Name _____ Date _____

8. Check Your Memory Bank

The twenty statements below come from the stories you have read. Read each statement below and decide if you agree with it or not. Write *Yes* if you remember it is true, and write *No* if your memory tells you it is not true.

	YES	NO
1. A walrus swallows whole clams without chewing them.		
2. A mouse's front teeth grow for its whole life.		
3. Siberian tigers can pounce or leap over 30 feet.		
4. Flying squirrels flap their wings to fly over trees.		
5. Elephants carry their babies inside for about two years.		
6. Monarch butterflies often migrate thousands of miles.		
7. The robin got its name from its habit of robbing nests.		
8. Black bears got that name because they're very black.		
9. Hares need longer ears and legs than common rabbits.		
10. Ladybugs are beetles that are very helpful to people.		
11. Opossums and kangaroos are called marsupials.		
12. The camel's hump is full of water to use in the desert.		
13. Chipmunks dig burrows for their safe homes.		
14. Sea turtles lay hundreds of eggs to hatch in the sand.		
15. Ravens are small, foolish, black birds related to crows.		
16. Coyotes never bother any livestock or housepets.		
17. Short-horned grasshoppers are also called locusts.		
18. People in California aren't allowed to own gerbils.		
19. No species of female deer has antlers or horns.		
20. None of the canine (dog) species can climb trees.		

Name _____ Date _____

9. Animal Puzzle Pieces

Each animal below is a puzzle piece with the title of a book about the animal and the **author** of it. Glue this page on a backing paper. Cut out all animals carefully and fit them **together.** (*Hint:* All letters are upright.)

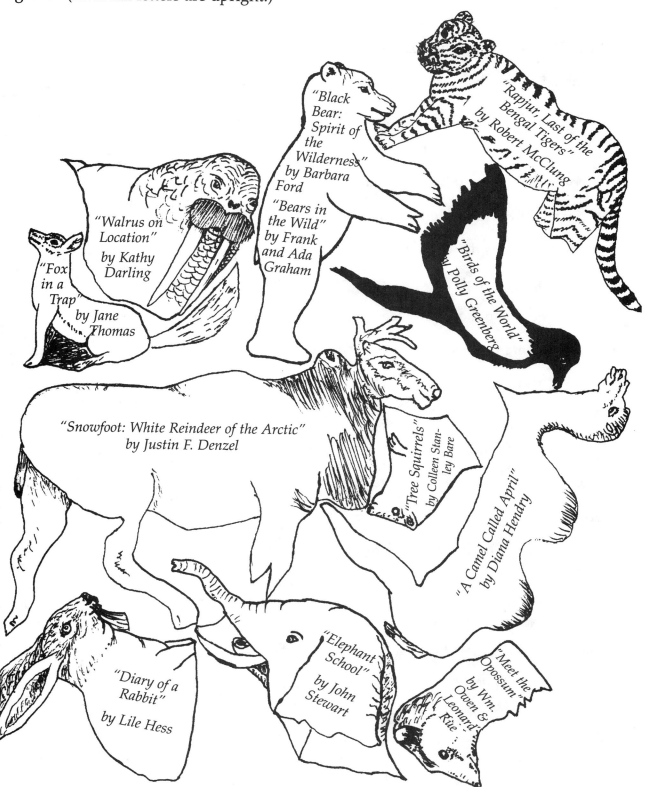

"Rapjur, Last of the Bengal Tigers" by Robert McClung

"Black Bear: Spirit of the Wilderness" by Barbara Ford

"Bears in the Wild" by Frank and Ada Graham

"Walrus on Location" by Kathy Darling

"Fox in a Trap" by Jane Thomas

"Birds of the World" by Polly Greenberg

"Snowfoot: White Reindeer of the Arctic" by Justin F. Denzel

"Tree Squirrels" by Colleen Stanley Bare

"A Camel Called April" by Diana Hendry

"Diary of a Rabbit" by Lile Hess

"Elephant School" by John Stewart

"Meet the Opossum" by Wm. Owen & Leonard Rue

10. Crazy Captions

You wrote some captions in early lessons and know that a caption tells about a picture. The captions you write for the pictures below should tell what the animals are doing, feeling, thinking, or saying to us. Write what you feel the picture is saying, and please do not write anything bad about anyone. Make it interesting and have fun!

Name _____ Date _____

Reading Level 4

Before Reading the Story:
New Vocabulary and Questions to Ask

1. Save the Giant Panda

New Vocabulary:

bamboo	scientists
endangered	severe
extinct	shy
future	starved
leopard	

Questions to Ask:

Have any of you seen a giant panda?
What family of animals do they belong to?
Where do the wild giant pandas live?
What do they like to eat?
Why are they an endangered species?

2. Hold on, Sea Horse

New Vocabulary:

aquarium	protrude
dorsal	rigid
emerge	shallow
prehensile	snout

Questions to Ask:

What sea creature's head is like a horse's?
What chess piece do sea horses look like?
What do you think sea horses eat?
Did you know the males have the babies?

3. I Wouldn't Eat that Cucumber

New Vocabulary:

cylinder	temperate
extract	tentacles
organisms	tropical

Questions to Ask:

Have any of you seen sea cucumbers?
Who thinks they are animals? Plants?
How do you think they eat?
Do you think they have any enemies?

4. Our Most Popular State Bird

New Vocabulary:

brood	migrate
crest	nuisance
incubates	popular
mate	

Questions to Ask:

What bird is a state bird in seven states?
Why is the cardinal so popular?
"Cardinal" is also a color. What color?
Where could they get food if snow falls?

5. The Really Big Bird

New Vocabulary:

comparison	predator
durable	scarce
gizzard	stride
plume	viciously

Questions to Ask:

What is the biggest bird in the world?
Do humans use ostriches for anything? What?
What do you think ostriches eat?
Do you think ostriches are endangered?

6. The Greatest Marsupial

New Vocabulary:

arid	mobs
dingo	pasture

Questions to Ask:

Do you know what a marsupial is?
Where do the wild kangaroos live?

| joey | ranchers | Why would people there call them pests? |
| marsupial | unofficial | What's a joey, and what's odd about it? |

7. A Cute Australian

New Vocabulary:		*Questions to Ask:*
dense	nursing	How much do you know about koalas?
eucalyptus	pelt	How many of you think koalas are bears?
groves	slaughtered	How are koalas like kangaroos?
hint	survive	What do you think koalas eat?
minerals	tourist	Why have koalas become endangered?

8. The Smallest, Brightest Birds

New Vocabulary:		*Questions to Ask:*
beak	nectar	Have you ever watched hummingbirds?
camouflaged	pollen	What did you see that amazed you?
cobweb	ranges	Have you ever seen a hummer's nest?
dart	slender	Does anyone know what hummingbirds eat?
hover		What do people put in hummingbirds' feeders?

9. The World's Tallest Animal

New Vocabulary:		*Questions to Ask:*
cud	nurse	What is the tallest animal in the world?
forelegs	savanna	Do giraffes all look pretty much alike?
gait	strands	What is their main food?
mane	tawny	How would a giraffe defend itself?

10. Watch Out for Jellyfish!

New Vocabulary:		*Questions to Ask:*
biologist	medusa	How many of you have seen jellyfish?
colony	minnow	What do they look like?
diameter	plankton	Are jellyfish dangerous? How?
hazard	toxin	What do you think they eat?
marine		Do you know of Portuguese man-of-war?

11. Whose Stomping Ground Is It?

New Vocabulary:		*Questions to Ask:*
carrion	musk	Are skunks good or bad creatures?
dye	nocturnal	Do they have any enemies?
emit	species	Can baby skunks spray you?
glands	whiff	Do you know how to get rid of the smell?
hibernate		What is a safe "no spray" distance?

12. A Prickly Mammal

New Vocabulary:

barb	quills
herbivore	rodents
marten	thrash
perspiration	

Questions to Ask:

Have any of you seen a porcupine?
What do you know about porcupines?
Do porcupines have any enemies?
Can they really throw quills at us?

13. The Horse Tigers

New Vocabulary:

colt	mare
filly	native
foals	plains
graze	ranch
mane	stallion

Questions to Ask:

What are some wild horses called?
How many of you think zebras all look alike?
Where do wild zebras live?
Who are the zebras' main enemies?
How can zebras be saved from extinction?

14. Barn Owls Don't Hoot

New Vocabulary:

down	roost
pellet	rotate
prey	symbol
rodents	talons

Questions to Ask:

How many of you have ever seen an owl?
What things do you know about owls?
What do owls eat, and how do they catch it?
What sense is most important for owls?

15. Is He Washing for Dinner?

New Vocabulary:

colonists	myth
coop	observation
fend	quest
gestation	survive

Questions to Ask:

What critter has a mask and rings on its tail?
What is so cute about raccoons?
What stories or myths have you heard?
What are baby raccoons called?
Do baby raccoons have the masks and rings?

16. King of the Beasts

New Vocabulary:

admire	mane
habitat	pregnant
lioness	prey
litter	pride

Questions to Ask:

What animal is "King of the Beasts"?
Do you think lions are the kings? Why?
What's a pride? Do other cats live in prides?
Are lions an endangered species?

17. Warts Can Be Beautiful

New Vocabulary:

boar	sow
diurnal	suckle

Questions to Ask:

What kind of animal is Pumbaa?
Where in the world do wild wart hogs live?

huddle	tasseled	Why do people feel wart hogs are ugly?
safari	theory	Why do you think wart hogs crawl to eat?
sounder	visible	Why do you think people hunt wart hogs?

18. Beep-beep!

New Vocabulary: *Questions to Ask:*

alert	fangs	How many of you like the roadrunner cartoons?
crude	maximum	How do roadrunners escape predators?
design	streamlined	What do roadrunners usually eat?
diet	zigzag	How do you think roadrunners got their name?

19. Could a Woodchuck Chuck Wood?

New Vocabulary: *Questions to Ask:*

alfalfa	rumpled	Do you know a woodchuck tongue-twister?
chuck	shrill	What other name is used for woodchucks?
complex	superstition	What do woodchucks eat? In the winter?
excavate	torpor	How do woodchucks sound an alarm signal?
haunches	venture	Do farmers dislike woodchucks? Why?

20. A Great Fish Story

New Vocabulary: *Questions to Ask:*

adapted	koi	Have any of you ever seen carp? Goldfish?
barbels	mussels	Have carp been in America a long time?
bask	probe	How big do you think carp get? Goldfish?
fry	spawn	Why do many people who fish dislike carp?
import	value	Have you ever eaten carp? Would you?

1. Save the Giant Panda

I want you to meet a giant panda. She lives in a bamboo forest in China. You may have seen stuffed teddy bears that look a lot like her. These giant pandas are often called bears because of their looks, walk, and those teddy bears. They really belong in the raccoon family, not the bear family. Most people are very surprised when they find out pandas are not bears. Bears eat meat, but giant pandas do not. Giant pandas have a thumb very much like the raccoon's. They can use this thumb to grasp bamboo to eat it more easily.

Giant pandas are in danger of becoming extinct (ek stingkt), which means no more of them would be living. People call this an endangered species. There are only a few hundred pandas left now. The main reason so few of them are still living is because of the poor food supply. As I told you, they eat bamboo. Many of their bamboo forests have been turned into farmland for Chinese people to grow food for themselves. Some new bamboo forests are way on the other side of China's villages and farming valleys. The pandas are afraid to cross those areas to get to that new bamboo. Each panda spends fifteen hours a day eating about 25 to 40 pounds of bamboo. There isn't enough bamboo now to feed many of them. They eat a few bird eggs and berries, but there isn't enough food to keep all of them alive.

The giant pandas can climb trees very well to escape leopards and brown bears that want to eat them. They depend on their great hearing to know when any enemies are trying to sneak up on them. You may

(Save the Giant Panda, *continued*)

have noticed their large ears. They can hear even the softest paws sneaking through the forest. If they hear any strange sound, they stand their full 4-1/2 feet tall and listen and sniff carefully. They can get up a tree to safety pretty fast. They also have a thick fur coat that helps them move quietly. That waterproof fur also helps them stay warm in the cold, wet forest.

The panda at the left is only ten months old. We call him Spunky because he is so brave and is not shy like most pandas. Like most giant panda babies, he was only the size of his mom's ear when he was born. He was 6 inches long and weighed 3 ounces at birth. Spunky will stay with his mom for about a year and a half until he is big enough to take care of himself. That means giant panda mothers can only have one baby every two years. Some of the giant pandas that were taken to live in a zoo have not had any babies.

The people of China have set aside special areas of bamboo forest for more giant pandas to be safe. They are also being very severe with any people they catch hunting for pandas. Scientists are working on getting pandas across the valley to the new forests before too many pandas starve. Their current bamboo forest is likely to be gone by the year 2030. Now you know more about giant pandas and the reasons they are an endangered species. Perhaps you know a way to help Spunky and other young pandas to grow up.

Save the Giant Panda

Vocabulary Checkup Write the words from the box on the correct blanks.

bamboo	endangered	extinct	future	leopard
scientists	severe	shy	starved	

1. The time that is to come after the present is the _____.

2. A wild cat-like animal is the _____.

3. Animals no longer living are _____.

4. _____ means in danger of being extinct.

5. _____ means strict or harsh treatment.

6. Bashful or timid around others is to be _____.

7. _____ are people who are experts in science.

8. A tree-like plant with hollow stems is _____.

9. _____ means to have suffered and died from hunger.

Comprehension You may need to look back at the story to answer the questions correctly.

1. Giant pandas belong in the same family with _____.

2. The main food eaten by giant pandas is _____.

3. Giant pandas eat _____ to _____ pounds of bamboo each day.

4. Giant pandas tell when an enemy is coming by using their _____.

5. To escape from enemies, pandas _____.

6. Newborn baby pandas are about the size of their mother's _____.

7. Pandas have a _____ to keep them warm and dry.

8. The giant pandas' natural home is in the country of _____.

Name _____ Date _____

Save the Giant Panda

Thinking About Giant Pandas Think carefully before answering these questions.

1. If pandas are so shy, how do you think they are being studied for this story?

_____

_____

_____.

2. Why do you think most people believe giant pandas are bears?

_____

_____

_____.

3. What do you believe scientists should do next to save the giant pandas?

_____

_____

_____.

4. Why do you think it is so bad for any animal species to become extinct?

_____

_____

_____.

Check It Out Find out about
  Bamboo
  Red pandas
  Kinkajous
  Ringtail or cacomistle

Name _____ Date _____

2. Hold on, Sea Horse

Is that a chess piece in your aquarium? Oh, sorry, but I can see now that you have one of those sea horses. I heard that the sea horse belongs in the fish family with other pipefish. It is called a sea horse because its head looks like that of a little horse. There are about fifty species of sea horses in the shallow, warmer waters of the oceans. They range in size from 1 to 12 inches (5 to 30 centimeters) long and have spiny plates covering their body. These bony plates are rigid enough to protect them. Some can change from black and gray to purple and yellow to blend with their surroundings in a few seconds to hide from predators. They are so bony that crabs are about the only real enemies they have. Of course, some people take a few to put them in aquariums.

Sea horses have a long tail that they use to grab sea plants. This is called a prehensile tail. They can stay in one place by wrapping that prehensile tail around seaweed and holding on. They beat their dorsal fin as fast as thirty-five times per second in order to keep their body in an upright position. Sea horses are very poor swimmers, but they can wiggle their dorsal fins to move around. They must depend on the current if they have to travel a long distance to get food. They have a small mouth at the end of their long snout. They usually eat by sucking water into their mouth and filtering out plankton, which is their main food. They can also suck up tiny fish that swim within a couple inches of their mouth.

The crazy eyes of the sea horse protrude (stick out) from the sides of its head so it can spot prey or predators from behind it as well as in front. The eyes can move different directions at the same time to help the sea

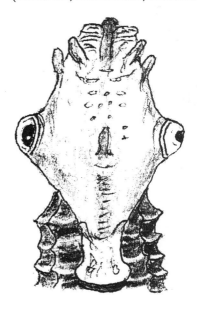

horse see in a full circle. Even the 1-inch-long pygmy sea horse has eyes like that. The 14-inch-long Australian sea horse's eyes look weird as they protrude and look around.

The most amazing thing about the sea horse is not its looks, however. The male sea horse lets the female snuggle up beside him to lay her eggs in his pouch. The female lays as many as 100 eggs into a pouch on the belly of the male. Females will fight over the males to see who gets to lay her eggs in the male's pouch. The male will carry the eggs for two weeks until they hatch. The babies then feed inside his pouch as he carries the bulge of about fifty or more babies around. It seems strange to me, but the male is the one who looks pregnant. He is! When the babies are ready to emerge from his pouch, he gives them a little squeeze out through the same opening where the female put the eggs in a few weeks ago. The squeeze helps the babies as they emerge to make it to the top of the water to take a gulp of air to fill their swimming bladder. The half-inch-long babies look a lot like their parents when they emerge, and they are on their own already. They may eat thousands of tiny baby shrimp each day, so they will be fully grown before they are one year old. Soon the males will be carrying babies in their own pouches, so it looks like we are in no danger of running out of these cute little "horses of the sea."

Hold on, Sea Horse

Vocabulary Checkup Write the words from the box on the correct blanks.

aquarium	dorsal	emerge	prehensile
protrude	rigid	shallow	snout

1. Something that is stiff and doesn't bend easily is _____.

2. A long nose and jaw area on an animal is called a _____.

3. To come out into view is to _____.

4. To stick out farther than the surrounding area is to _____.

5. Tails that grab and hold on are _____.

6. A glass-sided container for organisms is an _____.

7. Water or anything lacking depth is called _____.

8. A fin or anything located along the back is _____.

Comprehension You may need to look back at the story to answer the questions correctly.

1. Why do sea horses depend on the current to move?

_____

2. The sea horse got its name from

_____.

3. The main sea predators of sea horses are _____, but the sea horses can hide from them by _____.

4. A sea horse can spot prey in all directions because

_____.

5. A sea horse can even catch tiny sea animals by

_____

_____

Name _____ Date _____

Hold on, Sea Horse

Thinking About Sea Horses Think carefully before answering the questions.

1. What did you find odd about the body of sea horses?

   _____

   _____

   _____

2. Why do you think people want sea horses for their salt water aquariums?

   _____

   _____

   _____

3. What is very unusual about the way sea horses produce their babies?

   _____

   _____

   _____

4. What do you think is the sea horse's most important defense against predators?

   _____

   _____

   _____

5. Think of at least two good reasons why sea horses aren't likely to become extinct.

   _____

   _____

   _____

Check It Out Find out about

    Pipefishes

    Shrimp

    Sticklebacks

    Plankton

Name _____ Date _____

3. I Wouldn't Eat that Cucumber

I learned about strange critters called sea cucumbers while I was scuba diving near Hawaii. I thought they looked like pickles or big cucumbers as they laid on their side on the bottom of the sea. Their bodies look like cylinders or tubes. They are in the same group with sand dollars, sea urchins, and starfish. It is hard to believe sea cucumbers are related to starfish since they look so different. About 500 different species (kinds) live in the ocean. Scientists say the temperate species grow less than a foot long. The tropical species I saw were at least 3 feet (91 centimeters) long. There are hundreds of them if you dive about 100 feet deep.

I have noticed that sea cucumbers have a mouth at one end surrounded by about twenty arms or tentacles. I saw some reach out with their stretchy tentacles to grab bits of food and push it into their mouth. I have even seen one shove mud and sand into its mouth. Scientists say sea cucumbers can extract (pull out) very small organisms from the mud. I just thought they were quite lazy, lying around eating whatever little critters floated by or landed on the sea floor. Then I saw some sea cucumbers creeping along the sea floor. They have developed five double rows of tube feet down their side and can use them to walk slowly, searching for food. Next I saw a cucumber drop something that looked like eggs onto the bottom. When I checked a few days later, I saw that the eggs had hatched into some little worm-like sea cucumbers. Then they began moving around on the bottom eating.

There were many different colors of sea cucumbers around. Some were half buried on the bottom with the tentacles sticking up. I saw some floating along on the current and wondered if they could actually swim. I asked some other divers if any of them had ever eaten one of those sea cucumbers. One told me how she had tried once, but it tasted bitter and

was too prickly and tough. She also told me that her brother had heard that in China they dry sea cucumbers and use them in soup. We figured out that sea cucumbers probably don't have many enemies in the sea, so they will be around for a long time.

The more I looked at the sea cucumbers, the more I wondered if these strange things were plants or animals. I got a book and found out that they have a system for breathing by taking water in and getting oxygen from it before spitting it out. They have nerves in a ring around the mouth although they don't seem to have a brain to control them. They have blood which is pushed through the cucumber to carry oxygen and food to all of the cells. There are male and female cucumbers, and they do produce babies that grow up to look like their parents. I know cucumbers can move their tentacle-like arms to feed themselves. I read about how some sea cucumbers can even spit out their breathing sacs, digestive tubes, and other organs if a predator disturbs them. The predator eats those organs and leaves the rest of the sea cucumber alone. In a few days the sea cucumber grows new organs inside itself and lives on. Now I can see why scientists decided that these sea cucumbers that look like plants are really amazing animals.

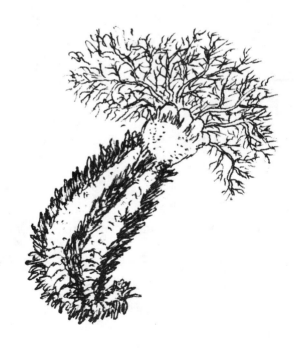

I Wouldn't Eat that Cucumber

Vocabulary Checkup Write the words from the box on the correct blanks.

cylinder	extract	organisms	temperate
tentacles	tropical	unique	

1. Some animals' long, flexible arms are called _____.

2. Individual plants or animals are called _____.

3. A _____ is tube shaped.

4. To _____ is to pull, draw, or separate out.

5. Anything that is unusual or one of a kind is _____.

6. A mild climate without being too hot or cold is _____.

7. Anything in the climate near the Equator is called _____.

Comprehension You may need to look back at the story to answer the questions correctly.

1. What do sea cucumbers look like? _____

_____

_____

2. Do any animals eat sea cucumbers? _____ What?

_____

_____

3. Two ways that sea cucumbers eat are to _____

and _____

_____.

4. What are three other animals in the same group with the sea cucumbers?

_____

_____

Name _____ Date _____

I Wouldn't Eat that Cucumber

Thinking About Sea Cucumbers Think carefully before answering the questions.

1. What made divers think sea cucumbers were lazy?

   _____

2. Why aren't sea cucumbers very likely to become extinct?

   _____

3. Do you think you would like dried sea cucumbers in your soup? _____
   Why? _____

4. Explain how you think sea cucumbers would swim.

   _____

5. Why are sea cucumbers classified as animals even though they look like plants?

   _____

Fact or Opinion Print an **F** for facts and print an **O** for opinions.

_____ 1. Sea cucumbers have tentacles around their mouth.

_____ 2. Sea cucumbers can't crawl very well.

_____ 3. Sea cucumbers are in the same science grouping with starfish.

_____ 4. Sea cucumbers are very strange animals.

_____ 5. Sea cucumbers' bodies are shaped like a cylinder or tube.

_____ 6. Sometimes sea cucumbers shove mud in their mouth.

_____ 7. Sea cucumbers look like big pickles.

Check It Out Find out about
Starfish
Sea urchins
Sea lilies
Sea anemones

© 2000 by The Center for Applied Research in Education

Name _____ Date _____

4. Our Most Popular State Bird

Cardinals are a popular American songbird usually seen more on the east side of the Mississippi River. They get their name from the red color of the robes of Catholic cardinals. The males are cardinal red with a black mask around the eyes and black beard under their beak. Females are more difficult to spot since they are brown with a touch of red on the wing and tail feathers. A crest of feathers on both looks like a pointed hat. Cardinals can raise and lower that crest of feathers anytime they want to. At about 8 inches (20 centimeters) long, they are the largest members of the finch family.

The song of the cardinals may begin with a simple, sharp *chip-chip*. Then you may hear *pret-tee, pret-tee, wheeet-wheeet, watch here-watch here, chip.* Cardinals are greatly appreciated birds for their beautiful singing as well as their color. The male and female mate for life and sing well together. The male may begin a song; then his mate will finish the second part. Then it is her turn to sing the first part and his turn to finish the song. Sometimes they will sing a solo.

Cardinals eat many insects that humans consider a nuisance or pest. They eat beetles, caterpillars, grasshoppers, worms, and even a few slugs, too. Cardinals love seeds from weeds, flowers, and fruits. They eat wild berries and fruit that is too ripe. Since they don't migrate south in the winter, they depend on feeding stations and waste grains in farm fields.

They seem to like to eat the sunflower seeds and corn from the birdfeeder first.

The pair of cardinals works together to build a nest out of grass, weeds, and old leaves in brush or briar patches. The female lays three to five eggs and incubates them for almost two weeks. It is a good thing the female is not bright red because she remains on the nest for those two weeks. The male brings his mate food during this time and seems to give her a kiss with each bite. Both parents feed their brood until the young are old enough to leave the nest. The pair may raise two or three broods in a nesting season.

These beautiful birds are now protected from hunters by laws, but people used to trap them to sell as songbirds or to harvest the bright red feathers to decorate women's hats. Cardinals are so pretty and such beautiful singers that seven states have chosen the cardinal as their state bird.

Now you know what cardinals look like, what their habits are, and what the song of the cardinal sounds like. You could attract cardinals to your school or your own back yard. One way to invite them to come close is by placing a feeder with cracked corn and sunflower seeds in a good spot. It is a good idea to hang the feeder so squirrels and cats can't get to it. Another good way to invite cardinals and other songbirds to come close is with pinecone feeders. Mix some oatmeal, seeds, or corn meal with peanut butter and stuff the mix into spaces in a pinecone. You may want to push some sunflower seeds into the cracks, too. Tie a string to the end of your pinecone and hang it where the birds can find it. You may want to check out some books to identify all of the different kinds of birds you will see coming to your new feeding stations.

Our Most Popular State Bird

Vocabulary Checkup Write the words from the box on the correct blanks.

brood	crest	incubates	mate
migrate	nuisance	popular	

You can see the _____ of feathers on the female as she sits on the nest and _____ the eggs to raise another _____ of young. Her _____ brings her some of the bugs that are a _____ or pest to people. It is easy to see why cardinals are _____ and well liked.

They will not _____ south this winter, so please feed them.

Fact or Opinion? Print **F** besides statements that can be proven true or as fact. Print **O** besides statements that are just a belief or opinion.

_____ 1. The cardinal is a large member of the finch family of birds.

_____ 2. Cardinals are the most popular songbirds in seven states in America.

_____ 3. Cardinals always eat the sunflower seeds from the feeder first.

_____ 4. Cardinals are useful to people in several ways.

_____ 5. Cardinals may be more useful than barn owls.

Comprehension You may need to look back at the story to answer the questions correctly.

1. What are two reasons that people used to catch cardinals?

_____

_____

2. What are some ways cardinal parents work together to raise their brood?

_____

_____

_____

Name _____ Date _____

Our Most Popular State Bird

3. How are cardinals of benefit to people?

_____

_____

4. What would be the best foods to use in a feeding station to attract cardinals?

_____

_____

Thinking About Cardinals Think carefully before answering the questions.

1. How is it easy to tell which is the male cardinal?

_____

_____

2. Why is it a good thing that the female cardinal isn't so brightly colored?

_____

_____

3. It is important for people to have birdfeeders in winter because

_____

_____.

4. The cardinal is the state bird in ___ states. Why do you think so many states chose it?

_____

_____

Name _____ Date _____

5. The Really Big Bird

I've always admired the ostrich, the largest living bird. They are so large and strong that people ride them in races! Some of them stand as tall as 10 feet (3 meters), and they can weigh over 345 pounds (156 kilograms). Wild ones live in flocks on plains and deserts in Africa. They are the only birds that have just two toes on each foot. Their long neck, long legs, and small head have only some little hair-like feathers. The female's body, tail, and wings have dull brown feathers. The male's body has black feathers, while the small wings and tail have plumes of white feathers on them. Both males and females have keen eyesight and hearing, but their sense of smell is not very good, although they somehow find water even in desert areas. People who live there often follow ostrich tracks to find water.

Ostriches cannot fly because their wings are so small in comparison to their body weight. They don't hop like most birds. They walk much like we do, but their long legs enable them to take 15-foot (4.6-meter) strides. They can reach speeds up to 43 miles per hour (70 kilometers per hour) to escape predators, and they can run 30 miles per hour (50 kilometers per hour) for twenty or thirty minutes. If the predator corners them, they can kick viciously using the claws on their toes as weapons. Adult ostriches have killed hyenas and young lions by kicking and slashing with that claw. If a predator threatens a nest of eggs or ostrich chicks, the father and mother will fight fiercely to defend them. Those strong leg muscles can send a hyena flying through the air. Young chicks are easy prey for young lions, but if the mother is nearby the cub risks being slashed open by her kicking claw. Ostriches have even been known to attack Jeeps and trucks if they thought they were after their chicks.

There is an old story about ostriches burying their head in the sand when they get scared. I think the story started when people saw ostriches grazing from a distance and couldn't see their heads. They can hide somewhat by lying down and stretching their long neck out flat on the sand, as shown below. They also teach chicks this trick.

I learned that a male ostrich usually has three wives. Males can make a roaring sound like a lion during mating season, but with a hissing sound added to it. The male also makes the nest for his wives by digging a shallow hole in sandy soil. His wives each lay as many as ten eggs in it. One ostrich egg is as big as twenty chicken eggs. The ostrich has a large body to cover those eggs, but some eggs on the edge of the nest will not be kept warm enough to hatch. A male incubates the eggs all night, and his wives keep them warm during the daytime. In about six weeks the babies hatch and start running. By one month old, a baby can run as fast as an adult. Several broods of babies will join together and be protected by a couple of large adults while they search for seeds, leaves, buds, and bugs to eat. Ostriches will eat mice, and as they swallow the lumps go down their neck. A baby has a gizzard like its parents, so it also eats dirt and pebbles for grinding up food in the gizzard for easier digestion in the stomach.

There were huge flocks of ostriches running around Africa and Asia hundreds of years ago. People took their eggs to eat and killed ostriches for their feathers, which reduced the flocks some. About 100 years ago, ostrich plumes became popular on women's hats and clothing. The ostrich disappeared totally in Asia, and flocks became scarce in Africa. Many farmers began raising them in Africa to harvest feathers twice a year from live birds. When demand for plumes disappeared, farmers still raised them for their skin, which is used to make durable leather boots and purses. A few farmers in the United States and Canada have begun to raise these big birds for meat and leather. Farm ostriches have lived to be seventy years old. Scientists fear that all wild ostriches may disappear someday since there are less than 150,000 left in Africa.

The Really Big Bird

Vocabulary Checkup Write the words from the box on the correct blanks.

comparison	durable	gizzard	predator
plume	scarce	stride	viciously

1. Ostriches can savagely, ferociously, or _____ attack.

2. A single long step is called a _____.

3. An especially large feather used for decorating is a _____.

4. An animal that preys on others for food is a _____.

5. Something _____ is likely to last and not wear out easily.

6. Anything _____ is rare since there are not enough of them.

7. The _____ is where a bird's food is ground up.

8. We find likeness and difference to make a _____.

Comprehension You may need to look back at the story to answer the questions correctly.

1. Exactly where do wild ostriches live? _____
   _____

2. How and why did wild ostriches become so scarce about 100 years ago?
   _____
   _____

3. Ostriches can run twice as fast as any person. What is the main reason ostriches can run so fast?
   _____
   _____

4. Why can't ostriches fly? _____
   _____

Name _____ Date _____

The Really Big Bird

Fact or Opinion? Print **F** besides statements that can be proven true or as fact. Print **O** besides statements that are just a belief or opinion.

_____ 1. The ostrich is the largest living bird people know about.

_____ 2. Ostriches are the most handsome birds on our planet.

_____ 3. Ostriches can make some sounds at times.

_____ 4. Ostrich eggs can be as much as twenty times as big as chickens' eggs.

_____ 5. The male helps sit on as many as thirty eggs at a time.

_____ 6. An ostrich hides its head in the sand when it gets scared.

_____ 7. Ostriches can sprint over 40 miles per hour.

Thinking About Ostriches Think carefully before answering the questions.

1. Why do you think the story got started about an ostrich hiding its head in the sand?

   _____

   _____

2. Why were ostrich feathers very popular on women's clothing 100 years ago?

   _____

   _____

3. Think of a good way to hatch more eggs from an ostrich nest.

   _____

   _____

4. Tell why ostriches should (or should not) be protected today.

   _____

   _____

Check It Out Find out about

Rheas

Emus

Cassowaries

Kiwi

Moas

Name _____ Date _____

6. The Greatest Marsupial

Many people would love to go to Australia to see the wild kangaroos. About fifty species of kangaroos live in Australia and on nearby islands. The tiny rat kangaroos are the size of a small rabbit. Red and gray kangaroos may stand 7 feet (2 meters) tall and weigh nearly 200 pounds (80 kilograms), but the female is much smaller than the male. Some say their small head looks like a female deer's head. All have large powerful hind legs, small forelegs, and a strong tail used for balance and hopping. They have four toes on their hind feet. The two little toes are used as a comb to groom their hair. The two larger toes on the outside have sharp claws used in battles.

Kangaroos live in groups called mobs on the arid (or dry) interior. People often see as many as 100 of them in a mob. They graze on grass and leaves in the coolness of night. Kangaroos use their front feet to put food into their mouth. They rest in the heat of the day in holes they scrape out under shrubs or trees. They pant and lick themselves to cool off.

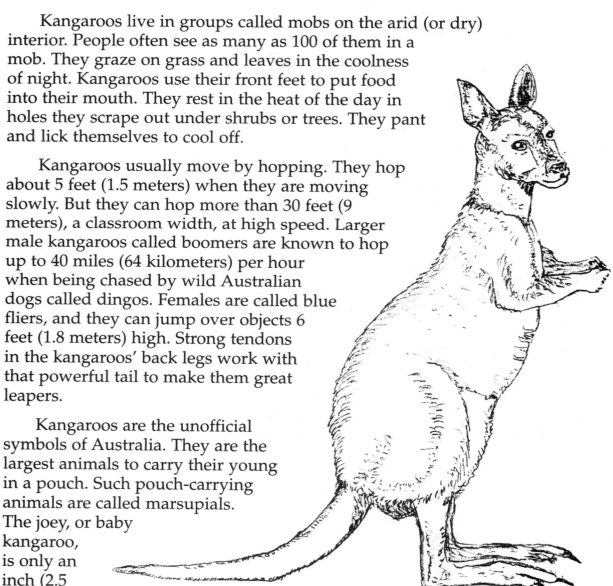

Kangaroos usually move by hopping. They hop about 5 feet (1.5 meters) when they are moving slowly. But they can hop more than 30 feet (9 meters), a classroom width, at high speed. Larger male kangaroos called boomers are known to hop up to 40 miles (64 kilometers) per hour when being chased by wild Australian dogs called dingos. Females are called blue fliers, and they can jump over objects 6 feet (1.8 meters) high. Strong tendons in the kangaroos' back legs work with that powerful tail to make them great leapers.

Kangaroos are the unofficial symbols of Australia. They are the largest animals to carry their young in a pouch. Such pouch-carrying animals are called marsupials. The joey, or baby kangaroo, is only an inch (2.5

centimeters) long when it's born. That is no bigger than your thumb! Mothers usually have a gestation period of one month, so the joey looks like a baby mouse when it is born. Its legs are strong enough to help it crawl up into the pouch, where it feeds on the mother's milk for the next seven or eight months. Sometimes a joey will return to its mother's pouch for safety until it is nearly a year old, but there is usually a new joey in there before that.

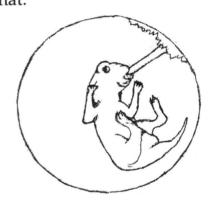

Humans are the only other major enemy kangaroos have (other than those dingos). Kangaroos were hunted for their meat to use in dog food and their hides to make shoes and purses years ago. Many ranchers killed kangaroos because they thought they were eating too much of the grass needed by their sheep or cattle. They couldn't find a way to fence the kangaroos out of the pasture. Scientists proved that ranchers didn't need to kill kangaroos to save their grasslands. Australia passed a law in 1973 stopping the export of any kangaroos or their parts so they wouldn't become extinct. Now they live as long as eighteen years in the wild and twenty-five years in zoos.

The Greatest Marsupial

Vocabulary Checkup Write the words from the box on the correct blanks.

arid	dingo	joey	marsupials
mobs	pasture	ranchers	unofficial

1. A _____ is an Australian wild dog.

2. A _____ is a baby kangaroo.

3. All _____ carry their babies in a pouch.

4. People raising livestock animals for a living are _____.

5. Not properly declared or claimed is _____.

6. Very dry land with little rainfall is called _____.

7. Large groups of kangaroos are called _____.

8. Grassy area where animals graze is a _____.

Comprehension You may need to look back at the story to answer the questions correctly.

1. What are the two statements of opinion in the first paragraph of the story?

   _____

   _____

2. Why do joeys stay in the mother's pouch for so many months?

   _____

   _____

3. Why do kangaroos eat mostly at night? _____

   _____

   _____

4. Large male kangaroos are called _____, and the
   female kangaroos are frequently called _____.

Name _____ Date _____

The Greatest Marsupial

Thinking About Kangaroos Think carefully before answering the questions.

1. Why do you think kangaroos stay in large groups called mobs?

   _____

2. How do you figure the scientists convinced ranchers that it wasn't necessary to kill kangaroos to save grassland for their cattle and sheep?

   _____

3. How do you think you could keep kangaroos from eating your animals' pasture?

   _____

   _____

4. How do you think a kangaroo would defend itself when attacked?

   _____

   _____

5. In your opinion, what is the most amazing thing about the kangaroo?

   _____

   _____

Reading Concepts Circle the letter of the correct answer.

Kangaroos are mammals because
   (a) they have long ears and strong tails.
   (b) they have hair and feed on mother's milk.
   (c) they have four legs and females have a pouch.

Check It Out Find out about

   Wallabies
   Rock kangaroos
   Tree kangaroos
   Marsupial wolves
      (thylacines)
   Marsupial moles

Name _____ Date _____

7. A Cute Australian

While I was talking to people from "down under" (which means from Australia), I asked them about the koala. It is a marsupial mammal since newborn are carried in a pouch. Some call it the pouched bear, but it isn't really a bear. It has a very short snout and large ears. Its dense (or thick) fur is light gray outside with white underneath. Koalas only have a hint of a tail. Adults grow to about 30 inches (76 centimeters) long, and weigh up to 30 pounds (14 kilograms). See the long fingers with claws for climbing?

The only food koalas eat is leaves and bark of the blue gum or eucalyptus (yoo ka lip' tis) tree. I learned that they can't survive without it. They eat about 2 pounds of eucalyptus leaves daily. They have cheek pouches like chipmunks and store some leaves to be chewed up later. The natives named them "koala," which means "no water." They never drink any water! They must get all of the water their body needs from those eucalyptus leaves.

The koalas stay high in their eucalyptus trees all of the time. When people have seen them on the ground, they noticed how awkwardly koalas waddled along. They move so slowly that some people thought they were members of the sloth family. They often hang upside down from limbs like a sloth does. Koalas sleep all day in the top of the eucalyptus tree and eat during the night. They are so slow and have no means of defense, so it's a good thing they stay in the tree most of the time. They will come to the ground to cross over to new feeding trees or to lick certain rocks for minerals. Unfortunately, sometimes tourist cars run over koalas at parks set up to protect them.

I learned koalas have one baby every other year. The baby is born after only a month inside its mother. It is not cute when it is born since it has no hair and is blind. At birth the baby is the size of your thumb nail. It will spend the next six months nursing and growing inside its mother's pouch. The tiny baby will nurse continually for the first few weeks. The baby will eat some of the mother's half-digested droppings until it can begin chewing on some of the eucalyptus leaves. The cub will spend another six months riding on its mother's back learning to find more leaves to eat.

Koalas nearly became extinct around 1900 due to a disease. Their soft fur was so valuable that hunters also slaughtered millions of them. More than 2 million koala pelts were sold in 1927 alone. Koalas are protected from being killed now, but they are threatened by the loss of eucalyptus trees in eastern Australia. Many brush fires destroy their habitat, and those fires are often set on purpose just to clear the land. People have also cleared away many eucalyptus groves for homes. I learned that it's difficult to raise koalas in zoos unless you can find just the right kind of trees to feed them. People are really worried about saving these cute critters for the future.

A Cute Australian

Vocabulary Checkup Write the words from the box on the correct blanks.

dense	eucalyptus	groves	hint	minerals
nursing	pelts	slaughtered	survive	tourist

1. Natural substances, not plants or animals, are _____.

2. Very thick or close together is _____.

3. The skins or hides of animals are called _____.

4. Killed in great numbers is _____.

5. The blue gum tree is also called the _____.

6. Small orchards or woods are also called _____.

7. A person going to an area to visit and see sights is a _____.

8. Babies drinking the milk of their mothers is called _____.

9. A helpful suggestion is a _____.

10. To continue to live through something is to _____.

Fact or Opinion? Print **F** besides statements that can be proven true or as fact. Print **O** besides statements that are just a belief or opinion.

_____ 1. Koalas look a lot like teddy bears.

_____ 2. Koalas have dense, grayish-white fur.

_____ 3. Koalas get very tired of eating nothing but eucalyptus leaves.

_____ 4. The koala is a marsupial because it has a pouch for its young.

_____ 5. The koala feels very safe up there in its eucalyptus tree.

_____ 6. Baby koalas are not cute at all.

_____ 7. Koalas don't drink water like most mammals.

Name _____ Date _____

A Cute Australian

Comprehension You may need to look back at the story to answer the questions correctly.

1. The name "koala" means _____.

2. The reason mother koalas can climb so well even with a baby on their back is due to

   _____.

3. The baby koala is quite helpless the first six months because _____

   _____.

4. What were the two main reasons koalas were endangered in the early 1900s?

   _____

5. The most recent threat to the koala species is the _____

   _____.

Thinking About Koalas Think carefully before answering the questions.

1. I think the reason koalas stay up in the eucalyptus trees all of the time is due to

   _____.

2. I think koalas probably learned to live on the water from the leaves because _____

   _____.

3. Why is Australia called "the land down under"? (*Hint:* See where it is on a map.)

   _____

4. How do you think you could convince people that koalas are not really bears?

   _____

Check It Out Find out about
Tasmanian devils
Bandicoots
Dasyure
Australia

Name _____   Date _____

8. The Smallest, Brightest Birds

Did you know hummingbirds only live in the Western World, meaning North and South America? There are more than 400 kinds of these brightly colored birds, but only 19 kinds are in the United States and Canada. Most of them live west of the Mississippi River. I've heard that humming coming from their wings as they move as fast as seventy beats per second. It's easy to figure out where hummingbirds got their name.

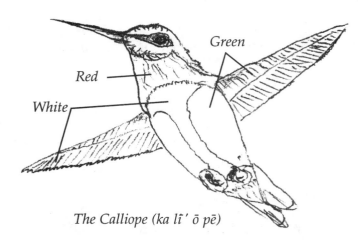

The Calliope (ka lĩ' ō pē)

The body of some hummingbirds is no larger than that of a bumblebee. Weight ranges from 0.1 ounce (3 grams) to 0.7 ounce (20 grams). The U.S. hummers are as short as 2 inches (5 centimeters) up to the length of 5 inches (13 centimeters). They more than make up for their small size with their bright red, orange, green, and blue colors that seem to change in the sunlight. Some species have only the males with these bright colors, but in many species the females are also colorful.

Hummingbirds could easily win any flying contest. They can fly in place (hover), dart sideways, and even fly backward when they want because their wings can beat 60 to 70 times per second. Their heart must beat about 600 times per minute, which is about eight times as fast as your heart is beating now. This energy used means they need to eat quite often. Their main food is nectar from the center of flowers, but they do eat some insects as well. Hummers grab insects while hovering, or they may find them inside the flower. Their beak is long and slender to reach deep inside the flower, and their tongue is forked to help them suck juices out. Many people hang hummingbird feeders out with one part sugar to four parts water to help feed them. Because hummingbirds transfer a dust of pollen from blossom to blossom, they help plants produce more fruit.

(The Smallest, Brightest Birds, *continued*)

Hummingbird nests are tiny works of art like the birds themselves. The nest is built from shreds of bark, grass, leaves, and other plant materials held together with cobwebs borrowed from spiders. The nest is camouflaged to blend in so well that a person or a predator could hardly see it. And the male is fearless in protecting the female sitting on their two eggs for two or three weeks. He will attack birds as large as hawks and crows if they get too near. The young leave the nest about three weeks after hatching. It is their turn to join the humming crowd pollinating flowers and giving everyone so much enjoyment.

This hummingbird nest is shown at its actual size. The two eggs are also the real size for a ruby-throated hummingbird. There is barely room in the nest for mother and two eggs. She could never feed more than two babies at a time anyway.

Hummingbirds spend most of their time eating nectar so they will have enough energy to fly around to find more nectar. They do find time to take several baths in a day, however. They also find time to chase each other and play-fight. Scientists feel they are playing more than they are really fighting since they never hurt each other. A hummingbird will use its bill to poke bigger birds threatening its nest. Hummingbirds take great care to not stick or injure each other during their chases and play-fighting.

The Smallest, Brightest Birds

Vocabulary Checkup Write the words from the box on the correct blanks.

beak	_____ threads spun by a spider
camouflaged	_____ a bird's bill
cobweb	_____ to move suddenly and rapidly
dart	_____ blended into scenery, hidden
hover	_____ the fine dust inside flowers
nectar	_____ very thin and long
pollen	_____ to fly in one place
ranges	_____ sweet fluid from flowers
slender	_____ varies or extends in a direction

Comprehension You may need to look back at the story to answer the questions correctly.

1. Hummingbirds get their name from _____

   _____

   _____

   _____.

2. All of the hummingbirds of the world live on the continents of _____

   _____.

3. Only _____ species of hummers live in the United States and Canada.

4. Hummingbirds help produce more fruit by spreading _____
   around from flower to flower.

5. Hummingbirds get nectar from flowers and eat a few _____, too.

© 2000 by The Center for Applied Research in Education

Name _____ Date _____

The Smallest, Brightest Birds

Thinking About Hummingbirds Think carefully before answering the questions.

1. The word "brightest" in the story title means _____
   _____.

2. The important ingredient hummers get from a feeder is _____.

3. What do you think makes hummingbirds brave enough to attack larger birds?
   _____
   _____
   _____

4. Why do you feel hummingbirds appear on so many things that are sold as art?
   _____
   _____
   _____

5. Why do you think hummingbirds chase and play-fight but don't stick each other
   with their bills?
   _____
   _____
   _____

Reading Concepts   Circle the letter of the best choice to complete the statement.

Hummingbirds are valuable little birds because

   (a) they fly very fast and attack big birds.

   (b) they are pretty, can hover, and are tiny.

   (c) they eat insects, pollinate flowers, and are
       fun to watch.

Name _____   Date _____

9. The World's Tallest Animal

Many of you probably thought of a giraffe as the tallest animal. At 18 feet (5 meters) tall, it is taller by 5 feet than the African elephant. The neck is 6 feet long, and the legs make up half of the height below the neck. Male giraffes only weigh about 3,000 pounds (1,400 kilograms), which means it would take four of them to equal an African elephant.

The giraffe's tawny (brownish-yellow) coat has patches of darker brown all over it. The markings on each giraffe are different, and scientists have yet to find two that look alike. These patches help camouflage giraffes as they stand in the shadows between trees. Giraffes have two or three bony bumps that look a little like horns on top of their head. They have a short-haired mane running down the ridge from the back of the head to the shoulders. Their 3-foot-long (91 centimeters) tail ends in long strands of black hair. Their hooves are split like those of a deer or a cow.

Giraffes live on the grassy plains called savannas in central Africa. They live in large groups but don't form permanent herds. Their main food is the leaves of the trees scattered on the savanna. A giraffe's tongue is over 17 inches (43 centimeters) long to help it reach leaves and pull them into its mouth. Giraffes can reach leaves that other animals can't. With their neck and tongue stretched as high as they can go, giraffes can reach well above the ceiling of most gymnasiums. The giraffe can wrap its tongue around small limbs and strip all of the leaves off into its mouth. Giraffes chew a cud like cows do. A cud is food that has gone to the stomach and been brought back up to be chewed longer. The male usually eats the leaves that are the highest. He saves the lower leaves for his wife and children. What a gentleman!

Giraffes split the forelegs apart so their long neck and tongue can reach the water to take a drink of water. Those long legs that make it difficult to drink the water are helpful in making the giraffe a fast runner. When giraffes are scared, they can gallop over 30 miles (48 kilometers) per hour. Their gait, or running style, makes them look like they're running in slow motion. Giraffes sleep standing up most of the time, but they can rest lying down.

The female giraffe carries her baby inside her for a year and three months. The calf may weigh 150 pounds (68 kilograms) and stand 6 feet (1.8 meters) tall at birth. The baby calf will nurse on the mother's milk for more than a year. The mothers often leave the whole group of calves alone in the brush while going in search of food for themselves. It is sad that about half of the calves will die before they are six months old because they aren't fast enough to escape lions, hyenas, and leopards. After calves are a year old, very few of them can be caught by the predators.

We have learned how giraffes use their great height and sharp eyes to watch for predators and escape. Lions sometimes kill big giraffes if they can catch them lying down. Giraffes can outrun lions or use their sharp hooves to defend both themselves and their calves. People of Africa have killed many giraffes for food and to make tools and ornaments. A few African ranches even raise giraffes for the meat and to supply zoos around the world. Giraffes can live to be twenty years old in captivity, even though their average lifespan in the wild is only five years.

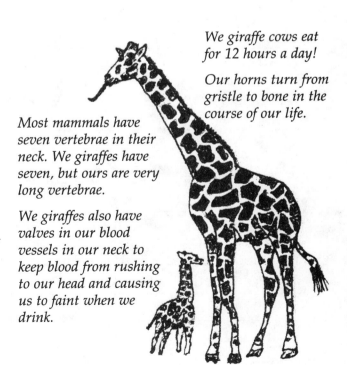

We giraffe cows eat for 12 hours a day!

Our horns turn from gristle to bone in the course of our life.

Most mammals have seven vertebrae in their neck. We giraffes have seven, but ours are very long vertebrae.

We giraffes also have valves in our blood vessels in our neck to keep blood from rushing to our head and causing us to faint when we drink.

The World's Tallest Animal

Vocabulary Checkup Write the words from the box on the correct blanks.

cud
forelegs
gait
mane
nurse
savanna
strands
tawny

_____ longer hair on the back of the neck

_____ to drink the mother's milk

_____ food chewed for a second time

_____ a running or walking style

_____ brownish-yellow color

_____ strips or threads of hair or fiber

_____ grasslands in central Africa

_____ an animal's front legs

Comprehension You may need to look back at the story to answer the questions correctly.

1. How do you know the giraffe is a mammal?

   _____

   _____

   _____

2. Why do giraffes seem to be running in slow motion?

   _____

   _____

3. What are the two biggest threats to a giraffe's life?

   _____

   _____

4. What are the main defenses of a giraffe? _____

   _____

   _____

5. Why does the giraffe need special valves in its neck to control blood flow?

   _____

   _____

Name _____ Date _____

The World's Tallest Animal

Thinking About Giraffes Think carefully before answering the questions.

1. Why do you think giraffes sleep standing up? _____

   _____

2. Why is it important that calves are 6 feet tall when they are born? (*Hint:* It has something to do with eating.)

   _____

   _____

3. Why did it say the males were being gentlemen? _____

   _____

   _____

Reading Concepts Circle the letter of the correct answer.

1. The main reason giraffes need to be tall is

   (a) to gallop faster than you think.   (b) to reach the leaves they eat.

   (c) to be the tallest animal.

2. The main food for giraffes is

   (a) bark.   (b) grass.   (c) leaves.

3. The markings on giraffes are all

   (a) the same.   (b) different.   (c) coming off.

4. The giraffe is a

   (a) carnivore.   (b) herbivore.   (c) omnivore.

Check It Out Find out about

Savannas

Okapis

Ossicorns (horns)

Acacia trees

Rumination

Front   *Hind*

Name _____   Date _____

10. Watch Out for Jellyfish!

The jellyfish is one of nature's strangest sea creatures. Marine biologists call them medusa, but we call them jellyfish because of the jelly-like material between the outer skin and inner organs. Many of them are colorless, but some are pale blue, pink, or light orange colored. Most jellyfish range in size from species no larger than a peanut to some in the Arctic regions that reach 8 feet in diameter (across), weigh almost 2,000 pounds, and have arms hanging down almost 200 feet long. However, there are also jellyfish as small as a pinhead.

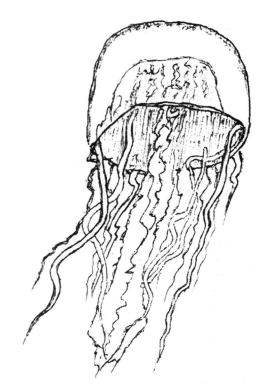

Most jellyfish are shaped like an umbrella or a lightbulb. Many will have tentacles hanging from the bottom edge. The mouth is underneath the center, and there are usually four arms around it to push food into the mouth. The jellyfish can move by expanding the edge of the umbrella, where the tentacles are, and then squeezing it back together again. This action pushes water out from under a jellyfish, moving it upward. Jellyfish usually just drift with a current to catch small creatures like minnows, plankton, and other jellyfish that get too close to the tentacles. They have stinging cells on the tentacles that shoot a toxin (poison) into their prey and paralyze it. The arms then push the prey into the mouth to be eaten.

Jellyfish frequently show up along the beaches in July and August and become a swimming hazard. There are many species that are harmless to people, but some of the species, like the sea wasps, can give people a deadly sting. The sea wasps live by the Philippine Islands and north coast of Australia. They can sting with a toxin deadlier than most snakes and have killed swimmers in less than five minutes.

Some jellyfish, called sea nettles, are found near North America and can sting and cause a rash. The Portuguese man-of-war, found in tropical waters and the Gulf Stream, has a more painful, deadly sting. Its toxin is strong enough to give a person large, red sores, and its poison has even been known to kill a person. The Portuguese man-of-war really is a colony or group of jellyfish hanging onto a floating bag of air or gas. There are several poisonous tentacles as long as 50 to 100 feet hanging down. The tentacles sting fish that come too close, and then the colony has fish to eat. One kind of fish is not bothered by its sting, and it hangs around to feed on the meat of the Portuguese man-of-war.

Jellyfish have several different ways to produce baby jellyfish. The common, harmless jellyfish you may have seen washed up on the beach produces a larva that simply splits into many tiny jellyfish that grow into adults. Some jellyfish produce eggs that attach to sea plants and grow into young jellyfish later. Portuguese man-of-war has some kinds that have eggs and other kinds that produce larva that splits apart.

Those jellyfish you find washed up on the beach may or may not have stinging tentacles, so you want to be careful. Mark the spot where you see one on the beach and watch for a few hours. You will find it has "melted" down, leaving nothing but a damp spot on the sand. Strangely, the jellyfish is 95 percent water, so there is only a little goo left when it melts.

The jellyfish does not want to run into people, and swimmers should also try to avoid the jellyfish whenever possible. Sure, many of them are harmless blobs of jelly, but you don't want to take a chance on getting your day at the beach ruined.

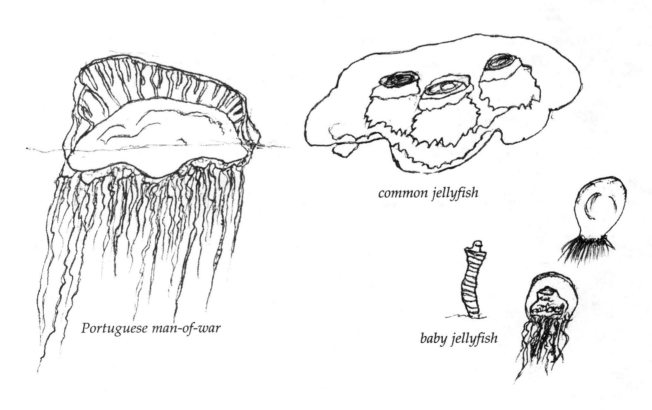

Portuguese man-of-war

common jellyfish

baby jellyfish

Watch Out for Jellyfish!

Vocabulary Checkup Write the words from the box on the correct blanks.

biologist	

_____ group of animals living closely together

_____ anything to do with the sea

_____ scientific name for the jellyfish

_____ a very small fish

_____ a person studying plants and animals

_____ the distance across a thing

_____ a risk, danger, or obstacle

_____ a poison

_____ small organic life floating in the sea

Box words:
- biologist
- colony
- diameter
- hazard
- marine
- medusa
- minnow
- plankton
- toxin

Comprehension You may need to look back at the story to answer the questions correctly.

1. Why do most people call the medusa a jellyfish?

_____

_____

2. What are some ways jellyfish can move?

_____

_____

3. What are some ways jellyfish can be different?

_____

_____

4. What are the steps jellyfish go through to eat?

_____

_____

5. What should you do if you see a jellyfish?

_____

_____

Name _____   Date _____

Watch Out for Jellyfish!

Thinking About Jellyfish Think carefully before answering the questions.

1. Why do you think the author didn't say anything about the enemies of a jellyfish?

   _____

   _____

2. Why do you think jellyfish have to paralyze their prey?

   _____

   _____

3. Why should people avoid jellyfish if some of them are quite harmless?

   _____

   _____

4. Why do you think people near the Philippines would ever risk swimming at all?

   _____

   _____

Reading Concepts Circle the letter of the best choice to complete the statement.

I should avoid the medusa or jellyfish because:

   (a) some of them are pretty big.

   (b) they have many tentacles and eat small fish.

   (c) I don't know if it will sting and cause pain and a rash.

Check It Out Find out about

   Hydra
   Sea anemone
   Coral
   Cassiopeia jellyfish
   Lucernaria jellyfish

Name _____   Date _____

11. Whose Stomping Ground Is It?

When you see the white stripes and get a whiff of the odor, you know what it is. It is one of the most easily recognized and unpopular creatures in America. Raise your hand if you have seen (or smelled) this animal before, and know why you should stay far away from it. Yes, it is the common striped skunk. Predators don't usually try to catch one, either. They know that they may go hungry for a long time if they get that skunk's scent on them.

Skunks can spray you if you are within 12 feet of them, and it will take a long time to get rid of the odor. People usually throw away or burn clothes that get sprayed by a skunk. Taking a bath in tomato juice or vinegar may help get the smell off you or your pet. Predators have to live with that smell for months.

Our most common skunk, the striped skunk, grows to about 11 to 15 inches (28 to 37 centimeters) long and weighs 1.5 to 5.5 pounds (0.75 to 2.5 kilograms). These furry, black and white critters are members of the weasel family. They got their name from a Latin word that means "poisonous mist." Skunks with two white stripes down the back are the most common in the United States and Canada, but there are also spotted skunks and hog-nosed skunks in the United States. All species have glands under their tail that emit the awful smelling spray, called musk, when they are scared or in danger. They usually give a warning growl, foot stomping, or tail-high warning before spraying. Skunks aim for the eyes of their attacker. Their spray can cause temporary blindness. They can spray seven or eight times in a row, which is more than enough to drive an enemy away. They give new meaning to the saying, "Turn your back on your enemy."

As you might guess, skunks don't get attacked by too many animals, but great horned owls or hungry bobcats sometimes grab a skunk for a meal. They must be really hungry! Can you think of a way they might catch skunks without getting sprayed?

All skunks use their sharp claws to dig out grubs, insects, beetles, and worms to eat. They also eat grasshoppers, crickets, mice, and carrion (dead, decaying flesh). They can also be a nuisance by eating the fruit, grains, eggs, or other produce people want to eat. They are primarily nocturnal and prefer to sleep during the day. They will build a nest of dry leaves in a burrow made by another animal. Even though they don't really hibernate, many skunks will sleep for several weeks when it gets very cold. The females give birth to four or five babies in the springtime. The baby skunk, or kit, is born with no fur and is blind. The kits nurse for several weeks in the den before following their mother to learn what else to eat. Kits can spray when they are very young.

In many places, believe it or not, skunks are hunted for their fur. People usually dye the fur all black before using it on coats, gloves, hats, etc. Now, all fur items have to be labeled as to what animal the fur comes from. Since most people won't buy fur if it is from a skunk, hunters and trappers don't hunt them much anymore.

Skunks live to be about seven years old in the wild. Of course, many are killed by cars on the road. They will not back down and seem to think they can spray a car and make it go away. I've heard that people sometimes make fine pets out of baby skunks. I'm sure they remove the musk glands first, and they probably don't have much company at their house!

Whose Stomping Ground Is It?

Vocabulary Checkup Write the words from the box on the correct blanks.

carrion	_____ organs to make special liquids
dye	_____ to give off
emit	_____ another name for skunk spray
glands	_____ dead, rotting flesh
hibernate	_____ to change the color
musk	_____ active mostly at night
nocturnal	_____ to go into a deep sleep all winter
species	_____ a quick smell of an odor
whiff	_____ a certain kind or type of living thing

Comprehension   You may need to look back at the story to answer the questions correctly.

1. What does a skunk do to warn that it's about to spray?

_____

_____

2. What are three main species of skunks in the United States and Canada?

_____

_____

3. How can you get rid of skunk odor on you or your pet?

_____

_____

4. What are some of the foods that skunks like to eat?

_____

_____

Name _____   Date _____

© 2000 by The Center for Applied Research in Education

Whose Stomping Ground Is It?

Thinking About Skunks Think carefully before answering the questions.

1. What do you think "turning your back on your enemy" means in this story?

   _____

   _____

   _____

2. Why do skunks seem to have so few enemies?

   _____

   _____

3. How would you capture a skunk and deliver it to your local zoo if you had to do it?

   _____

   _____

   _____

4. Why do many skunks get killed crossing roads?

   _____

   _____

   _____

Reading Concepts Explain how skunks are both beneficial to humankind and a nuisance to us.

_____

_____

_____

Check It Out Find out about
   Polecats
   Hog-nosed skunks
   Spotted skunks
   Weasels
   Minks

Name _____   Date _____

12. A Prickly Mammal

Porcupines are fairly large rodents (gnawing animals) that live in wooded areas across most of the United States and Canada. They have sharp bristles of hair, called quills, that make them look like their hair is all messed up. Many of the North American porcupines grow 2 or 3 feet long, including the tail. Males can weigh as much as 40 pounds, but females are closer to 25 pounds. Their color varies from yellowish-brown to a greenish-black. They have sharp claws on all of their feet and are great tree climbers.

Porcupines do not run away when you get close to them. As a matter of fact, they are really very slow-moving critters. They waddle along slowly, and may stop and sit quietly if anything comes near. They don't need to run for protection since they have those quills for defense. Quills are less than an inch long on the face, but they're more than 4 inches long on the back and tail. Porcupines can't really throw these quills, but they can thrash their tail around and stick quills into their enemy. Many of these quills have a barb (back-pointing hook) that make them difficult to pull out. The quills can get stuck in a predator's mouth and prevent it from eating for a long time. Porcupines often have as many as 25,000 quills and grow new ones when they lose some. The quills are hollow, so the porcupine can swim very well.

Porcupines are herbivores (plant-eaters) that prefer to eat grass in spring. In the summer they eat buds, leaves, berries, and seeds. When fall and winter arrive, they move into the pine forest to eat twigs and tree bark. They kill trees by stripping the bark. Logging companies have gotten desperate enough to bring in one of the porcupine's worst predators, the pine marten. These weasel-like creatures love to eat porcupine, and they

© 2000 by The Center for Applied Research in Education

(A Prickly Mammal, *continued*)

are so quick that they can attack the face of a porcupine. They have to watch out for the thrashing tail of the porcupine the whole time. When they kill the porcupine, they flip it over and eat from the spineless belly. These pine martens (called fishers) have reduced porcupine populations quickly in some areas. Of course, this made the logging companies very happy.

Porcupines mate in the fall, and females have one soft-haired porcupette in the spring. Within hours of its birth the soft hairs dry and the porcupette can defend itself. It nurses for about a month but can eat leaves when it's only ten days old. It will stay with the mother all summer before going away to make its own home territory in the fall.

Porcupines may nest in pine trees sometimes, but they usually have dens in rock piles or old hollow logs. They don't really hibernate in the winter, and they don't often wander very far from their den to eat some bark and pine needles. They love to eat salt and have made some people mad by chewing up the handles of tools to get the salt left from human perspiration (sweat). Rangers in some campgrounds have to trap porky and move him to other areas to keep him from gnawing all of the tables. A porcupine sleeps all day and can't see very well, but may walk right up to you at night. Porcupines are gentle creatures, but you should stay a safe distance away and just watch these strange animals. Please don't get too close to that prickly tail.

A Prickly Mammal

Vocabulary Checkup Write the words from the box on the correct blanks.

barbs	herbivores	marten	perspiration
quills	rodents	thrash	

1. Animals that eat only plant materials are _____.

2. Gnawing animals are often called _____.

3. Sticky, hairlike projections on porcupines are called _____.

4. Porcupines have backward hooking, sharp _____ on their quills.

5. Sweat containing salt is also called _____.

6. To beat or wave around wildly is to _____.

7. A predator of a porcupine is named the pine _____.

Comprehension You may need to look back at the story to answer the questions correctly.

1. Why are porcupines considered to be rodents?

_____

2. Where do porcupines usually build their den?

_____

_____

3. Porcupines are good climbers because of _____

_____.

4. Why are quills often hard to pull out? _____

_____

5. What serious problems can happen to animals who get a mouth full of quills?

_____

_____

Name _____ Date _____

A Prickly Mammal

Thinking About Porcupines Think carefully before answering the questions.

1. Why do you think logging companies are happy when martens kill porcupines?

   _____

   _____

   _____

2. It is important that porcupine quills are hollow because

   _____

   _____

   _____.

3. What do you think makes some people believe porcupines can throw their quills?

   _____

   _____

   _____

4. What makes the quiet, peaceful porcupine a nuisance to humans in some areas?

   _____

   _____

   _____

5. What did you think was the most interesting thing you learned about porcupines?

   _____

   _____

   _____

Check It Out Find out about
   Pine martens
   Hedgehogs
   Capybaras
   Old World porcupines
   Prehensile-tailed porcupines

Name _____ Date _____

13. The Horse Tigers

The wild horses of Africa we call zebras used to be called "horse tigers" by natives. The zebra looks like a horse in many ways and does belong to the horse family, equus (ee-kwis). Zebras are shorter than horses, have bigger ears, and have a mane that stands straight up along their neck. The main difference you can see right away is the zebra's stripes. Stripes are everywhere: on the tail, the ears, the face, and even into the mane. A zebra at 950 pounds weighs just a little less than most horses.

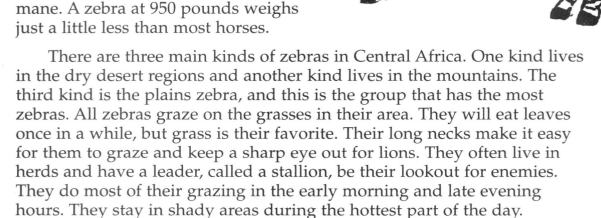

There are three main kinds of zebras in Central Africa. One kind lives in the dry desert regions and another kind lives in the mountains. The third kind is the plains zebra, and this is the group that has the most zebras. All zebras graze on the grasses in their area. They will eat leaves once in a while, but grass is their favorite. Their long necks make it easy for them to graze and keep a sharp eye out for lions. They often live in herds and have a leader, called a stallion, be their lookout for enemies. They do most of their grazing in the early morning and late evening hours. They stay in shady areas during the hottest part of the day.

Zebras can be fierce fighters, biting and kicking at their enemies. However, the first thing they choose to do is to outrun lions and hyenas. A zebra can run as fast as 35 miles per hour for long distances. Zebras usually run in a tight grouping with the baby zebras in the center. Zebras have great eyesight and a wonderful nose, but their large ears, which can twist in all directions, are a big help in locating enemies that stalk them by sneaking through the tall grass. The braying sounds and barking noises warn the herd that an enemy is close, and the lookout stallion will lead them to safety.

Scientists have never found any two zebras with the same striping. Just as no two humans have exactly the same fingerprints, each zebra has its own pattern of stripes. Scientists think the stripes help the zebra to hide in the shadows, but it has not been proven that lions can't see them due to those stripes. We do know that zebras can tell each other apart by the striping. They also recognize the braying and barking sounds of different

(The Horse Tigers, *continued*)

members of their herd. Zebras use certain looks to tell other zebras how they feel. When they pin their ears back and bare their teeth, they are mad. If their ears are forward and lips curled to show their teeth, they are scared. When their mouth is relaxed and their ears are pointing up, they are being friendly. People have not been able to be friendly with zebras, however. They are very hard to tame or train.

The female, or mare, usually has her baby (foal) in the spring. The male foals are called colts. The female foal is called a filly. The foals usually have a mane that runs all the way down their back to their tail. Foals may have brownish-colored stripes instead of black ones until they get a few months older. Foals weigh about 60 pounds at birth and stand up right away. Believe it or not, within a few hours they can run as fast as the adults. Their parents soon teach them to take a bath by rolling in a mudhole with them. The mud will dry so they can shake it off leaving just some dust on the skin. Mothers also lick the mane and face of their foal to clean them and show their love.

Millions of zebras used to live in Africa. People killed many of them for eating or for their beautiful striped skin. There are still over 300,000 zebras in Africa, and they are protected better from hunters now. The main reason the zebra population has not grown more is because humans have taken away much of the zebras' grassland to grow food and build ranches. The future of the zebra depends on people giving it enough safe areas to live in and remain wild and free.

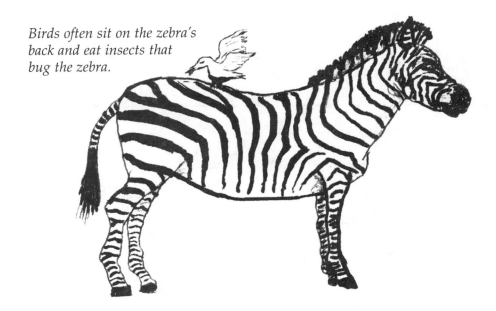

Birds often sit on the zebra's back and eat insects that bug the zebra.

The Horse Tigers

Vocabulary Checkup Write the words from the box on the correct blanks.

graze
mane
plains
ranch
native
foals
colt
filly
mare
stallion

All newborn zebra babies are called _____.

A kind of farm where animals are raised is a _____.

To eat grass that is growing is to _____.

The ridge of hair along an animal's neck is called a _____.

A large area of level country, often with no trees, is _____.

A person born in a country or a place is a _____.

A male zebra or horse is called a _____.

The young male (boy) zebra is called a _____.

The young female (girl) zebra is called a _____.

The mother zebra is called the _____.

Comprehension You may need to look back at the story to answer the questions correctly.

1. What are two ways zebras are like horses?

_____

_____

2. What are two ways zebras are different from horses?

_____

_____

3. Why do zebras graze in early morning and late evening hours?

_____

_____

4. What are the two main ways zebras give messages to each other?

_____

_____

Name _____ Date _____

The Horse Tigers

Thinking About Zebras Think carefully before answering the questions.

1. Why is it so hard for lions to catch most zebras?

   _____

   _____

   _____

2. How do you think zebras can tell each other apart?

   _____

   _____

   _____

3. Circle the sense you think is most important to zebras: smell   sight   hearing

   Why do you think so? _____

   _____

   _____

4. What do you think is most unusual about zebra foals?

   _____

   _____

   _____

5. Why aren't there millions of zebras anymore?

   _____

   _____

   _____

Check It Out Find out about
   Mountain zebras
   Grevy's zebra
   Grant's zebra
   Mongolian wild horses

Name _____ Date _____

14. Barn Owls Don't Hoot

This is a picture of a barn owl we recently found living in the top of my hay barn. My kids found owl pellets on the floor first. There are ten different kinds of barn owls, and they live in every part of the world except the coldest regions. Some people call them monkey-faced owls, but I'm sure they don't really like that name very well. For some strange reason, not many creatures like being told they look like a monkey. Owls probably do like being the symbol of wisdom just because their eyes make them look so wise.

Curoo!

There is another family of owls called the typical owls. You may have heard of some of them, like the great horned owl, screech owl, snowy owl, burrowing owl, barred owl, and short-eared and long-eared owls. The elf and pygmy owls are some of the smallest, at 5 or 6 inches long. The largest are the eagle and great gray owls, at 28 to 30 inches long with wingspans of 5 or 6 feet.

The barn owls are medium sized, at a little over a foot long and about 5 pounds. I know they look heavier than that, but it's probably due to their soft, fluffy feathers. Their feathers are not very brightly colored, but those dull colors help them hide better. They fly pretty fast, and those fluffy feathers also help them swoop down to surprise their prey very quietly at night. Since they hunt at night, they are definitely nocturnal animals. You probably noticed their sharp talons and hooked beaks for tearing apart larger prey, like rabbits. They eat smaller prey whole, and then spit out a pellet with the fur, bones, or feathers in it later at their daytime roost. Scientists like to examine owl pellets to see the skeletons of what the owl has been eating. It may be easier to see barn owls by first finding the pellets, like my kids did. You can't find barn owls by listening for hoots because they don't give a hoot.

Barn owls have large eyes that are pointing forward instead of on the side, like most birds. This means barn owls can use both eyes to look at objects like people do, but they can't move their eyes, so they have to rotate their head to see things moving. They rotate their head about three-fourths of the way around, so some people think they can spin it all the way around. They can't do that, but they can turn their head completely upside down. Some people think that owls can't see in the daytime. They can, but they actually see better at night because they have sensitive eyes for seeing in very dim light.

All owls have terrific hearing, and they depend on their ears to find their prey first. Their ear openings are found behind and to the side of their eyes. It is a good thing that feathers cover the ear openings or the owl would look funny. The barn owl has one ear above an eye toward the forehead. The other ear is lower than the opposite eye. Scientists think this helps the owl zero in on the exact location of prey. The dish-shaped face helps the owl hear a mouse moving in the grass. It hears the mouse, closes in on it, sees it, and hardly ever misses it with its talons.

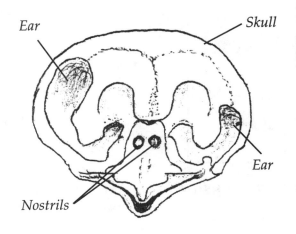

Barn owls are not good nest builders. The male and female mate for life, but the female lays her eggs in the dark near where the pellets have dropped. She often waits two or three days between laying eggs. The eggs hatch in about a month in the order they were laid. This makes it easier for the male to feed the chicks. He will bring a rodent to the chicks and use his beak and talons to tear small pieces for them to eat. His mate will help later, as all four or five hungry owlets need to be fed for about two months. Owlets are covered with a white down shortly after being hatched. They don't get the darker flight feathers until they are about five or six weeks old.

Barn owls are very valuable birds since they eat lots of rodents, like mice and rats, that damage farmers' crops. Modern farming methods have reduced the number of barn owls. Adults only live a couple of years and only hatch out two broods. We hope that barn owl we have in our barn gets a mate and raises some owlets.

Barn Owls Don't Hoot

Vocabulary Checkup Write the words from the box on the correct blanks.

down
pellet
prey
rodents
roost
rotate
symbol
talons

_____ an animal hunted by another for food

_____ a place where birds settle to sleep

_____ the soft feathers on some birds

_____ to turn or revolve

_____ a small, rounded ball

_____ sharp claws on birds of prey

_____ gnawing animals like mice and rats

_____ it stands for something else

Comprehension You may need to look back at the story to answer the questions correctly.

1. Why are barn owl feathers such dull colors?

   _____

   _____

2. Farmers like owls because _____

   _____

   _____.

3. Explain how barn owls usually find and catch their prey. _____

   _____

   _____

4. You might find _____ in an owl pellet.

5. Owls can surprise their prey quietly because _____

   _____

   _____.

Name _____ Date _____

Barn Owls Don't Hoot

Thinking About Owls Think carefully before answering the questions.

1. Would you like being called a "monkey face"? _____ Why? _____
   _____
   _____

2. Why do you think owls are used as symbols of wisdom? _____
   _____
   _____

3. Why do some people believe owls can turn their head all the way around?
   _____
   _____

4. I think the most unusual thing about barn owls is _____
   _____
   _____.

5. Why do you think some people believe that owls can't see at all in the daytime?
   _____
   _____

6. What can you think of that has changed on modern farms to reduce the owl's food supply?
   _____
   _____

7. From this list of typical owls, circle the ones you have heard of before now:

   great horned owl   screech owl
   snowy owl   burrowing owl
   barred owl   short-eared owl
   long-eared owl   elf owl   pygmy owl
   great gray owl   eagle owl

   You may want to find out more about these owls.

Name _____ Date _____

15. Is He Washing for Dinner?

One of the best-loved small mammals in America is not understood very well despite its popularity. Nearly every person recognizes the ring-tailed, black-masked raccoon. You may have seen the curious and clever masked thief in your own neighborhood. Raccoons are able to live just about everywhere, but they don't like desert regions or the high mountain areas. They are familiar to people from the southern part of Canada clear down into southern Mexico. The adult 'coon will be about 2 feet long with a tail another foot long. It can weigh as much as 50 pounds, but the average is about 25 pounds. Raccoons have five finger-like toes on each foot and use them to hold things, like monkeys do. Raccoons are very nocturnal, so perhaps you've only seen their tracks in the snow or mud.

Hind   *Front*

People have spread several myths or legends about raccoons. One myth says that raccoons like to eat around the water but don't like to swim. They are excellent swimmers and will even use rivers and lakes to escape predators. Dogs that attack a raccoon in the water may lose their life if the raccoon is big enough to pull the dog under and drown it. Another myth is that raccoons always wash their food before they eat it. Science experiments and observations have been done to see if this is true. It was discovered in those experiments and observations that raccoons did dunk food if water was available, but food wasn't cleaned much. Scientists believe that they dunk the food to moisten it or because they catch lots of food in water. The raccoons often eat food when no water is around. They even eat from garbage cans without washing!

Another myth that some people believe is that raccoons live much of their life in the trees. They are excellent tree climbers and even build dens in hollows in some trees. Their nightly food quests are done almost entirely on the ground, however. They use caves and abandoned burrows to sleep in during the day as often as they do trees. But they have been seen sunbathing high up in a tree. One last myth that you should learn about is the one about raccoons making good pets. Baby raccoons can be tamed and are intelligent enough to learn tricks. When they are about a year old, you would want to release them because they get large, turn wild, and can really bite and scratch. Then you will have the problem of how to teach them to survive on their own.

Raccoons will eat just about anything they can catch. They love to eat fish, frogs, clams, turtles, mice, birds, bugs, eggs, fruit, nuts, corn, and other grains. They even eat slugs, snails, snakes, worms, and bees or wasps. They will sneak into a farm chicken coop and have a feast. A 'coon will fight other animals over food and will even fight with its own family. Raccoons often put on extra weight in the fall in cold areas so they can sleep when food is scarce. They do not actually hibernate, though.

The female will raise a litter of three to five young, called kits, that are born after a nine-week gestation. A nest of leaves in a hollow log or tree is a normal den. The kits are born with a little fur but are blind for the first three weeks. They don't have a mask or rings on the tail until their eyes open. The kits stay with the mother even after they are weaned at about three months. She teaches them how to find food and climb to safety at a young age. The mother chases the father away, as she seems to prefer to raise her kits alone. Sometimes the kits stay with her through most of the next winter before going away to fend for themselves.

People have hunted and trapped raccoons for their furs and meat for hundreds of years. Colonists in America used raccoon pelts as money. Raccoon fur made some of the best hats and coats. When the movies of Davy Crockett and Daniel Boone were made about fifty years ago, nearly every boy in America wanted a coonskin cap. Many hunters like to use 'coon dogs to tree the raccoon, and people say the meat is tasty. In spite of all this, the raccoon is in no danger of becoming extinct.

Is He Washing for Dinner?

Vocabulary Checkup Write the words from the box on the correct blanks.

colonists	coop	fend	gestation
myth	observation	quest	survive

1. A legend, story, or unproven belief of people is a _____.

2. A pen or building to house birds is often called a _____.

3. To live through something is to _____.

4. People who settled and built colonies were called _____.

5. A search or adventurous trip is a _____.

6. Being independent and managing your life is to _____ for yourself.

7. What you see or notice is an _____.

8. The time babies are carried inside the mother is _____.

Reading Concepts Circle the correct answer to complete each sentence.

1. A raccoon's paw is a lot like a person's   foot   hand   knee.

2. Raccoons often dip food into water to   wash   taste   moisten   the food.

3. Baby raccoons are born without a   mask   tail   tongue.

4. Raccoons are very good   runners   readers   swimmers.

5. Quite often raccoons are pests to   teachers   farmers   bankers.

6. A full-grown raccoon can weigh as much as   5   15   50   pounds.

7. Raccoons are most likely to steal from   gas stations   supermarkets   corn fields.

8. You would see raccoons most often at   night   noon   dinner.

9. Adult raccoons have rings around their   fingers   bathtubs   tails.

10. Raccoon babies are raised on milk, so they must be   reptiles   mammals   birds.

Name _____   Date _____

© 2000 by The Center for Applied Research in Education

Is He Washing for Dinner?

Comprehension You may need to look back at the story to answer the questions correctly.

1. What uses have humans found for raccoons?

   _____

   _____

2. Why shouldn't people try to make pets out of baby raccoons?

   _____

   _____

3. What were the two reasons given for raccoons to dip their food into water?

   _____

   _____

Thinking About Raccoons Think carefully before answering the questions.

1. What evidence do you think showed that raccoons don't wash food before eating?

   _____

   _____

2. Why do you think it would be difficult to recognize newborn kits?

   _____

   _____

3. Why do you think many farmers consider raccoons as pests?

   _____

   _____

4. Why do you think people like raccoon hats and coats?

   _____

   _____

Check It Out Find out about

    Ring-tailed cats   Coatimundis

    Kinkajou   Red pandas

    Giant pandas

Name _____ Date _____

16. King of the Beasts

I watched several movies recently and began to wonder about lions. I questioned if they were really "king of the beasts." I also wanted to know more about the lion cubs. Do lions only live in Africa? I checked out some books on these big cats to look for answers to my questions.

The first thing I learned was that the wild lions in the world do live in the middle part of Africa. Lions used to live in most parts of the world. They even lived in North America until about ten thousand years ago. There are a few lions still left in India. You may have seen some lions in a zoo or circus.

I found out that people called the lions king of the beasts because they admire their looks and great strength. Lions are also called king of the jungle, but they don't live in the jungle. They live out on the grasslands of central Africa. The mane of hair on the proud-looking male does give him the look of a king. It is the only cat that has a mane, and scientists say the mane helps to make him look bigger to his enemies and protect him some in battles. The old lion may have a black mane since the mane gets darker with age. These males get to be about 500 pounds and are around 9 feet long to the tip of the tail. The lionesses are about 300 pounds. Only the Siberian (Si beer' e un) tiger is larger than the lion in the cat family.

The two most obvious weapons of the lions are the teeth and the claws. The pointed teeth are for killing prey and tearing meat apart. The lion doesn't have teeth for chewing its food, so it swallows it in chunks.

Lions are the only cats that live in family groups called prides. A pride of lions usually has twenty to thirty members. There will be several lionesses with their cubs and at least one male. If there is more than one male in the pride, they are very likely to be brothers. Isn't that how it was in the *Lion King* movies? It really helps the lions to live in a pride as a big family. They all help to take care of the cubs and protect them. The males are the guards in charge of defending the pride against enemies. The lionesses work together and do all of the hunting. Lions have great hearing and eyesight to help them hunt at night. They like zebra and wildebeest the best but will eat just about any meat when hungry. One of their favorite tricks is to lie near a watering hole and wait for their prey. The lioness can leap more than 30 feet through the air to catch the prey. Lions only kill when they are hungry. Sometimes the zebra and other animals ignore nearby lions. They just seem to know when lions have eaten and aren't going to attack them.

A lioness usually has from three to five cubs in a litter. The 3-pound babies are born blind and can hardly crawl to the mother to get milk. They are born with a spotted coat to help them hide better in the tall grass. All of the mothers in the pride will feed each other's babies at times. The cubs will stay with their mother for a couple of years until she is pregnant with a new litter. The young females may stay with the pride, but the males are driven out of the pride's territory to set up prides of their own. The males may have to fight some other pride leader to try to take over his pride.

I hope you learned as many new facts about lions as I did. I learned another important fact: The greatest threat to the lion population is for them to run out of territory because humans have been taking over the lions' habitat. Many African parks are helping provide safe lion habitat. I sure hope the *Lion King* movies help people know the lions are worth saving.

King of the Beasts

Vocabulary Checkup Write the words from the box on the correct blanks.

admire	habitat	lioness	litter
mane	pregnant	prey	pride

1. The female lion is called a _____.

2. A _____ is a group of lions living together like a family.

3. The long hair around the neck of the male lion is called a _____.

4. To _____ is to think of with wonder, respect, or high regard.

5. An animal being hunted for food is called the _____.

6. A _____ is a group of babies born to a mother in one birthing.

7. A mother with young developing in her body is _____.

8. The natural environment of an animal is its _____.

Comprehension You may need to look back at the story to answer the questions correctly.

1. Where do most of the wild lions of the world live? _____

_____

2. What is the main job of the male lions in the pride? _____

_____

_____

3. What jobs do the lionesses have? _____

_____

_____

4. What are three things a lioness has that help make her a great hunter?

_____

_____

Name _____ Date _____

© 2000 by The Center for Applied Research in Education

King of the Beasts

Thinking About Lions Think carefully before answering the questions.

1. Why do you think the lion is called king of the beasts around the world?

   _____

   _____

   _____

2. Why shouldn't lions be called king of the jungle anymore?

   _____

   _____

   _____

3. Why do you think the zebra and wildebeest are the favorite prey of lions?

   _____

   _____

   _____

4. How do you think the zebra and wildebeest can tell when lions aren't going to attack?

   _____

   _____

   _____

5. Think about whether you would choose life as a male or female lion, and explain your choice.

   _____

   _____

Check It Out Find out about
   Leopards
   Jaguars
   Housecats
   Retractile claws
   Lion training

Name _____ Date _____

17. Warts Can Be Beautiful

One of the most unusual-looking creatures has to be the wart hog of Africa. It gets its name from the four large warts on the sides of its face. Scientists are not sure why those warts are there, but one theory is that they may protect wart hogs during battles with other wart hogs. The four warts together with the four tusks give the poor wart hog a beauty only another wart hog could love. The warts are useful in distinguishing the males from the females since you can hardly see the warts on the females.

Male wart hogs, called boars, weigh over 200 pounds, are 4 feet long, and stand about 30 inches tall. The female is called a sow and is slightly smaller than the boar. Wart hogs have a rough gray skin with some bristles of hair sticking out. The long legs and short neck combined with the flattened head really don't help improve the looks of this strange creature. The wart hog's lower tusks are barely visible, but those two long, curved tusks above them make the wart hog look fierce. Those top tusks can get up to two feet long and are used as weapons in battles, mostly between two boars. Wart hogs also use them to rip at their main enemies, the leopards and lions.

Wart hogs prefer to roam the grasslands of Africa as a family herd, called a sounder. There are usually a boar, a sow, and their seven to nine piglets in a sounder. Wart hogs like to wallow in mud holes to cool off, so they may not look gray at times if the mud has red or yellow in it. They need water and mud to cool down since they can't perspire (sweat). They are diurnal (active in daytime), and will sleep at night in dens made under rocks or abandoned aardvark dens. The boar backs into the den last so his tusks are ready to defend the family.

Sounders of wart hogs spend the day grunting along the grasslands munching on grasses and roots of shrubs. Wart hogs have to crawl around on their front knees since their neck is too short to graze like many

(Warts Can Be Beautiful, *continued*)

other animals do. Their eyes are high on their head, enabling them to watch for predators as they eat. They will eat some leaves, too, and even gobble up birds' eggs from nests they find. They can run surprisingly fast, at 30 miles per hour, to chase down small mammals to eat. They sure look funny running across the fields with their 18-inch, tasseled tail held straight up in the air.

A pregnant sow will look for a new den that isn't being used when it is time to deliver her new litter. She may have as many as seven little

pinkish-gray piglets, but three or four piglets is a more likely number. The newborn usually will huddle together in the den to stay warm during the day while their mother is out feeding. She will come back to suckle and warm them up a few times and will spend the night there, too. Within a week the young will be wandering out on the grasslands during the day. The boar will help their mother protect them.

Wart hogs are not an endangered species. They have strong numbers roaming the African savanna south of the Sahara Desert. Farmers try to control the number of wart hogs in their fields. Many tribes in Africa hunt the wart hogs for food. Hunters also shoot them for sport and mount the unique trophy after an African hunting trip called a safari.

175

Warts Can Be Beautiful

Vocabulary Checkup Write the words from the box on the correct blanks.

boar	diurnal	huddle	safari	sounder
sow	suckle	tasseled	theory	visible

1. The family group of wart hogs is called a _____.

2. The female wart hog is called a _____.

3. The male wart hog is called a _____.

4. A scientific guess or belief is often called a _____.

5. To crowd or draw together closely is to _____.

6. _____ means having threads or hairs hung on a tip.

7. A _____ is a hunting trip or expedition.

8. _____ means to be active in the daytime.

9. _____ means it can be seen or is in your sight.

10. _____ means to nurse milk from the mother.

Comprehension You may need to look back at the story to answer the questions correctly.

1. What features make the wart hog look unusual? _____

_____

_____

2. What are some ways wart hogs defend themselves? _____

_____

_____

3. What do wart hogs eat, and what is unusual about the ways they eat?

_____

_____

Name _____   Date _____

Warts Can Be Beautiful

4. Why do wart hogs have to wallow in the mud? _____

_____

_____

Thinking About Wart Hogs Think carefully before answering the questions.

1. Why did the author say "wart hogs have a beauty only another wart hog could love"?

_____

_____

2. What do wart hogs do that you found strange or funny?

_____

_____

3. Why do you think wart hogs haven't become endangered even though they are hunted?

_____

_____

4. What other purpose do you think those warts could have?

_____

_____

5. Why do you think a cartoon maker chose a wart hog and meerkat as partners for stories?

_____

_____

Check It Out Find out about
Wild boar
Javelinas (Peccaries)
Bushpigs
Pigs

Name _____ Date _____

18. Beep-beep!

The curious roadrunners live in desert areas of the southwestern part of the United States and Mexico. They are the state bird in New Mexico. It seems strange that a bird that can fly is one of the fastest runners. It can run at speeds up to 25 miles per hour. That is as fast as the fastest humans can run! Those roadrunners got their name back when they ran beside the horses and wagons on the earliest roads. The roadrunner is about 2 feet long, including its 8-inch-long tail. The crest of feathers on top of the head is raised straight up when the roadrunner is curious or alerted.

The roadrunner is a pretty clumsy bird when it comes to flying. People have only seen them fly a little ways. Their body seems to be designed better for running than for flying. They have a long, thin body that gets more streamlined to reach maximum speed. The neck is stuck far out in front, and the long tail works like a rudder to zigzag or change direction quickly. Their legs are so strong and quick that they take twelve steps per second when running fast. They really are not faster

than the coyotes they always get away from in the cartoon, however. They simply change directions so fast that the coyote can't zigzag fast enough to catch them. The real-life coyote usually gives up when he finds out how quickly roadrunner dodges this way and that.

The roadrunner has a very interesting diet. It eats many desert insects from shrubs and cactus, but a lot of its diet is made up of snakes and lizards. Roadrunners can outrun the lizard, grab it by the tail, and quickly beat it against the ground to kill it. The roadrunner is more famous for the way it catches snakes. It runs in a circle around the snake until it gets behind it. The roadrunner is always

(Beep-beep!, *continued*)

careful to stay out of reach of a snake's fangs. At just the right moment, the roadrunner darts in and grabs the snake behind the head. It beats the snake's head against the ground until it is dead. Roadrunners can even kill a fairly good sized rattlesnake in this manner. If a snake or a lizard has tough skin, the roadrunner keeps smacking it on the ground until it can eat it. The roadrunner also eats a few small birds and some rodents.

Female roadrunners build a crude nest out of twigs and grass in a shrub or on a cactus. They will usually lay three to five white eggs in the nest in March or April. They will incubate the eggs for three weeks. The chicks have no feathers at birth, and their skin is black. Both parents feed them, so they grow quickly. The parents know chicks need extra water, so they pretend to be giving them food and then spit up into the chick's beak. The chicks are able to run around the desert at less than three weeks of age. They are independent by the time they are a month old.

The roadrunner does another strange thing when it sleeps. Even though it gets cold in the desert at night, the roadrunner lowers its body temperature to save energy. Scientists say it comes close to going into a condition a lot like hibernation every night. This seems to be dangerous, but very few roadrunners get caught by predators. A black patch of skin behind the wings soaks up the sun's heat to warm the bird at dawn. Roadrunners are probably in greater danger trying to outrun cars along the desert highways. Beep-beep!

Beep-beep!

Vocabulary Checkup Write the words from the box on the correct blanks.

alert	crude	design	diet
fangs	maximum	streamlined	zigzag

1. The foods usually eaten are part of your _____.

2. Making sharp turns left and right in a path is to _____.

3. To be fully aware, watchful, and prepared is to be _____.

4. The long teeth of snakes are called _____.

5. Anything roughly made or not well finished is _____.

6. Smooth design so air flows easily is _____.

7. To plan and form skillfully is to _____.

8. The highest amount or upper limit is the _____.

Comprehension You may need to look back at the story to answer the questions correctly.

1. Roadrunners live in the _____ in the United States and are the state bird in _____.

2. The roadrunner got its name from _____ _____.

3. Coyotes can't catch roadrunners because _____ _____ _____.

4. Roadrunners kill rattlesnakes to eat by _____ _____ _____.

Name _____ Date _____

Beep-beep!

5. The roadrunner uses its long tail to _____

_____

_____.

Thinking About Roadrunners Think carefully before answering the questions.

1. Why do you think roadrunners choose to run more than they choose to fly?

_____

_____

2. Why do you think roadrunners take the risk of catching rattlesnakes?

_____

_____

3. Why do those strange birds try to outrace cars along the roads?

_____

_____

4. What did you think was the most unusual thing done by the roadrunners?

_____

Why? _____

_____

5. Why do you think so many people (including adults) love roadrunner cartoons?

_____

_____

Check It Out Find out about
Black-billed cuckoos
Yellow-billed cuckoos
Lesser roadrunners
Roadrunner cartoons
Torpor

Name _____ Date _____

19. Could a Woodchuck Chuck Wood?

The tongue-twister goes like this: "How much wood could a woodchuck chuck if a woodchuck could chuck wood?" Woodchuck is another name for the only marmot family member found in the east part of North America. It is commonly called the groundhog. Since chuck means to throw, groundhogs (or woodchucks) would not chuck any wood at all. They are in the squirrel family and can climb trees, but they don't throw wood. They prefer to spend most of their time eating, sleeping, and digging burrows. They get their name from the Native American word *wuchak*. We can enjoy that tongue-twister anyway, can't we?

Woodchucks look a lot like a small beaver except for their tail. The woodchuck is about 15 to 20 inches long and weighs from 5 to 10 pounds. The fluffy tail is 6 to 8 inches long. The woodchuck has reddish-brown, rumpled fur that has some gray in the head and shoulder area. Since this type of marmot is in the squirrel family, it also sits up on its haunches like a squirrel. Its front claws help excavate complex burrows with compartments for sleeping. The long front teeth are also used to dig and come in handy for chewing through tree roots. A groundhog peeks out of its burrow very cautiously, then comes out on top of its mound, sits up on its haunches to sniff the air, and looks all around. If it senses danger, it may sound a shrill whistle to warn other groundhogs. The groundhog will immediately begin to eat if there is no danger. It will never venture far from the entrance to its burrow, however. You can often tell where a groundhog's home is by looking for large circles of grass that are shorter than the surrounding field of hay. Groundhogs especially love clover, alfalfa, and timothy, but they will eat many other grasses to fatten themselves before winter arrives.

The woodchuck eats so much in the late summer months that it sometimes doubles its weight. It may weigh 11 or 12 pounds instead of its spring weight of 5 or 6 pounds. It has stored extra fat on its body to help live through a long hibernation from September until spring. It curls up in its underground room which it lined with grass and leaves. The woodchuck's body goes into a condition known as torpor during the five- or six-month hibernation. The woodchuck slows its heart down and lowers its body temperature from 97 to 39 degrees in the torpid condition. During hibernation it may only take one breath every six minutes. It will wake up once in a while to go to the bathroom.

Legend has it that the woodchuck will come out on February 2 (Groundhog Day) to check the weather. If it sees its shadow, it is supposed to go back to sleep for six weeks until winter is over. If the sun isn't shining and it can't see its shadow, then winter must be over. Of course, many people believe this is all superstition since it is not based on good scientific facts. It is fun for people to think about such legends, and it gives the groundhog its own special day to be recognized in a positive light.

The groundhog usually mates right after it comes out of hibernation looking skinny again. The babies that are born four to five weeks later have no hair and their eyes are closed. Woodchucks can have as many as six in a litter, but three or four is a more normal size litter. The babies are nursed for the first two months, and then they are expected to fend for themselves by finding their own spot to fatten up and dig a burrow for the winter.

The woodchuck is not very popular with farmers, as you might have already figured out. Their holes and mounds make fields so rough that it is very hard on farm equipment. Farmers are not very happy when they look out in their hay fields and see big circles of hay or soybeans eaten down to the ground. So farmers will even pay some hunters for the tail of each woodchuck they shoot. The woodchuck's habit of sitting up on its haunches to check for danger can make it an easy target. The other dangerous habit it has is sunbathing on a mound or big rock on sunny days. The woodchuck is not in any danger of becoming extinct, however.

Could a Woodchuck Chuck Wood?

Vocabulary Checkup Write the words from the box on the correct blanks.

alfalfa	chuck	complex	excavate	haunches
rumpled	shrill	superstition	torpor	venture

1. _____ means to throw or toss.

2. _____ is the sluggish, slowed condition in hibernation.

3. _____ is a type of grass often used as hay for animals.

4. _____ sounds are high-pitched whistles or screams.

5. _____ are the rear parts an animal can sit upon.

6. _____ means to travel or risk going forth.

7. _____ is a belief with no scientific basis.

8. _____ is involved or complicated with many parts.

9. _____ means to dig out to make a hole.

10. _____ is wrinkled, creased, or bumpy.

Comprehension You may need to look back at the story to answer the questions correctly.

1. Where did the name for the woodchuck come from? _____

_____

2. What are some ways that a woodchuck is different from a beaver?

_____

_____

3. Why do groundhogs eat and eat to get fat in the late summer?

_____

_____

Name _____ Date _____

Could a Woodchuck Chuck Wood?

4. What does a woodchuck change during torpor?

_____

_____

5. What are two reasons that farmers don't like groundhogs?

_____

_____

Thinking About Woodchucks Think carefully before answering the questions.

1. Why do you think woodchucks are also named groundhogs?

_____

_____

2. Why does the author say "a woodchuck could chuck no wood"?

_____

_____

3. Why do you think the woodchuck never ventures far from its burrow?

_____

_____

4. Why do you think the woodchuck is skinny in the spring?

_____

_____

5. How could it be both good and bad that woodchucks sit up on their haunches?

_____

_____

6. Do you think the legend about the groundhog's shadow is correct? _____

Why? _____

Check It Out Find out about

Whistling marmots	Alpine marmots
Groundhog Day	Prairie dogs
Punxsutawney Pete	

Name _____ Date _____

20. A Great Fish Story

Thousands of years ago there was a fish that only lived in Asia. Many people from the Caspian Sea to China and Japan loved this fish. Some of the people began raising these fish to eat on special feast days. Japanese and Chinese raised them for their beautiful colors and learned to produce fish with gleaming colors of gold, purple, red, yellow, blue, and silver or white. The palaces had ponds with these ornamental fish, over a foot long swimming around. Other countries of the world began importing the fish for its beauty or its food value. East European countries served these fish as the main dish for Christmas dinner. African countries imported them to feed hungry people. The beautiful fish were trained to pull ropes to ring bells to signal when they were hungry at a palace in France. In the 1870s, they were brought to California and have spread to many rivers all over North America. Those fish have now spread to every continent except Antarctica and South America.

This freshwater family of fish is the carp. Japanese call them koi, and some people who raise them there claim they have a few koi that are nearly 200 years old! Scientists say that you can tell the age of a carp by counting the rings on its scales, and they have found many carp over 50 years old. Many of the carp in fish aquariums are simply called goldfish. Yes, goldfish are also members of the carp family, but they are not always gold. The wild carp in our rivers are named mirror, leather, and scaled carp. They can quickly reach 20 pounds at 30 inches of length. Some old carp have weighed as much as 90 pounds and are as long as many fourth graders! Most wild species have bluish backs and golden brownish-yellow sides with large scales.

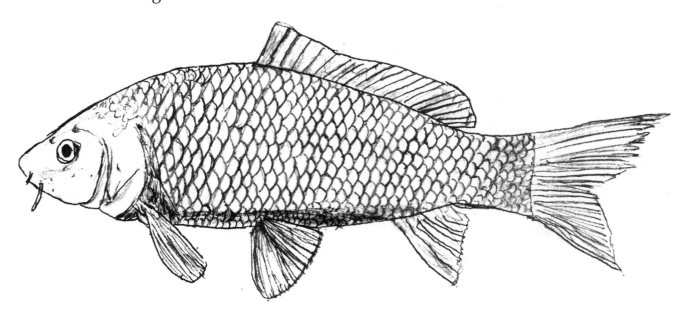

Carp in the rivers are mostly bottom feeders. They have four thread-like feelers, called barbels, on the sides of their mouth. They use them to probe around in soft mud to find food. They eat many nymphs, snails, worms, mussels, shrimp, crawdads, and a few small water plants. Since the carp has no teeth, it crushes the food in shells as it goes down the throat. Then it swallows the meat part and ejects the shells and mud it scooped up. Carp like the slower moving and shallower parts of the stream better than the swifter waters. They also like to bask in the sun just under the surface on hot days. Those carp that come to the surface will make a sucking sound as they eat floating insects like mosquitoes. It may sound a lot like a person slurping soup.

Carp also prefer to lay their eggs in those shallow, slow-moving, sunlit waters. A 20-pound carp can lay anywhere from 60,000 to 2,000,000 eggs in one spawning. She usually sticks the eggs on aquatic plants to hatch out in the sunlight. The young hatchlings, or fry, hatch in about a week and stay close to the river bank to grow up. The fry frequently are eaten by many other fish, even other carp. Many fry will escape and grow up quickly to produce young of their own in a couple of years.

Carp are both useful and harmful fish. Even though most people in America do not like to eat carp, they are of great value as food in many countries. The Soviets are growing carp that gain about 9 pounds each year and are valuable food fish. You are already aware that carp are considered delicious in many parts of the world and are now served on holidays. Millions of people serve them fresh baked or smoked, and they are even canned to eat in the winter. They are also valuable as ornamental fish in ponds and aquariums since so many beautiful colors have been developed. Carp have adapted too well in many streams, however. When they take over a stream, they may reduce the population of fish many people prefer. Carp suck food up from the mud and destroy the eggs and spawning areas of fish like trout, pike, and bass. Many people who fish have been trying to get rid of the carp in their streams. They have found out that it is a lot easier to get carp started in a stream than it is to get rid of them. Carp are famous for being tough survivors. They can live a long time trapped in very little water or totally out of water. People's attempts to poison or trap carp to get them out of streams have not worked very well. So I suppose we'd better learn to enjoy them more.

A Great Fish Story

Vocabulary Checkup Write the words from the box on the correct blanks.

adapted	barbels	bask	fry	import
koi	mussels	probe	spawn	value

1. _____ means to bring in from another country or area.

2. _____ are bivalve mollusks similar to clams.

3. _____ means adjusted to new conditions.

4. _____ is a colorful, Japanese carp.

5. _____ are the thread-like feelers by a carp's mouth.

6. _____ means to search or examine, often by feeling.

7. _____ means to lie in the sun for the warmth.

8. _____ is a measure of worth or importance of a thing.

9. _____ are the newly hatched baby fish.

10. _____ is when fish deposit eggs to produce fry.

Comprehension You may need to look back at the story to answer the questions correctly.

1. What were the two main reasons people imported carp?

   _____

   _____

2. How can scientists find out how old a carp is? _____

   _____

   _____

3. What are the names of three species of carp mentioned?

   _____

   _____

Name _____ Date _____

A Great Fish Story

4. How do carp find food buried in the mud? _____

_____

_____

5. One way carp are useful is _____

_____

_____.

6. One way carp are harmful is _____

_____

_____.

Thinking About Carp Think carefully before answering the questions.

1. Why do you think people have brightly colored carp swimming in palace ponds?

_____

_____

2. Why do you think carp like the slower, shallower water?

_____

_____

3. Why don't Americans like to eat carp?

_____

_____

4. Why don't carp jam-pack our rivers if millions of eggs hatch?

_____

_____

5. Why do you think many people who fish don't want carp in their streams?

_____

_____

Check It Out Find out about

Goldfish colors   Koi
Fish spawning   Record carp caught
Your local stream fish
How to cook carp

Name _____ Date _____

Answer Key for Activity Sheets

Panda *(Save the Giant Panda)*

Vocabulary—1) future 2) leopard 3) extinct 4) endangered 5) Severe 6) shy 7) Scientists 8) bamboo 9) starved.

Comprehension—1) raccoons 2) bamboo 3) 25 to 40 4) ears/hearing 5) climb trees 6) ear 7) thick fur coat 8) China.

Thinking—1) Perhaps a hidden camera or captured pandas helped. 2) Their walk, size, and appearance. 3) Suggestions: Capture them and fly them to new bamboo forest, or botanists find out how to regenerate bamboo better. 4) Answers will vary, but you may want to point out that they can't restart extinct species.

Sea Horse *(Hold on, Sea Horse)*

Vocabulary—1) rigid 2) snout 3) emerge 4) protrude 5) prehensile 6) aquarium 7) shallow 8) dorsal.

Comprehension—1) Sea horses are very poor swimmers. 2) Its head looks like a horse's. 3) Crabs; changing color. 4) Its eyes protrude on both sides. 5) Sucking water in and filtering it.

Thinking—1) Head or tail or pouch, etc. 2.) Answers may include unique looks. 3) He gets to carry eggs and raises babies. 4) Probably camouflage colors. 5) May mention few enemies or number of young born.

Sea Cucumber *(I Wouldn't Eat that Cucumber)*

Vocabulary—1) tentacles 2) organisms 3) cylinder 4) extract 5) unique 6) temperate 7) tropical

Comprehension—1) Big pickles. 2) Yes; people in China. 3) They grab food as it swims by with tentacles and also shove mud in their mouth to filter food out. 4) Sea urchins, starfish, and sand dollars.

Thinking—1) They lie around eating. 2) May mention bitter taste. 3) Answers will vary. 4) May say they wave tentacles or jet about. 5) Answers will vary.

Fact or Opinion—1) F 2) O 3) F 4) O 5) F 6) F 7) O.

Cardinals *(Our Most Popular State Bird)*

Vocabulary—crest, incubates, brood, mate, nuisance, popular, migrate.

Fact or Opinion—1) F 2) O 3) O 4) F 5) O.

Comprehension—1) To sell as songbirds or sell the red feathers for hats. 2) Both build nest, he feeds her as she is sitting on eggs, and both feed brood. 3) They eat insects. 4) Sunflower seeds are their favorite, but they also like corn.

Thinking—1) He is bright red. 2) She can hide on the nest better. 3) Cardinals don't migrate and need food. 4) 7; may mention beauty, song, insects eaten, etc.

Ostrich *(The Really Big Bird)*

Vocabulary—1) viciously 2) stride 3) plume 4) predator 5) durable 6) scarce 7) gizzard 8) comparison.

Comprehension—1) On plains and deserts of Africa. 2) They were killed to get their plumes for hats and clothing. 3) They have long legs and take 15-ft. strides. 4) Their body is too heavy for wing size.

Fact or Opinion—1) F 2) O 3) F 4) F 5) F 6) O 7) F.

Thinking—1) Answers may include how it looks that way when seen grazing from a distance. 2) May say fashion trend or beauty of feathers. 3) Maybe taking outer ones off to an incubator. 4) Answers will vary.

Kangaroo *(The Greatest Marsupial)*

Vocabulary—1) dingo 2) joey 3) marsupials 4) ranchers 5) unofficial 6) arid 7) mobs 8) pasture.

Comprehension—1) Many people would love to go to Australia. Their small head looks like a deer's head. 2) They are born early and very small, so they mature as they nurse in the pouch. 3) It is cooler. 4) Boomers; and blue fliers.

Thinking—1) Probably for safety. 2) May mention experiments done. 3) May say a tall fence. 4) They would use their strong hind legs to kick hard. 5) Answers will vary.

Reading Concepts—(b) They have hair and feed on mother's milk.

Koalas *(A Cute Australian)*

Vocabulary—1) minerals 2) dense 3) pelts 4) slaughtered 5) eucalyptus 6) groves 7) tourist 8) nursing 9) hint 10) survive.

Fact or Opinion—1) O 2) F 3) O 4) F 5) O 6) O 7) F.

Comprehension—1) No water. 2) Their strong claw-like grip. 3) They are defenseless, tiny babies. 4) Disease and killed for the soft furs. 5) Loss of many eucalyptus trees.

Thinking—1) May say they are safer there. 2) They found it was dangerous to get on the ground. 3) Students should say Australia is south of the equator. 4) Answers will vary.

Hummingbird *(The Smallest, Brightest Birds)*

Vocabulary—cobweb, beak, dart, camouflaged, pollen, slender, hover, nectar, ranges.

Comprehension—1) humming of their wings. 2) North and South America. 3) 19 species. 4) pollen. 5) insects.

Thinking—1) Brightly colored. 2) Sugar. 3) May say how fast they are and how they fly so well. 4) Answers vary, but may mention their beauty or size. 5) Answers will vary, but they don't want to injure that bill which is important for eating.

Reading Concept—(c) They eat insects, pollinate flowers, and are fun to see.

Giraffe *(The World's Tallest Animal)*

Vocabulary—mane, nurse, cud, gait, tawny, strands, savanna, forelegs.

Comprehension—1) They have live babies and nurse them. 2) They have long legs and their long gait looks slow. 3) Predators like lions, and people poaching them. 4) Camouflage and ability to run fast. 5) To keep blood from rushing to head and fainting.

Thinking—1) It is hard for them to get up and down, and they're safer. 2) So they can reach their mother's milk. 3) He politely saved lower leaves for wife and children.

Concepts—1) (a) Reach leaves they eat. 2) (a) Leaves. 3) (b) Different. 4) (b) Herbivore.

Jellyfish *(Watch Out for Jellyfish!)*

Vocabulary—colony, marine, medusa, minnow, biologist, diameter, hazard, toxin, plankton.

Comprehension—1) It has a jelly-like material under its skin. 2) Drift with the current or expand and contract umbrella of tentacles. 3) Size, color, and poison level. 4) They grab prey, sting it, and arms push it into mouth. 5) Observe it but don't touch it.

Thinking—1) They don't have any. 2) To catch it since they can't outswim it. 3) You can't tell which ones sting. 4) Fun, job, attitude, etc.

Reading Concepts—(c) I don't know if it will sting and cause pain and a rash.

Skunks *(Whose Stomping Ground Is It?)*

Vocabulary—glands, emit, musk, carrion, dye, nocturnal, hibernate, whiff, species.

Comprehension—1) It stomps its feet, growls, and raises its tail high. 2) Striped, spotted, and hognose. 3) A bath in vinegar or tomato juice. 4) Grubs, insects, beetles, worms, mice, carrion, fruit, grain, eggs, and people food.

Thinking—1) They have to turn their tail end toward the enemy to spray. 2) They aren't willing to be sprayed. 3) Answers will be interesting! 4) They must think their spray can keep cars away.

Reading Concepts—Eat many pests, but create bad odor.

Porcupine *(A Prickly Mammal)*

Vocabulary—herbivores, rodents, quills, barb, perspiration, thrash, marten.

Comprehension—1) They gnaw. 2) A rock pile or hollow log or tree. 3) Sharp claws. 4) They have barbs on them. 5) They starve since they can't eat; infection, too.

Thinking—1) They kill many trees. 2) They are lighter to carry and swim with. 3) Maybe they didn't notice the thrashing tail. 4) Hard on forests and gnaw tools. 5) Answers will vary.

Zebras *(The Horse Tigers)*

Vocabulary—1) foals 2) ranch 3) graze 4) mane 5) plains 6) native 7) stallion 8) colt 9) filly 10) mare.

Comprehension—1) Same body style, food, and some behaviors. 2) Zebras are striped, have bigger ears, an erect mane, weigh less, and are shorter. 3) It's too hot, so they're in the shade the rest of the day. 4) Braying and barking and with certain looks.

Thinking—1) Lookouts warn the herd and they can outrun lions. 2) By the stripes and by close association. 3) Probably hearing, but students may justify another. 4) How fast they run, brown stripes, mane, mudrolling, etc. 5) Humans have killed some and encroached.

Barn Owls *(Barn Owls Don't Hoot)*

Vocabulary—1) prey 2) roost 3) down 4) rotate 5) pellet 6) talons 7) rodents 8) symbol.

Comprehension—1) Hide better. 2) They eat rodents. 3) They hear it and then see it and swoop in. 4) Fur, bones, and feathers. 5) Their fluffy feathers muffle sound of flight.

Thinking—1) Most dislike looking like a monkey. 2) Eyes maybe. 3) They can turn their head 3/4 the way around. 4) Students might mention hearing, head swivels, flying silently, etc. 5) May say they never see them. 6) Pupils may need help knowing that farmers didn't use to remove some cover for rodents and open grain bins have disappeared, too. 7) Answers will vary.

Raccoon *(Is He Washing for Dinner?)*

Vocabulary—1) myth 2) coop 3) survive 4) colonists 5) quest 6) fend 7) observation 8) gestation.

Reading Concepts—1) hand 2) moisten 3) mask 4) swimmers 5) farmers 6) 50 lbs. 7) corn fields 8) night 9) tails 10) mammals.

Comprehension—1) Fur for hats and coats; hunting sport and eating. 2) They will have to return to the wild when they get about one. 3) To moisten it, and food caught in water.

Thinking—1) They eat from garbage cans and eat when no water is around. 2) They're born without masks. 3) Grain is eaten and poultry raided. 4) Answers will vary.

Lions *(King of the Beasts)*

Vocabulary—1) lioness 2) pride 3) mane 4) admire 5) prey 6) litter 7) pregnant 8) habitat.

Comprehension—1) Mid-Africa on the Savanna. 2) Guard the pride and fight off enemies. 3) All of the hunting and caring for the cubs. 4) Sharp claws, teeth, great hearing and eyesight, and perhaps their stealth and cunning.

Thinking—1) Probably will say it's the strength and "kingly" looks with the mane. 2) They don't live in the jungle, they live on the savanna grasslands. 3) Maybe it's the taste or the ease of catching them. 4) Maybe it's their relaxed posture or look in the eye. 5) Answers will vary.

Wart Hogs *(Warts Can Be Beautiful)*

Vocabulary—1) sounder 2) sow 3) boar 4) theory 5) huddle 6) tasseled 7) safari 8) diurnal 9) visible 10) suckle.

Comprehension—1) The 4 warts on its face and 4 tusks sticking out of its mouth on a long head with eyes set up high. 2) Ripping enemies with the tusks, also running fast. 3) Grass and leaves, also eggs and small mammals; graze by crawling on the front knees. 4) They can't sweat and wallow to cool off.

Thinking—1) Probably because they look good to themselves but ugly to everyone else. 2) May say crawling on knees, or mud wallowing, or running with tail erect. 3) Maybe because they hide in dens, run fast, or have enough babies. 4) Answers will vary. 5) Maybe because they both look strange.

Roadrunners *(Beep-beep!)*

Vocabulary—1) diet 2) zigzag 3) alert 4) fangs 5) crude 6) streamlined 7) design 8) maximum.

Comprehension—1) Southwest or desert; New Mexico (it needs to be emphasized as a state). 2) Its habit of running down the road beside or in front of vehicles. 3) They run fast, but the main thing is the zigzag action eludes coyote. 4) Carefully grabbing them behind the head and hitting them on the ground. 5) Steer with, changing direction fast.

Thinking—1) They don't fly well, food is on the ground, and legs are strong and fast. 2) Maybe snakes are plentiful, and the skill of roadrunners decreases the risk. 3) That will elicit interesting answers! 4) Racing cars, or killing snakes, etc. 5) Answers will vary.

Woodchuck *(Could a Woodchuck Chuck Wood?)*

Vocabulary—1) chuck 2) torpor 3) alfalfa 4) shrill 5) haunches 6) venture 7) superstition 8) complex 9) excavate 10) rumpled.

Comprehension—1) A Native American word, *wuchak*. 2) No flat tail, much smaller, its fur isn't nice like a beaver, and food and homes are different, too. 3) To carry them through the winter hibernation. 4) Its body temperature, heart rate, and breathing. 5) They eat hay crop and burrows ruin equipment.

Thinking—1) Perhaps burrowing and eating habits gave them the name. 2) They don't gnaw wood or carry it, so they sure don't throw it. 3) It is its safe haven. 4) It burned the fat and didn't eat all winter. 5) They can see better, but sadly they become easy targets. 6) There is no scientific basis for the tale, so I hope most say no for that reason.

Carp *(A Great Fish Story)*

Vocabulary—1) import 2) mussels 3) adapted 4) koi 5) barbels 6) probe 7) bask 8) value 9) fry 10) spawn.

Comprehension—1) For their beauty and for food (eating). 2) They count rings on the scales (one ring for each spawning). 3) Mirror, leather, scaled, and koi. 4) They feel for it with their barbels. 5) As food, or as ornamental fish. 6) They reduce the population of favored fish and take over the whole stream.

Thinking—1) Probably because they enjoy looking at the beautiful fish. 2) It has more silt or mud to find food in and it is the warmer water, too. 3) Maybe because they are used to the taste of other fish, or don't know how to cook carp. 4) Probably because the fry are eaten by so many fish including the adult carp. 5) They are not a great gamefish and deplete supplies of better gamefish.

Enrichment Activities: Teaching Ideas and Answer Key

1. **Pretend You Are the…:** You could copy the page, write the name of an animal on the top, and have students fill in the blanks regarding whatever animal you chose. You could have individual students, partners, or small groups choose what animal to answer the questions about.

2. **Animal Information on…:** You can write an animal's name on the blank and have every student or group fill in the sections on that animal, or you could allow students or groups to choose an animal to summarize.

3. **Word Search:** The word search could be done by individuals, or partners can learn cooperation and decision-making skills. The three animals done diagonally are CARP/PANDA beginning with third letter in top row, and LION starts at ninth letter over in third row down. The answers for blanks top to bottom are H, O, O, O, H, H, H, O, H, C, O, H, H, C, O, C, H, C, H, O.

4. **Picture Puzzle:** I suggested to students that they glue the puzzle pieces to a sheet to save it. If it is a one-time activity, they could skip backing it and just glue it to a sheet as they unscramble it. The four animals from North America are sea horse, cardinal, carp, and roadrunner. Lion and wart hog = Africa and kangaroo = Australia while panda = Asia.

5. **Drawing Favorite Animals:** You may need to illustrate how students can draw within each right-hand square the reverse lines of left-hand squares. I did this with students by making an overhead transparency to illustrate the process. You may wish to make enough small grid transparencies for students to overlay other pictures to draw on graph paper.

6. **Secret Word Puzzles:** Instructions should be self-explanatory, but you may want to assist a few students by filling in some letters for them. Answers (top to bottom): kangaroo, cardinal, ostrich, zebra, jellyfish, Africa, sea horse, koalas, and secret word = giraffes; barn owl, woodchuck, raccoon, panda, wart hog, porcupine, skunk, lion, sea cuke, carp, and secret word = roadrunner.

7. **Animal Crossword Puzzle:** *Across:* 2) skunk 4) zebra 5) caw 7) La 8) lion 9) carp 12) ostrich 14) owls 15) he 16) oyster. *Down:* 1) gerbil 2) sea horse 3) koalas 6) wart hog 9) coon 10) prey 11) fox 13) cat.

8. **Look in Your Memory Bank:** This page could be a pretest/posttest or a discussion sheet. Answers: 1) giraffe 2) carp 3) roadrunner 4) lion 5) jellyfish 6) raccoons 7) equus 8) marsupial 9) 12 10) tail 11) hearing 12) False 13) pride 14) boar 15) herbivore 16) sea horse 17) tentacles 18) ostrich 19) cardinal 20) koala 21) second 22) carnivores.

9. **Crazy Captions:** This is a good opportunity for students to use their imagination and have fun writing. Guide students to ensure that the captions are fun and not negative in tone.

10. **Name That Animal:** You can use the list on page 206 to help with this activity.

1. Pretend You Are the _____

1. Draw a small picture of your animal species in the box.

2. Where do you and your relatives live? _____
_____

3. What can you do now that you couldn't do as a human?
_____

4. What is your species' most important feature? _____
Why? _____

5. What looks would you change about your species?
_____

6. What is your species' most boring activity?
_____

7. What are you most afraid of as one of these animals? _____
How do you defend yourself? _____
_____

8. What is the most fun being this animal? _____
_____

9. Would you like to become human again? _____
Why? _____

© 2000 by The Center for Applied Research in Education

Name _____ Date _____

2. Animal Information on _____

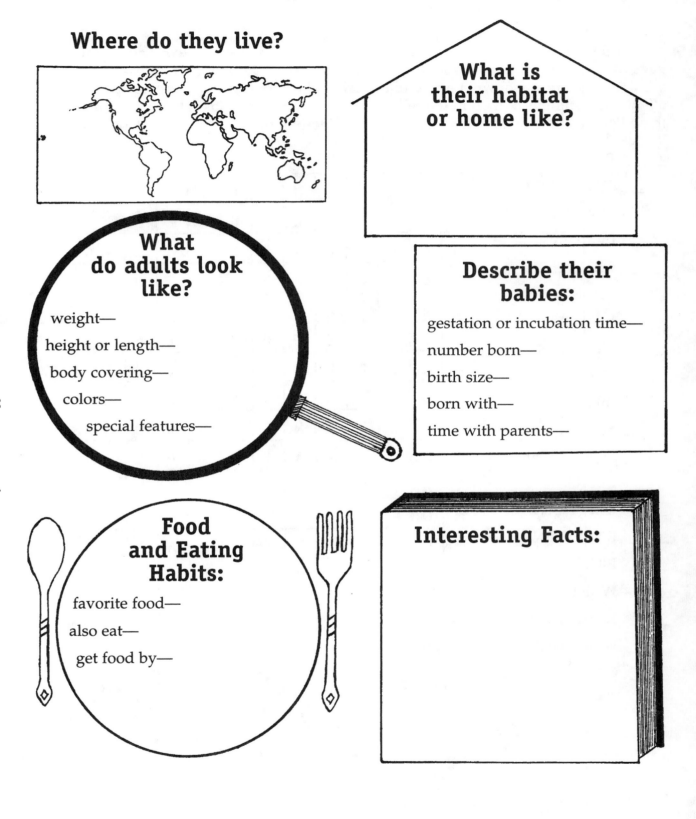

Where do they live?

What is their habitat or home like?

What do adults look like?

weight—

height or length—

body covering—

colors—

special features—

Describe their babies:

gestation or incubation time—

number born—

birth size—

born with—

time with parents—

Food and Eating Habits:

favorite food—

also eat—

get food by—

Interesting Facts:

Name _____ Date _____

3. Word Search

Find the names of the animals listed in the box in the word search. Three animals have their names written diagonally, but nine are written horizontally across and eight are written vertically down. Be careful to stick to the list of twenty because there are also a few other animals hidden in the search. When you have found all twenty animals, print these letters on the blanks: **C** = Carnivore, **H** = Herbivore, **O** = Omnivore. Good luck!

_____ PANDA

_____ SEA HORSE

_____ SEA CUCUMBER

_____ CARDINAL

_____ OSTRICH

_____ KANGAROO

_____ KOALA

_____ HUMMINGBIRD

_____ GIRAFFE

_____ JELLYFISH

_____ SKUNK

_____ PORCUPINE

_____ ZEBRA

_____ BARN OWL

_____ RACCOON

_____ LION

_____ WART HOG

_____ ROADRUNNER

_____ WOODCHUCK

_____ CARP

S	A	C	K	A	N	Z	D	O	N	K	E	Y	S
T	Y	R	A	C	C	O	O	N	E	W	T	S	A
U	A	S	N	R	A	S	B	L	A	C	K	E	Y
R	B	U	G	O	P	E	A	Z	I	B	R	A	T
P	E	T	A	W	W	A	R	T	H	O	G	C	I
O	S	T	R	I	C	H	N	E	L	R	N	U	C
R	K	E	O	L	W	O	O	D	C	H	U	C	K
C	U	C	O	O	S	R	W	R	A	T	H	U	G
U	N	C	L	E	N	S	L	U	R	O	O	M	I
P	K	O	A	L	A	E	B	A	D	G	E	B	R
I	H	U	M	M	I	N	G	B	I	R	D	E	A
N	O	G	R	O	A	D	R	U	N	N	E	R	F
E	M	I	L	Y	Z	E	B	R	A	S	U	R	F
J	E	L	L	Y	F	I	S	H	L	U	C	Y	E

© 2000 by The Center for Applied Research in Education

Name _____ Date _____

4. Picture Puzzle

You might want to glue this page to a backing paper before you cut out the blocks and put the puzzle together. Print **N.A.** in the circle under the four animals pictured that are commonly found in North America. Print the first three letters of the names of the continents where the other four animals are found.

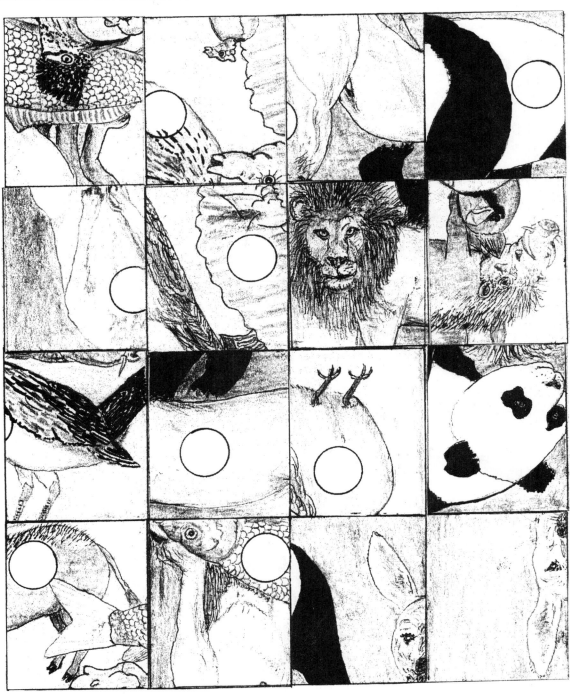

5. Drawing Favorite Animals

Use the grid to draw the other half of the kangaroo. Then use the same method to draw another animal.

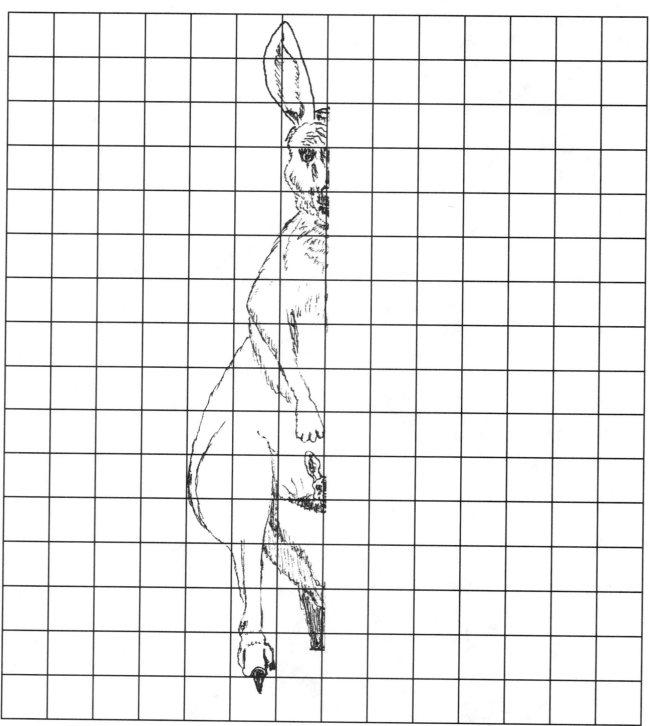

Name _____   Date _____

6. Secret Word Puzzles

Use the clues to fill in the missing letters in each line. Then look for the secret words down the middle of the puzzles.

She has a baby named Joey.

State bird in seven states sees red.

Bird that can run up to 43 miles per hour.

No two striped equus the same.

Sea nettles can be painful.

Continent where lionesses catch buffaloes.

Prehensile tail holds on for pregnant males.

Australian cuties not bears.

The secret animals in this puzzle are the _____.

Check our pellets for barn rodents.

"I saw my shadow! Goodnight all!"

Newborns don't have rings or masks yet.

China "bear" is not a bear.

Tusks are not their ugliest feature.

Pine marten eats them.

Stomp, tails up; get back!

We really have our pride.

The pickle of the sea isn't tasty. *(nickname)*

Beautiful koi, goldfish, and scales.

The secret animal in this puzzle is the _____.

Name _____ Date _____

7. Animal Crossword Puzzle

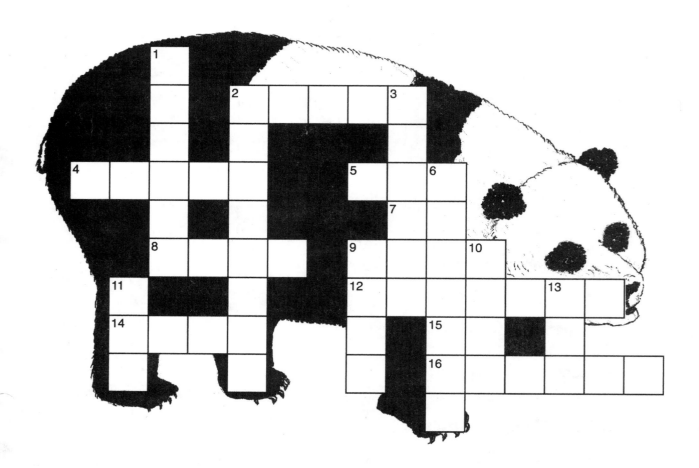

Across:
2. Stomps and sprays
4. Striped horse
5. Call of a crow
7. Do, Re, Mi, Fa, So, ___
8. King of beasts
9. Goldfish family
12. Fastest bird on land
14. Wise birds of prey
15. Male subject pronoun
16. Produces pearls

Down:
1. Earth color mouse-like pet
2. Male carries babies
3. Love eucalyptus
6. Pumbaa is a _____.
9. Ringtail's short name
10. Predator's quarry
11. Sly as a _____.
13. Lion or tiger

© 2000 by The Center for Applied Research in Education

Name _____ Date _____

8. Look in Your Memory Bank

Use your memory to answer these questions. A list of possible answers is shown at the bottom of this page, but you won't need all of them.

1. The tallest animal in the world is the _____.

2. The goldfish is a member of the family of fish called the _____.

3. The fastest running wild bird in the United States is the _____.

4. The _____ is king of the jungle but lives on Africa's grasslands.

5. Portuguese man-of-war and sea wasps are in a _____ family.

6. Giant pandas are in the same mammal family with _____ because of their grasping thumbs.

7. The zebra is an African mammal in the horse family called _____.

8. The kangaroo is a pouched mammal called a _____.

9. Skunks can spray you if you are within _____ feet of their raised tail.

10. Porcupines can't throw their quills, but they can hit with their _____.

11. Most owls depend primarily on their sense of _____.

12. True or False? Raccoons wash their food before they eat it. _____

13. Lions live in a family grouping called a _____.

14. A male wart hog is called a _____.

15. The woodchuck only eats plants, so it is an _____.

16. The male _____ seems pregnant because he has babies.

17. Sea cucumbers use _____ to put food in their mouth.

18. The biggest bird is also the fastest runner. It is the _____.

19. The red bird that is state bird in seven states is the _____.

20. The animal whose name means "no water" is the _____.

21. Hummingbirds' wings beat sixty to seventy times per second minute hour day. (Circle one.)

22. The lions primarily eat meat, so they are called _____.

   carnivores, herbivores, omnivores, giant panda, sea horse, sea cucumber, jellyfish, porcupine, carp, 10, 2, 12, 20, ostrich, giraffe, skunk, cardinals, lion, sounder, raccoon, roadrunner, sow, boar, kit, foot, tail, koala, equus, tentacles, squid, true, false, second, minute, hour, smell, sight, hearing, mandible, marsupial

Name _____   Date _____

9. Crazy Captions

You have learned that a caption tells about a picture. A caption should tell the readers what the illustration means. Study the illustrations on this page and write a caption to tell what you think the message in the picture should be. Your captions may tell what the animals are thinking, doing, hearing, seeing, or saying for us. Please make the captions interesting, but make sure they do not offend anyone.

Name _____   Date _____

10. Name that Animal

The format of this game may seem familiar to many. One or two students think of an animal that classmates should be familiar with. (You may want them to tell you what it is, or at least write it on a secret slip of paper.) They want the class to try to identify this animal by using information gathered by asking a set of "yes" and "no" questions. The following guidelines or rules are suggested:

- Students with a hand raised should be recognized to ask one question.
- The leader(s) will only be able to answer with a "yes" or "no."
- The class or teams may have two short conferences at any point in the questions to share thoughts and theories, or to formulate good questions to get data.
- The student or team to guess the correct animal is the winner and gets to be the leader(s) and provide another animal for the class to identify. If the class is stumped, then you may have the leaders choose who goes next.

You could limit the number of questions to twenty or twenty-five. You could also limit the time to ten minutes per animal, but leaders have to answer in a timely manner. I used to award five points to the leaders for incorrect guesses to discourage using up the twenty questions or time by guessing. I also found it helpful to limit students to one or two guesses per round. You may want to use the list of eighty animals or another limiting list. It is also important to decide ahead of time how specific answers must be. (Will any snake do, or does it have to be a cobra? Any dog or cat, or do they name the breed?)

You might want to encourage the asking of the following types of questions:

1. Is it a vertebrate? (This eliminates 955,000 or so species if it is!)
2. Is it a mammal, bird, fish, reptile, amphibian, or insect? (one at a time, of course)
3. Is it a carnivore, herbivore, or omnivore? (again, one at a time)
4. Is it found in our state? United States? Habitat questions are good. (desert, forest, arctic, plain)
5. Comparative size questions are often helpful.
6. Body coverings, colors, and other body features can be good clues, too.
7. Some may want to pursue the reproduction of this animal.
8. Knowing whether it is endangered or extinct may be helpful.
9. Speed, strength, or defense mechanisms may help solve what animal it is.

You may choose to play this game using a team format if you find friends share answers so they can monopolize the game. The team concept does provide for more "winners" and promotes cooperation on teams as well. If you dislike competition, then team formats won't work. The whole idea is to learn how animals are classified and to have fun socializing in an educational setting.

You could have the class brainstorm a list of potential animals to be used for the game, or you can use the list of "Eighty Animals in This Book" shown on the following page.

Eighty Animals in This Book

A	B	C	D
Robin	Giant panda	Blue whales	Dolphins
Black bear	Sea horse	Otters	Llama
Ladybug	Sea cucumber	Beavers	Alligators
Jackrabbit	Cardinals	Badger	Praying Mantis
Butterfly	Ostrich	Bald Eagle	Rhinoceros
Gerbil	Kangaroo	Electric eel	Gorillas
Flying squirrel	Koala	Armadillo	Canada goose
Tiger	Hummingbirds	Hippopotamus	Fur seals
Walrus	Giraffe	Octopus	Mountain lion
Elephant	Jellyfish	Black widow	Tarantula
Opossum	Skunk	Orangutan	Cheetah
Camel	Porcupine	Anaconda	Cobra
Chipmunk	Zebra	Giant anteater	Chimpanzee
Fox	Barn owl	Polar bear	Honeybee
Sea turtle	Raccoon	Mallard	Grizzly bear
Raven	Lion	Prairie dog	Vampire bat
Coyote	Wart hog	Bison	Emperor penguin
Grasshopper	Roadrunner	Snapping turtle	Great white shark
Reindeer	Woodchuck	Falcon	Wolves
Mouse	Carp	Orca (Killer whale)	Komodo dragon

Extra Animal List:

Dogs	Cats	Horse	Starfish	Guinea pig
Cow	Pig	Sheep	Flamingo	Grouse
Donkey	Frog	Goat	Python	Pheasant
Rat	Toad	Salamander	Cricket	Salmon
Clam	Crab	Lobster	Ants	Garter snake
Tick	Scorpion	Earthworm	Goldfish	Jaguar
Deer	Monkey	Antelope	Chickadee	Sparrow
Elk	Mosquito	Fly	Pigeon	Rattlesnake
Blue Jay	Trout	Bass	Chameleon	Moose

Reading Level 5

Before Reading the Story:
New Vocabulary and Questions to Ask

1. The Biggest Mammal

New Vocabulary:

baleen	inhale
blubber	mammal
buoyancy	migrate
exhale	plankton
extinct	sleek
flukes	species

Questions to Ask:

What is the biggest animal ever to live?
What group of animals do whales go into?
Is our gym long enough for a blue whale?
How do whales feed their babies?
Why are many whales endangered?
What do blue whales eat? How?

2. Playful River Otters

New Vocabulary:

aquatic	frolic
burrow	insulate
carnivore	nostrils
expert	submerge

Questions to Ask:

What mammal loves to go sliding on hills?
Why don't we see otters very often?
What do you think otters eat?
Why were otters nearly extinct at one time?

3. The Largest Rodent in North America

New Vocabulary:

ambitious	mature
forepaws	pioneer
fossils	steer
incisors	superb

Questions to Ask:

What do you recall a rodent as being?
What do you already know about beavers?
Have any of you seen some beavers (or signs
  of them)?
What would you like to know about beavers?

4. Dig Those Badgers

New Vocabulary:

badgering	habitat
fierce	hibernate
gestation	omnivore
gland	weaned

Questions to Ask:

Have you ever heard of badgering?
What are badgers like?
Where do badgers live?
Do we see badgers very often? Why?

5. The Great American Bird

New Vocabulary:

carrion	prey
keen	rare
majestic	salmon
osprey	soar
pesticides	talons

Questions to Ask:

What bird is our nation's symbol?
Is the male bald eagle bigger than the female?
What is the eagle's nest like?
What is the main food of bald eagles?
Why are bald eagles no longer so endangered?

6. A Real Shocking Story

New Vocabulary:

current	related
fry	stun
organs	surface
pollution	volts
radar	

Questions to Ask:

Have you ever heard of eels?
Do you know where electric eels live?
Can electric eels shock with much power?
How do electric eels catch their food?
Do you know of any enemy they have?

7. A Night in Armor

New Vocabulary:

armor	flex
buoyant	forage
burrow	litter
defense	nocturnal

Questions to Ask:

What animal wears a suit of armor?
Do any armadillos live in the United States?
What do armadillos eat?
What kind of home do armadillos build?

8. The River Horses

New Vocabulary:

aquatic	herbivorous
consume	moist
emit	protruding
fluid	seldom
gestation	tusks

Questions to Ask:

What is the second largest land mammal?
Where does the hippo live?
Why are hippos' ears, eyes, and nostrils high
    on the head?
What is the worst enemy of the hippo?

9. The Most Intelligent Invertebrate?

New Vocabulary:

eject	paralyzing
gills	pigment
inject	siphon
invertebrate	tentacles
mantle	

Questions to Ask:

What do you know about the octopus?
Do octopi have bones?
Do you know what a mollusk is?
Do many people eat octopus?
What do octopi like to eat?

10. Our Most Dangerous Spider

New Vocabulary:

abdomen	stressed
aggressive	venomous
arachnids	victim
distinguish	widow
fatal	

Questions to Ask:

What is the most dangerous U.S. spider?
Where are black widows often found?
How can you recognize black widows?
Are black widows a great danger to people?
Have any of you seen a black widow?

11. Man of the Woods

New Vocabulary:

ape	fossil
canopy	gestation

Questions to Ask:

Have you ever seen an orangutan?
Why are orangutans so popular in movies?

crude	habitat	Where in the world do wild orangutans live?
diurnal	legend	What do you think orangutans like to eat?
erect	lofty	Why do you think orangutans are endangered?

12. The Biggest Snake in the World

New Vocabulary: *Questions to Ask:*

anaconda	elastic	What do you think is the biggest snake?
brood	jaguar	Why are some snakes called constrictors?
coil	python	How do snakes eat their food?
constrict	venom	How many of you are afraid of snakes?

13. The Ant Bear

New Vocabulary: *Questions to Ask:*

camouflaged	lumber	Can any of you describe an anteater?
coarse	moisture	How do you think anteaters find ants?
defense	nocturnal	Where do you think wild anteaters live?
extract	probe	Do you think anteaters are dangerous?
larva(e)	rare	Have you ever seen an anteater at the zoo?

14. The Sea Bear

New Vocabulary: *Questions to Ask:*

Arctic	stalking	What do you know about polar bears?
food chain	triplets	Why are they such good swimmers?
kelp	tundra	What do polar bears eat mostly?
nostrils	webs	How can they survive the arctic cold?
nursery		How are their cubs raised in the Arctic?

15. Those Old Ducks

New Vocabulary: *Questions to Ask:*

dabblers	imprinting	What duck is the origin of all tame ducks?
descended	natal	How many of you know what mallards look like?
domesticated	preening	What are male ducks called? Females?
down	reservoirs	Why do ducks and other birds preen?
drake	speculum	What do ducks eat mostly?
flyways	staging	Are we close to one of the flyways? Which?

16. Where Has Little Dog Gone?

New Vocabulary: *Questions to Ask:*

acute	ferrets	Have any of you seen prairie dogs? Where?
boundary	imitate	What do prairie dogs look like?
chambers	lookout	What are they related to?
coterie	privilege	Why are they called prairie dogs?
detect	vision	Do you have any idea how prairie dogs spoil pups?
		Do you think prairie dogs are a pest to anyone?

17. Largest Land Animal in the United States?

New Vocabulary:

conservationists slaughter
dung stampede
rituals sunscreen
rumination tendons
significant vital

Questions to Ask:

What is the largest land animal in North America?
Why call them buffalo if the right name is bison?
What do you picture first when you think of bison?
Why were so many bison killed?
Are bison endangered? Why?

18. Watch Your Fingers!

New Vocabulary:

burlap groping
carapace lunge
devour lure
encounter plastron
flailing vertebrates

Questions to Ask:

Have you ever heard of snapping turtles?
Do snapping turtles live around here? Who saw one?
How big do snapping turtles get?
What scientific classification are snapping turtles in?
How are snapping turtle babies born (hatched)?

19. The Fastest Creature on Earth!

New Vocabulary:

banning mustache
efficient nickname
eyrie remote
falconry stoop
fledgling teasing

Questions to Ask:

What is the fastest animal in the world?
How fast can falcons go (80, 100, 200 miles per hour)?
Have any of you seen a falcon? Where?
What is the sport of falconry?
How did falcons almost become extinct?

20. The Beautiful Killer Whale

New Vocabulary:

breaching individual
communication nannies
distinct pod
echolocation romp
fertile zoologists

Questions to Ask:

What is the fastest-swimming mammal?
How many of you have seen an orca? Where?
What other name is used for orcas? Killer?
Why are orcas popular at marine parks?
Do you know how orcas communicate?

1. The Biggest Mammal

I was on a boat and saw some enormous sea creatures south of Florida. I was told they were baleen whales, which are much bigger than toothed whales. I know baleen whales have plates of material, called baleen, in their mouth. Baleen hangs from the roof of their mouth and is made of a material like your fingernails. It looks like a huge comb and is used to filter out plankton—drifting clumps of tiny animals and plants. Our ship's captain told me their feeding grounds are in the Arctic and Antarctic, where plankton is plentiful, but they migrate to the warm tropics to have their babies.

Blue whales are the largest of the baleen whales, and they are bigger than any other animal that has ever lived. They have been known to get to 100 feet (30 meters) long. That is as long as three classrooms together. They weigh over 300,000 pounds (135,000 kilograms), which is more than the weight of thirty elephants. A land animal can only become so big before the bones can't hold up the body weight. The support of water helps the blue whales grow much larger than land animals. Whales are long and sleek so it is easier to use their flukes (sideways tail fins) to move all that weight.

I learned that whales are mammals instead of fish. To prove that I must explain that they've lost some of their mammal looks, such as the hair and four legs. They still have a few stiff hairs on their head, and flippers took the place of front legs. You know fish breathe underwater with gills and have up and down tail fins. Well, whales have lungs to breathe air like we do and have sideways tail fins. Whales are warm-blooded, unlike most fish, which are cold-blooded. Whales give birth to live babies and feed them with milk from the mother. Most fish lay eggs and don't feed their babies. You can now see why whales are grouped with the rest of us mammals.

© 2000 by The Center for Applied Research in Education

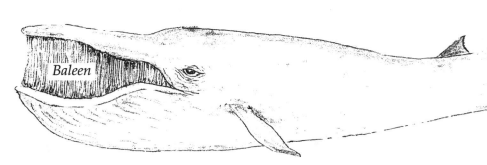

Flukes

Baleen

Average Man

Whales have a 6-inch (15-centimeter) layer of blubber, or fat, under their skin to help keep them warm and feed themselves when food is scarce. Blubber gives whales more buoyancy (floating lift) so it is easier for them to come up every 15 minutes or so to exhale (blow out) air through the blow holes on top of the head. They'll stay underwater for two hours when they need to, however. They inhale (breathe in) about 2,100 quarts (2,000 liters) of air. People usually only see a pod (herd) of whales as they come up and exhale, blowing spouts of water and vapors 20 feet into the air.

The father (bull) and mother (cow) usually migrate or move to warm water for the birth of their baby (calf), which is a big animal when it's born. Blue whale calves are 23 feet (7 meters) long and weigh 16,000 pounds (7,200 kilograms) when born. Since their mother's milk is so rich, they gain about 200 pounds (91 kilograms) a day during their seven-month nursing time. I was amazed to learn that the babies drink about 160 gallons of milk a day, but I've never seen that since they're fed underwater.

I found out that humans killed so many blue whales in the past that they're an endangered species. During 1930 and 1931, over 30,000 blue whales were killed. But in 1946, countries all over the world decided to protect the whales. They stopped all hunting of several species including blue whales. In 1971, the United States quit hunting whales and won't even buy any whale products. Scientists think that all species of whales have been saved for right now, but we will have to protect them for a long time to make sure they don't become extinct.

The Biggest Mammal

Vocabulary Checkup ~~Write the words~~ from the box ~~on~~ the correct blanks.

Draw a line *to*

baleen _____ warm-blooded and fed on mother's milk

blubber _____ a whale's sideways tail fins

buoyancy _____ means to move to another region

exhale _____ clumps of drifting sea plants and animals

extinct _____ a floating or lifting-up action

flukes _____ when animals breathe in

inhale _____ when animals breathe out

mammal _____ bony matter in some whales' mouth

migrate _____ no more of the species living

plankton _____ the fat on some animals

sleek _____ kinds or types of animals or plants

species _____ smooth and streamlined

Comprehension You may need to look back at the story to answer the questions correctly.

1. Two ways whales show they are mammals:

_____

_____

2. Describe how baleen whales eat. _____

_____

3. Whale calves grow fast because _____

_____

_____

4. Two ways blubber helps whales: _____

_____

5. Why do whales go to warm waters if there is more food in the Arctic?

_____

Name _____ Date _____

© 2000 by The Center for Applied Research in Education

214

The Biggest Mammal

Thinking About Whales Think carefully before answering the questions.

1. Why can whales get so much bigger than land animals?

   _____

   _____

2. How do you think fish are different from whales? _____

   _____

3. Why do you think people began hunting whales? _____

   _____

   _____

4. What did you think was the most amazing thing about the blue whales?

   _____

   _____

5. Do you think whales will ever become extinct? _____

   Why? _____

   _____

6. Would you like to go on a whale-watching boat? _____

   Why? _____

   _____

Check It Out Find out about

Bowhead whales   Right whales
Humpback whales   Toothed whales
Finback whales

Name _____ Date _____

2. Playful River Otters

I watched some otters playing on the river bank last night. They are the clowns of streams on every continent except Australia and Antarctica. These mammals are the aquatic members of the weasel family since they spend nearly all of their time in the water playing. They are expert divers and swimmers who love to frolic, wrestle, and swim in loops and circles in the water. They build slides on muddy or snowy stream banks to slide and slither down to their swimming hole.

I've heard that giant otters in South America can grow to 7 feet (2 meters) long, but the rest of the freshwater otters of the world average 3 feet long (1 meter) and weigh close to 20 pounds (9 kilograms). Their fur is a medium to dark brown and is oily to keep water away from their skin. The belly is a lighter brown, and there is usually a white patch on the throat. Even though they have claws, they have webbing between their toes to help them swim faster. Otters in colder regions also have a layer of fat under the skin that helps insulate them from the cold. They have muscles that close their ears and nostrils to make it easier to submerge underwater for three to four minutes. Otters' eyes remain open so they can spot prey. If the water is murky, they will dig on the bottom and use their front feet and their whiskers to find food.

River otters are carnivores, and fish is their favorite food. They are such fast swimmers that they can zoom in behind a trout and grab it in their sharp teeth. Most of the fish they eat are the slower swimmers like carp, suckers, and bullhead 6 inches or smaller. They eat shellfish like

(Playful River Otters, *continued*)

crayfish and clams, too. They also catch a frog, snail, turtle, or snake once in a while. They will travel several miles in a night to find food.

The female otter will find a burrow in the bank or any hollowed-out place under roots or rocks that is close to the water for a den. Her babies are born in February or March with their eyes closed and no teeth. It is a good thing they have a coat of fur at birth. Mother will nurse two to four pups or cubs for about two months. Then she will teach them to hunt for food with her. Strangely, these pups can't swim until they are a few months old and get a signal like a growl, squeak, or a nudge from their mom. They are finally off to play and eat on their own after nearly nine months of training.

Humans have trapped otters for their soft, valuable fur for hundreds of years. Now we regulate carefully how many are taken. Otters have become more nocturnal where humans have crowded them, playing and eating mostly at night. They are some of the most intelligent of the smaller mammals. We hope these playful, beautiful creatures will never become extinct.

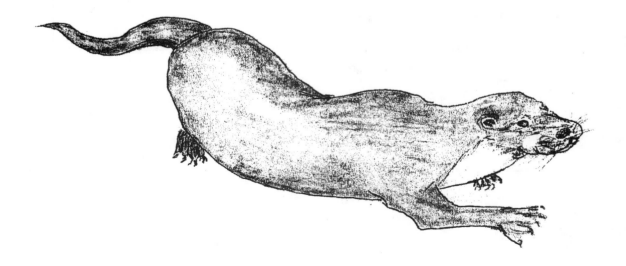

Playful River Otters

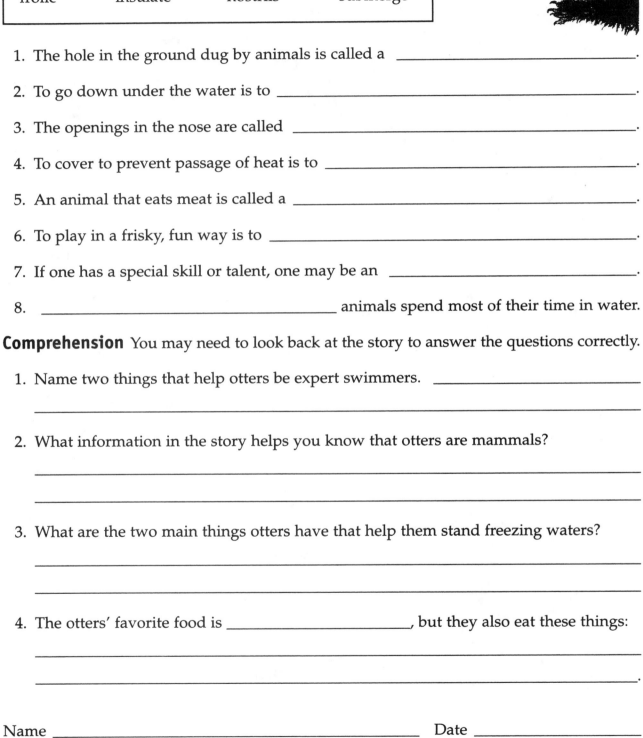

Vocabulary Checkup Write the words from the box on the correct blanks.

aquatic	burrow	carnivore	expert
frolic	insulate	nostrils	submerge

1. The hole in the ground dug by animals is called a _____.

2. To go down under the water is to _____.

3. The openings in the nose are called _____.

4. To cover to prevent passage of heat is to _____.

5. An animal that eats meat is called a _____.

6. To play in a frisky, fun way is to _____.

7. If one has a special skill or talent, one may be an _____.

8. _____ animals spend most of their time in water.

Comprehension You may need to look back at the story to answer the questions correctly.

1. Name two things that help otters be expert swimmers. _____
   _____

2. What information in the story helps you know that otters are mammals?
   _____
   _____

3. What are the two main things otters have that help them stand freezing waters?
   _____
   _____

4. The otters' favorite food is _____, but they also eat these things:
   _____
   _____.

Name _____ Date _____

Playful River Otters

Thinking About River Otters Think carefully before answering the questions.

1. Why do you think otters spend so much time playing?

    _____

    _____

2. Why have many otters become more nocturnal creatures?

    _____

    _____

3. What would you like most of all to watch the river otters do?

    _____

    _____

4. Do you think the mother otter raises the pups by herself? _____

    Why? _____

    _____

5. How can people help protect otters and make sure they don't become extinct?

    _____

    _____

Check It Out Find out about

    Sea otters

    European otters

    Sable

    Ermine

    Ferret

    Otter furs

© 2000 by The Center for Applied Research in Education

Name _____ Date _____

3. The Largest Rodent in North America

Did you know there are more beavers in the United States and Canada than anywhere else in the world? These large water rodents are famous for cutting down trees with their large front incisors. Since they always seem to be working, we often use sayings like "busy as a beaver," or "eager beaver," to describe hard-working, ambitious people. I wonder if those sayings began with the pioneers.

Mature North American beavers are about 4 feet (120 centimeters) long, including the tail. They can weigh about 60 pounds (27 kilograms). Beavers keep growing for all sixteen years of their life. A few old beavers have reached 100 pounds! Fossils of 700-pound beavers from 10,000 years ago have been found. The beaver's soft underfur traps air to help insulate its body even in cold, icy streams. Even though they can't see too well, beavers have keen senses of hearing and smell to warn them of danger. Their webbed feet help them swim a half mile (0.8 kilometer) underwater while holding their breath for fifteen minutes. They can use their forepaws like hands. Their long, flat tail is used to steer while swimming. It also balances them while they stand on their hind legs to cut trees. The tail smacks the water loudly to warn other beavers of enemies or danger.

Beavers have four strong, orange-colored front teeth that are used for gnawing. These teeth continue to grow their whole life, so they never wear out even though a beaver uses them constantly. As a matter of fact, they have to grind their teeth together to keep them from getting too large.

(The Largest Rodent in North America, *continued*)

Beavers cut trees for three reasons: (1) to build their homes called lodges, (2) to build dams to control water depth, and (3) for food to eat. A beaver can gnaw through a 4-inch tree in fifteen minutes! They eat the bark, leaves, and twigs of willow, birch, and poplar trees most of the time. They do not eat the actual wood like some people think. They also love water plants to eat in the warmer months.

Beavers live in their lodges as families. A family usually has the mother and father, two to four kits or pups born this year, and the two to four kits from last year. The parents mate for life. Kits are born with soft fur and eyes open in the spring and can swim a few hours later. The kits live with their parents until they are two years old. They help raise the next set of brothers and sisters and enlarge the lodge and dam. In cold areas they all spend the winter in the darkness of their lodge. They don't really hibernate the way you might think. They come out to get some of the branches they stored in the mud last fall. They will come out even under a frozen pond to drag branches into their underwater tunnels to feed the family several times each week.

The beaver is a fascinating critter because of its broad, flat paddle of a tail, its sharp, orange teeth, and its superb tree-cutting skills. Beaver fur was so valuable for hats and coats for pioneers that the beavers were almost extinct by the late 1800s. Today, beavers are protected by laws and their numbers have increased, so you may get a chance to see a lodge and watch a family of eager beavers at work someday.

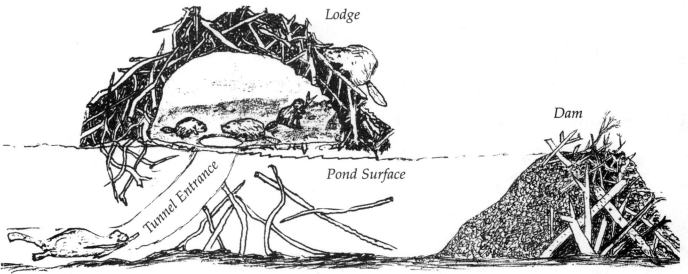

Lodge

Dam

Tunnel Entrance

Pond Surface

The Largest Rodent in North America

Vocabulary Checkup Write the words from the box on the correct blanks.

ambitious	forepaws	fossils	incisors
mature	pioneer	steer	superb

1. To guide or direct as with a rudder is to _____.

2. A _____ is a person who ventures into new territory.

3. To be _____ is to be fully aged or developed.

4. The four front teeth used for cutting are _____.

5. To be _____ is to be very fine or excellent.

6. The front feet on many mammals are called _____.

7. One who is _____ tries very hard with extra effort.

8. The remains or imprints left from living things are _____.

Fact or Opinion Print **F** beside statements that are true or fact. Print **O** beside statements that are opinions.

_____ 1. The two senses most important to beavers are smelling and hearing.

_____ 2. The beaver is a very large rodent.

_____ 3. Beaver fur made beautiful coats and hats.

_____ 4. The beaver has orange colored front teeth.

_____ 5. The United States and Canada have more beavers than any other countries.

Comprehension You may need to look back at the story to answer the questions correctly.

1. How do beavers warn others that danger is near? _____

_____

2. Why don't beavers' incisors wear out? _____

_____

Name _____ Date _____

© 2000 by The Center for Applied Research in Education

The Largest Rodent in North America

3. Why were beavers almost extinct at one time in the United States?

_____

_____

4. What are the three ways we read that a beaver uses its tail?

_____

_____

Thinking About Beavers Think carefully before answering the questions.

1. A beaver's life may be busy, but you may think it's dull and boring. How is that so?

_____

_____

2. Describe some ways a beaver lodge is like your own home.

_____

_____

3. What are some ways you can think of that beavers are helpful creatures?

_____

_____

4. What do you think is the most interesting thing about beavers?

_____

_____

Check It Out Find out about
    Capybarra
    Pocket gophers
    Whistling marmots
    Beaver dams
    European beavers

Front Foot   *Hind Foot*

Name _____ Date _____

4. Dig Those Badgers

Perhaps the best digger in the weasel family is the badger. Badgers dig burrows and dens deep into the ground. They dig so fast they can outdig moles and gophers. They eat those two as well as ground squirrels, mice, snakes, and other small animals. They love to dig so much that they will dig out a prairie dog or other burrowing animal and then continue digging to make that burrow another den for themselves. They are true omnivores as they also eat some plants. They are hard to see during the day even when they come out to sun themselves because they flatten out on the ground and look like a dry clump of grass. They hunt mainly at night since they are nocturnal. You may have seen one if you live on the plains or deserts of the West or Midwest in the United States or Canada. Many animals eat their fair share of mice, but they aren't willing to fight the fierce badger for them.

Badgers are about 2 feet (61 centimeters) long and weigh about 25 pounds (11 kilograms). They have flattened heads, short necks, and broad bodies with short, strong legs. They are clumsy runners and waddle when they walk. Their tail is about as long as your hand. Their short front legs end with five sharp claws that are great digging tools. Their fur has a silver-gray appearance. They have a white stripe running from their nose to their neck. Their face has a badge appearance, and that is probably where they got their name.

Badgers are somewhat shy and will hide if people get too close. However, they will fight when they are backed into a corner. You can understand why animals don't want to fight with them. Their sharp claws and teeth help make them ferocious fighters. Mean people used to put them in a box or barrel and send a dog in to get them just to watch the

(Dig Those Badgers, *continued*)

fight. This is probably where the the term *badgering* came from. It means to nag or tease in an unkind way. Badgers do have scent glands like their cousins, the skunks, and can give off unpleasant odors, so that is another reason most animals choose to leave them alone.

In the winter, badgers usually hibernate during the coldest months. The female will have a litter of about four young in the spring after a gestation period of six months. It is normal for one-fourth of the litter to die early, and only one out of the three that are left will live past three years of age. The mother will nurse her cubs for two months down in the den before taking them outside to learn to dig up their own food. They will probably not be totally weaned from the mother's milk until they are about eight months old. Mother is usually expecting a new litter before her cubs are weaned and off on their own.

Humans are the only natural enemy the badgers have. Many badgers are killed by cars as the badgers waddle around. Some people also hunt and trap badgers for their fur. Artists like paint brushes made from badger bristle. It has become more difficult to get a license to kill or catch badgers in recent years. A few people have caught the young and tamed them as unusual pets, but it is best to leave them in their natural habitat, where they will be much happier. You may remember what some mean people did with badgers they caught, so it is now against the law to keep any wild animal without a permit.

Dig Those Badgers

Vocabulary Checkup Write the words from the box on the correct blanks.

badgering	fierce	gland	gestation
habitat	hibernate	omnivores	weaned

1. Animals that sleep in winter are said to _____.

2. The natural surroundings where one lives is a _____.

3. Very violent, savage, or ferocious fighters are said to be _____.

4. A _____ time is how long babies are inside mom.

5. A _____ is any organ that makes special substances.

6. Animals that eat both plants and animals are _____.

7. When babies are taken off mother's milk, they are _____.

8. _____ means to nag or tease in an unkind way.

Comprehension You may need to look back at the story to answer the questions correctly.

1. What makes badgers such expert diggers? _____
   _____

2. When do badgers usually fight? _____
   _____

3. The badger probably gets its name from _____
   _____.

4. Where did we get the term *badgering*? _____
   _____

5. What are the ways humans are the main enemy of badgers? _____
   _____

Name _____ Date _____

Dig Those Badgers

Thinking About Badgers Think carefully before answering the questions.

1. What probably causes the badger to walk with a waddle and run so poorly?

   _____

   _____

   _____

2. Do you think animals ever attack badgers? _____

   Why? _____

   _____

   _____

3. Please think of why you should not try to adopt a baby badger as a pet.

   _____

   _____

   _____

4. Why do you think badgers would be out on the road where they can get run over?

   _____

   _____

   _____

5. Why do you think the government has made laws to protect badgers?

   _____

   _____

   _____

Check It Out Find out about
   Weasels
   Honey badgers
   American martens
   Mink
   Stoats
   Wolverines

Name _____ Date _____

5. The Great American Bird

The bald eagle looks so fierce and proud that these majestic birds were chosen as the national bird of the United States in 1782. They've been a symbol of freedom and power for centuries. Bald eagles have a wingspan of 7 feet (2 meters). Among the birds of prey, only the California condor is larger. Most birds of prey are small when compared with bald eagles. Eagle male adults weigh from 8 to 15 pounds (3.6 to 6 kilograms). The females are 25 to 30 percent larger than the males, so they can be about 3 feet long from the tip of their beak to the tip of their white tail. Females may weigh up to 20 pounds. Bald eagles aren't really bald, either. It just looks that way from a distance due to their white head. I'm sure they do not like being called "baldy" at all. I don't blame them—I wouldn't like it either.

Bald eagles' beaks are hooked at the end for tearing food apart. Their large eyes give them very keen eyesight to spot prey from high above. They use their strong, sharp claws, called talons, to grab the prey. Their long wings and broad tail make them seem awkward on the ground. When they soar in the sky, they can spread the tail and wing feathers to catch lots of air. These members of the hawk family are famous for their strength as well as their keen vision.

Bald eagles mate for life when they are about four years old. They build a large nest called an aerie (air' ee) near water in the top of tall trees. It is built mostly with sticks and twigs and lined with leaves or grass. The pair will use the same aerie each year, adding some more material where it's needed. The female will

lay two eggs in the nest and warm them for the next forty days. The male will bring her food and even warm the eggs while she takes a break. When the eggs hatch, it is rare for both eaglets to survive since the stronger one usually gets the most food and even attacks the weaker one. Eaglets stay in the nest for about three months and near it for a couple more months until they learn to hunt and care for themselves. It seems strange, but the eaglet will not have a white head or tail like the parents until it's more than two years old.

Bald eagles eat fish and carrion (dead animals) most of the time. They swoop down to catch fish in the water, or they may steal fish from osprey or other fish-eaters. They watch other fish-eating birds to find out where schools of fish are gathering, but they also know when and where salmon spawn. Bald eagles gather at spawning time to clean up the dying salmon after they spawn. Sometimes they may even eat other birds like ducks. They also eat small mammals and a few reptiles.

Over 100,000 bald eagles were killed in Alaska from 1920 to 1952 to protect the salmon fishing. All bald eagles have been protected by law in the United States since 1953. In recent years, pesticides (bug killers) got into eagles' systems and weakened the eggs until it seemed eagles may become extinct. New laws now control pesticide use better and the number of bald eagles is growing steadily. A group of scientists in 1999 counted the eagles along a river, and they found the numbers steadily increased. Just knowing that America's symbol is not becoming extinct makes us feel better.

The Great American Bird

Vocabulary Checkup Write the words from the box on the correct blanks.

carrion	keen	majestic	osprey	pesticides
prey	rare	salmon	soar	talons

1. _____ means regal, stately, or supreme greatness.

2. _____ are fish that often have a pink flesh.

3. _____ is the rotting flesh of dead animals.

4. _____ are the claws of birds of prey.

5. _____ are also birds of prey that feed on fish.

6. A _____ is an animal hunted by another for food.

7. To _____ is to glide and fly high in the sky.

8. _____ means uncommon or not found very often.

9. _____ are chemicals used to kill pests.

10. _____ means highly sensitive, sharp, or intense.

Comprehension You may need to look back at the story to answer the questions correctly.

1. Is the bald eagle the largest bird of prey? _____ Explain why.

   _____

   _____

2. What are the main reasons bald eagles are becoming more plentiful recently?

   _____

   _____

3. The eagles' nest is called an_____ and is built with

   _____.

Name _____ Date _____

The Great American Bird

4. Why does only one of the baby eagles in the nest usually survive?

_____

5. Describe how eagles can hunt so well. _____

_____

_____

Thinking About Eagles Think carefully before answering the questions.

1. Why do you think our country chose the bald eagle as its national bird?

_____

_____

2. Why do bald eagles build their nests so close to the water?

_____

_____

3. Why were they named bald eagles if they aren't bald?

_____

_____

4. Why were people fifty years ago wrong to kill eagles in Alaska to protect salmon fishing? (Think about what happens to spawning salmon.)

_____

_____

5. Why is it difficult to identify the young bald eagle before it is two years old?

_____

_____

Check It Out Find out about
    Golden eagles
    Harpy eagles
    African fish eagles
    Martial eagles
    Osprey

Name _____ Date _____

6. A Real Shocking Story

There is an electric eel in South America that is a freshwater fish, and it can be a shocking experience. Its olive-brown body makes it look like an eel or a snake, but it is really a fish. It is related to carp and catfish. Its eyes and mouth are far forward on its flattened head. It has no scales or regular fins like fish, but it does have a fin all along the very bottom of its snaky body. It can move that powerful fin to swim quite well. Electric eels get as long as 9 feet (2.75 meters) and weigh up to 100 pounds (45 kilograms). The organs that generate electricity are in the tail and make up about half of the eel's total weight.

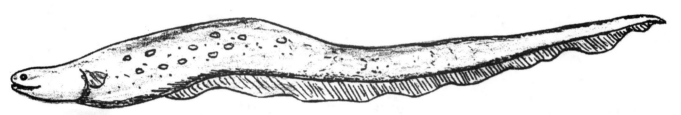

Inside of the electric eel is where they are very different. All of their organs lie in the front quarter of their body. The rest of the body is made up of thousands of plates that work like the plates in a battery to make electricity. The current flows from the positively charged head to the negatively charged tail. The electroplates can produce enough voltage to light a small lamp or run a small motor. The whole eel is like a bolt of lightning. Electric eels can send out as much as 650 volts of electricity, and that is enough to stun a horse!

These electric eels live in the Amazon Basin of South America. They don't get enough oxygen from the water they live in, so they have to come to the surface to gulp some air. They can't see very well in the muddy river water, so they send out weak electric pulses like radar to see if any prey is near. When a fish or frog comes near, the electric eel sends out shock waves that stuns or kills the prey instantly.

You may have already figured out that the electric eel doesn't have very many enemies. It seems there are no creatures in their area that are willing to risk such a shocking experience. The electric eels' blindness means they have to depend on their radar to tell them when an enemy is near. The eels are kind enough to send a little warning shock of a lower voltage first. If that doesn't convince any enemy to leave, a stronger shock will follow immediately. When the eels get very scared, they send out a series of powerful shocks in groups of three or five. Each shock may only last a hundredth of a second, but it is in the 200- to 300-volt range. The eels seem to be able to keep giving these shocks for a long time. Humans can be knocked out by electric charges that powerful, and it could kill them if they get hit by several bursts of electricity.

Male and female electric eels look exactly alike. Scientists don't really know how electric eels produce their young. They think they lay eggs when they disappear from their normal habitat for a short time each year. They come back soon with little eels about the length of your hand. Scientists are guessing when they say that the young (called fry) did hatch out from some eggs. They may be cute, but I wouldn't mess with them, unless you want your hair curled.

The only threat to the life of these unusual fish seems to be the loss of their habitat. Some rainforest areas have been cut down in the Amazon Basin, and this has caused great damage along the rivers. Pollution has increased also, and the supply of fish and frogs is disappearing in the murky waters where the electric eels live. Soon they may have nothing left to shock.

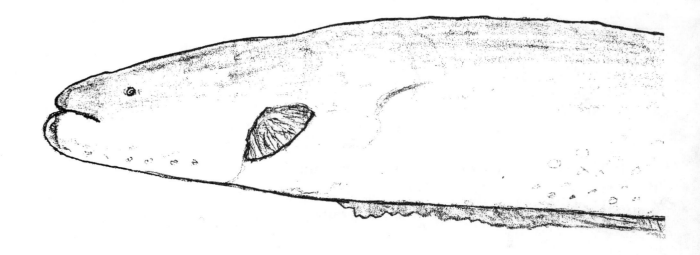

A Real Shocking Story

Vocabulary Checkup Write the words from the box on the correct blanks.

current	fry	organs	pollution
related	stun	surface	volts

1. Connected by family or common origin is to be _____.

2. Animal tissue groups that do a special job are called _____.

3. The flow of an electric charge is called the _____.

4. The units of force of an electric current are measured in _____.

5. To daze or knock senseless by the impact is to _____.

6. The young electric eels are called _____.

7. The top, outer layer of a thing is called the _____.

8. Dirty, foul, and harmful things in air or water are _____.

Fact or Opinion Print **F** for facts. Print **O** for opinions.

_____ 1. Electric eels can knock some large animals senseless or kill them.

_____ 2. The electric eel is the scariest animal in South American rivers.

_____ 3. Electric eels are really fish instead of eels.

_____ 4. The electric eel looks and acts more like a snake than a fish.

_____ 5. Electric eels look funny because of their long bottom fin.

Comprehension You may need to look back at the story to answer the questions correctly.

1. Why are electric eels placed in the fish family?

_____

_____

Name _____ Date _____

© 2000 by The Center for Applied Research in Education

A Real Shocking Story

2. Since they don't have good eyesight, how do they locate prey?

_____

_____

3. How much electric power can electric eels produce? _____

_____

4. Why is the electric eel in danger if there are no animals that threaten it?

_____

_____

Thinking About Electric Eels Think carefully before answering the questions.

1. Why do you think it really isn't known how baby electric eels are born?

_____

_____

2. Explain how you would catch an electric eel for the zoo. _____

_____

_____

3. (Circle your choice.) We   should   should not   try to save electric eels' habitat. Why?

_____

_____

4. Draw a cartoon on the back of this page showing an electric eel using its shocking powers.

Check It Out Find out about
   Electric catfish
   Torpedo rays
   Electric fish
   Moray eels
   Freshwater eels

Name _____   Date _____

7. A Night in Armor

One of nature's strangest creatures is the armadillo. Armadillos got their name, which means "small armored one," from some Spanish explorers. The area from Texas to Florida has a species of armadillo called the nine-banded armadillo. It's only found in that part of the United States. Their shell is made of nine jointed, bony plates covering the back. The plates have to flex for the armadillo to bend. Even the head and tail have bony scales covering them. The belly only has a few scraggly hairs covering it.

These common armadillos are about 30 inches (77 centimeters) long and weigh up to 18 pounds (8 kilograms). They have strong claws they can use to dig burrows or tunnels in the ground. Sometimes they will dig as many as a dozen burrows in the area in which they live. They usually hide in their burrow during the day or if enemies approach. They also can dig rapidly into the ground for defense. Armadillos can dig a hole very fast when enemies catch them in the open. If they are injured and can't dig a hole to escape, they tuck the head, feet, and tail in and roll into a ball so the predator cannot find anything to bite except that hard shell. Nine-banded armadillos are not so good at rolling into a ball as their cousins, the three-banded armadillos of Central and South America.

These nocturnal mammals eat a variety of small animals. They don't see or hear very well, so they depend on their nose as they forage. They poke their long snout into ant and termite nests. They have a sticky tongue to lick up termites, insects, and ants. They can eat as many as 40,000 ants for a meal. They can't bite very well since they only have very small teeth way back in their mouth, but they

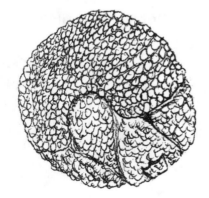

Three-banded armadillo rolled into a ball

© 2000 by The Center for Applied Research in Education

also eat frogs, worms, beetles, snails, and snakes. People in Florida and elsewhere have heard them snorting and sniffing their way through the brush and weeds looking for food.

Scientists say that nine-banded armadillos are the only type that can swim. They swallow a whole bunch of air into their stomach to make themselves buoyant enough to float and paddle across a river. Armadillos who can't do this can get across by holding their breath and walking on the bottom of the stream. Scientists discovered that armadillos can hold their breath for as long as six minutes. This also comes in handy to keep dirt and dust out of their nose when they dig burrows as deep as 12 feet underground. They build one or two nests and line them with dry grass to have their babies in underground safety.

The nine-banded female always gives birth to four babies in a litter. She always has four boy or four girl babies. Scientists have never found a litter with both boys and girls in it. The newborn have leathery, pink skin that turns into hard plates and scales after a few weeks. The young armadillos will nurse for a few weeks and then follow the mother as she

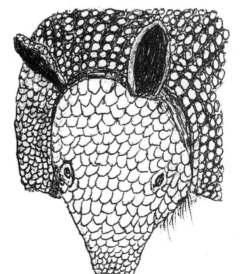

forages for food. They have to stay near the burrows for the first few weeks until the babies' armor gets hard enough to protect them better.

Farmers like the fact that armadillos eat many insects and bugs that can harm their crops, but they don't like having all of those burrows dug in their fields. People kill armadillos for their meat in some countries. Many are also killed to make baskets from the armor shells, using the tail for a handle. The shell is also used to make other items to sell, but these creatures are not endangered.

A Night in Armor

Vocabulary Checkup Write the words from the box on the correct blanks.

armor	buoyant	burrow	defense
flex	forage	litter	nocturnal

1. _____ means to be active mostly at night.

2. The protective plates covering the body are called _____.

3. A _____ is a hole or tunnel dug in the ground.

4. To be light enough to float is to be _____.

5. A _____ is a protection or resistance from attack.

6. A group of young born together is called a _____.

7. To wander and search or rummage for food is to _____.

8. To bend back and forth is to _____.

Comprehension You may need to look back at the story to answer the questions correctly.

1. Where in the United States are you most likely to find armadillos?

   _____

2. Why are they called armadillos? _____

   _____

3. What are the two ways armadillos get across streams? _____

   _____

   _____

4. What do armadillos like to eat? _____

   _____

   _____

Name _____ Date _____

A Night in Armor

5. Nine-banded armadillos always have _____ boys or _____ girls in a litter.

6. Farmers like armadillos because _____
_____.

Thinking About Armadillos Think carefully before answering the questions.

1. What feature do you find most unusual about the armadillo? _____
_____
_____

2. Farmers probably don't like the burrows armadillos dig because _____
_____
_____.

3. Why do you think armadillos dig so many burrows in their territory?
_____
_____

4. Why do you think some people would want a basket made from armadillo shell?
_____
_____

5. Why do you think only 1 out of the 20 different kinds of armadillos lives in the United States?
_____
_____

Check It Out Find out about

    Pink fairy armadillos   Three-banded armadillos
    Giant armadillos   Pangolin (not an armadillo)
    Pichi (pee' chee) armadillos

Strong, front digging claws!

Name _____ Date _____

8. The River Horses

I learned about the hippopotamus, or hippo, from visiting our zoo. However, the wild hippos are found in African rivers and get their name from two Greek words that mean "river" and "horse." These huge mammals spend most of their day in the river. They come out at night to feed on the grass, leaves, and fruit along the river bank. These herbivorous (hur biv' or us), or plant-eating, animals consume (eat up) about 120 pounds (59 kilograms) of plant matter each night. These mostly aquatic (a kwat' ik), or water-loving, creatures are excellent swimmers and can stay underwater up to six minutes. The hippo can shut its ears and nostrils to keep water out. Another unusual thing hippos can do is to emit, or give off, a special reddish-pink fluid to keep their skin moist when they are on land. This started the saying that hippos sweat blood.

Hippos have a long body, large head, and short legs. They are only about 5 feet (1.5 meters) tall, but they are twice as long as they are tall. Males weigh up to 7,000 pounds and females are half as big. Hippos have four webbed toes on each foot. Hippos can see, breathe, and hear with most of their head underwater due to the way their eyes, nostrils, and ears are sticking out, or protruding from their head. They don't see very well, but they have an excellent sense of smell. These grayish-brown creatures only have a few bristles of hair on the head and tail. Hippos have big front teeth and long side teeth that form ivory tusks, which they can use to fight even though they seldom get attacked.

The hippopotamus usually only has one baby at a time after an eight-month-long gestation (je stay' shon) or pregnancy period. The calf weighs about 100 pounds (45 kilograms) at birth and swims right away. The baby

may be born underwater and have to quickly swim up to get its first breath of air. It nurses on its mother's milk underwater and then crawls up on her back to sun itself as she floats around. The calf will only nurse for the first eight or nine months, but it will stay near the mother for protection for about three or four years. When they are on land, a mother hippo may have her last three young following her. They look like stairsteps with the youngest one close to Mom and the oldest one in the back.

Hippopotamuses (or hippopotomi) usually spend the whole day in the water. They can't spend too much time on land because they lose too much water through their skin. Sometimes people see birds, turtles, or baby crocodiles resting in the sun on the back of a big hippopotamus. If the hippo gets tired of those critters using its back for sunbathing, it can dive under and even take a walk on the bottom.

The adult hippos do not have to fear any enemies since they have such tough skin and are so large. However, hunters have killed many hippos for their valuable ivory tusks. Many farmers in Africa have taken the hippo feeding grounds to grow crops. Those farmers have to shoot some hippos to protect those crops. People also eat the meat and use the skin to make soup. Scientists have suggested to Africans that they should raise hippopotami for their tasty meat. Hippos are in no danger of becoming extinct. They have been known to live over thirty years in the wild and over fifty years in a zoo.

The River Horses

Vocabulary Checkup Write the words from the box on the correct blanks.

aquatic	_____ pregnancy period
consume	_____ to give off or send out
emit	_____ does not happen very often
fluid	_____ long, ivory teeth in the mouth
gestation	_____ liquid, not solid or rigid
herbivorous	_____ to take in or eat up
moist	_____ plant eating
protruding	_____ water loving
seldom	_____ sticking out
tusks	_____ slightly wet

© 2000 by The Center for Applied Research in Education

Comprehension You may need to look back at the story to answer the questions correctly.

1. What does the name *hippopotamus* mean according to natives of Africa?

   _____

   _____

2. What features help hippos swim underwater very well?

   _____

   _____

3. Why is it likely that hippos could become an endangered species before too long?

   _____

   _____

4. Why can't hippos spend too much time on land during the day?

   _____

   _____

Name _____ Date _____

The River Horses

Thinking About Hippopotamuses Think carefully before answering the questions.

1. Why do you think predators don't attack adult hippos very often?

   _____

   _____

   _____

2. What did you consider unusual about baby hippo behavior?

   _____

   _____

   _____

3. Why do you think some people say hippos really sweat blood?

   _____

   _____

   _____

4. What information surprised you the most about the big hippopotamuses?

   _____

   _____

   _____

Reading Concepts Circle the letter of the correct answer.

The hippopotamus is a herbivorous mammal since:

(a) it eats plants and lives near water.

(b) it eats plants and nurses its baby with milk.

(c) it eats plants and is second in size to the elephant.

Check It Out Find out about

Pygmy hippos   Tapir
Peccary   Tagua
Swine

Name _____   Date _____

9. The Most Intelligent Invertebrate?

You can learn about some eight-legged ocean critters that are nearly as smart as you are. A friend told me there are about 150 different species of octopuses in the sea. I have seen some as small as your fist, but a few are as large as 30 feet (10 meters). Those giant octopuses can spread their arms (or tentacles) to reach from one side of a classroom to the other.

The name *octopus* comes from Greek words that mean "eight feet." Those eight tentacles, large, shiny eyes, and sharp beak make the octopus look scary enough that some people call them devilfish.

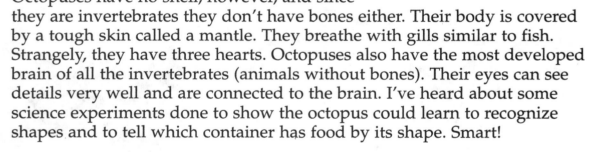

Octopuses make their homes in cracks in rocks in the shallow waters. People noticed how they often moved using suction cups on their tentacles to crawl along the ocean floor. They also saw them shoot water out of their siphon tube to propel themselves more quickly. Octopuses belong to a shellfish group called mollusks, which includes clams, snails, and oysters. Octopuses have no shell, however, and since they are invertebrates they don't have bones either. Their body is covered by a tough skin called a mantle. They breathe with gills similar to fish. Strangely, they have three hearts. Octopuses also have the most developed brain of all the invertebrates (animals without bones). Their eyes can see details very well and are connected to the brain. I've heard about some science experiments done to show the octopus could learn to recognize shapes and to tell which container has food by its shape. Smart!

It is difficult to say what color octopuses may be since they can actually change colors to match their surroundings. They have sacs of pigment (coloring material) that go from their skin to their nerves. When they seem nervous, they can change color to blend in with the surroundings. If they get really excited, they can turn blue, purple, red, white, or even striped! When an octopus is attacked by an enemy, it can eject (shoot out) a cloud of ink that darkens the water and hides the escape of the octopus. The ink has chemicals in it that make it hard to smell which way the octopus went. The pigment in those sacs was also some of the first ink people used to write.

Octopuses eat creatures like crabs, other mollusks, and crayfish that swim too close to the well-hidden carnivores. Octopuses grab them with their tentacles and inject a paralyzing poison into their prey. They can drill a hole in hard-shelled animals in order to inject the poison. They drill with sharp little teeth on their tongue. And if the prey happens to cut off one of the octopus's tentacles, a new one grows in its place.

A female octopus often attaches as many as 180,000 eggs to a rock. She stays to guard her eggs for about two months until they hatch. Since the mother will not leave the nest unguarded, she may starve to death during that time. The babies start catching their own food right away, so they are on their own even though they are not able to protect themselves very well yet. Many animals eat them. My friend says newborn octopus is delicious. So many people like the meat that in some ocean areas octopuses have been overfished and are scarce now.

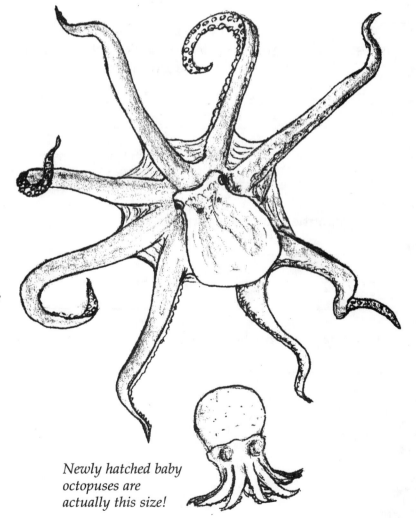

The octopus uses its eight arms to feel things, grip its prey, and crawl.

The suction cups have nerves to tell it what it's touching.

Newly hatched baby octopuses are actually this size!

The Most Intelligent Invertebrate?

Vocabulary Checkup Write the words from the box on the correct blanks.

eject	_____ animals that have no bones
gills	_____ Greek word meaning "eight feet"
inject	_____ making an animal unable to move
invertebrate	_____ to shoot out
mantle	_____ breathing organs like fish have
octopus	_____ to shoot in
paralyzing	_____ arms on some animals
pigment	_____ a tube to carry liquids
siphon	_____ coloring material
tentacles	_____ a covering like a skin

Comprehension You may need to look back at the story to answer the questions correctly.

1. Why have some people called the octopus devilfish?

_____

_____

2. What does the word *octopus* mean? _____

3. How can the octopus escape sharks and other predators? _____

_____

_____

_____

4. What have scientists discovered will happen if an octopus has a tentacle cut off?

_____

_____

_____

Name _____ Date _____

The Most Intelligent Invertebrate?

Thinking About Octopuses Think carefully before answering the questions.

1. How is an octopus different from most mollusks?_____

_____

_____

2. What makes us think the octopus is smart? _____

_____

_____

3. Why do you think some owners of fishing boats get upset when they catch octopuses in their nets?

_____

_____

_____

4. What do you think is the most fascinating thing about the octopus?

_____

_____

_____

Reading Concepts Circle the letter of the correct answer.

The octopus is an invertebrate and is intelligent because

(a) it has no shell, but it has a brain.

(b) it has no bones, but its brain is developed.

(c) it is a mollusk, but its eyes are keen.

Check It Out Find out about

Squid
Cuttlefish
Nautilus
Sea slugs
Naked sea butterfly

Name _____ Date _____

10. Our Most Dangerous Spider

Birds are hungry enough at times to eat insects, but they seldom eat spiders. They can distinguish spiders from insects the same way we can; we just count their legs from a safe distance. Insects only have six legs while spiders have eight legs. The legs have thousands of hairs that are used to sense movements. Spiders only have two sections to the body instead of three like insects. All spiders belong to the scientific group called arachnids, which also includes mites and ticks. Many spiders are poisonous, so most of the birds just don't take any chances with them.

The black widow spider is the most dangerous spider in North America. It is most common in the southern part of the United States, but it is also found in most of our states and in Canada. The female black widow is pictured in actual size above. She is shown lying on her back so you can see the red hourglass mark under her abdomen. You would not want to pick one up and flip it over to see if that red mark is there, however. Female black widows have a venomous bite that causes breathing problems and muscle twitching in their victims. Their bite has been fatal for some people, but most victims died from a combination of causes. The females usually are not aggressive unless they are guarding an egg sac or are stressed out from being caught in clothing or squeezed into a tight spot. Black widows like to hide in dark corners where people never go so they won't be bothered. They like to have a place where they can crawl in to hide so they can't possibly be reached. You may have guessed they're most dangerous when they can't hide or escape from people, so just leave them alone and you will be safe.

Black widows are carnivores that spin a web to catch insects (and other spiders) to eat. They have special organs, called silk glands, in their abdomen that can produce the silk to spin the webs. The spinnerets shown in the picture on the next page push the silk out the back of the abdomen and it sticks and dries immediately. The whole web usually takes less than an hour to make. The spider waits for an insect to move into the web. Even though spiders have eight eyes, they depend on feeling a prey in the web. They rush out to bite it and inject the poison that will kill it quickly. Spiders don't have jaws to chew up their food, so they also inject juice into the insect that can make the inside of the bug into a liquid. The spider then sucks the liquid up through a tube-like mouth into its stomach, leaving only the outside shell of the insect in the web.

Females lay many eggs in an egg sac to hatch. The male black widow spider is not seen very often, and scientists don't think he bites. He is much smaller than the female and has four pairs of red marks on his sides. The female often kills the male after mating, and this is where the name *black widow* comes from. This is also one of the times when you better stay away from the female since she will defend her egg sac to her death. The spiderlings begin to grow in the egg sac, and as they get larger they have to molt, or shed their outside shell. A spiderling may molt as many as fifteen times before it becomes an adult.

It is a good thing very few people get bitten by black widow spiders in the United States each year. The black widow spider's poisonous venom is stronger than rattlesnake venom. We should be thankful that they are shy arachnids and are not so big as rattlesnakes.

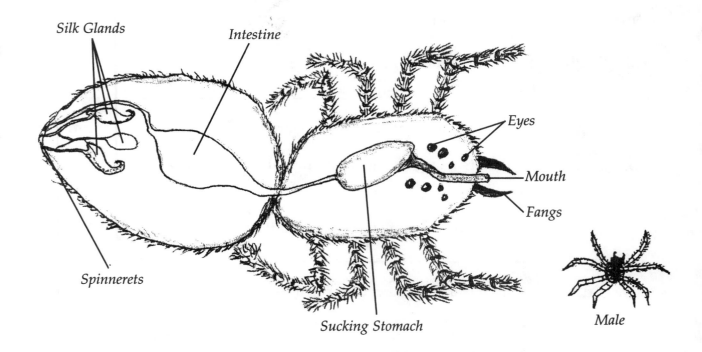

Silk Glands

Intestine

Eyes

Mouth

Fangs

Spinnerets

Sucking Stomach

Male

Our Most Dangerous Spider

Vocabulary Checkup Write the words from the box on the correct blanks.

abdomen	aggressive	arachnids	distinguish	fatal
stressed	venomous	victim	widow	

1. A female whose mate has died is a _____.

2. Anyone who is killed by the attack of another is called the _____.

3. The female has an hourglass on her _____.

4. Spiders belong to the scientific group called _____.

5. To see or point out the differences is to _____.

6. Anything that makes a poison or venom is _____.

7. To be put under pressure or tension is to be _____.

8. Anything that causes death to the victim is _____.

9. Really going after or attacking is being _____.

Comprehension You may need to look back at the story to answer the questions correctly.

1. Black widow females are usually dangerous only when they are

_____.

2. Black widow spiders got their name from their habit of

_____.

3. These dangerous spiders are not seen very often because

_____

_____.

4. You can tell the difference between insects and arachnids (especially spiders) by

_____

_____.

Name _____ Date _____

Our Most Dangerous Spider

5. Scientists can distinguish between male and female black widow spiders by the

_____

_____.

Thinking About Black Widow Spiders Think carefully before answering the questions.

1. How do you think birds know to leave spiders alone? _____

_____

_____

2. What is the best thing to do if you think you see a black widow spider?

_____

_____

_____

3. How do you think scientists learned a lot about black widow spiders?

_____

_____

_____

4. Why do you think female black widows often kill their mates?

_____

_____

5. We (circle one)   should   should not   live in fear of them because _____

_____

_____.

Check It Out Find out about
   Red or brown widow spiders
   Wolf spiders
   Mites
   Ticks
   Scorpions
   Trapdoor spiders

Name _____   Date _____

11. Man of the Woods

The only members of the great apes that don't live in Africa live in the southeast Asian country of Indonesia by the equator. The orangutan (oh rang' oo tan) lives in the forests of two island countries called Borneo and Sumatra. These island countries are located between India and Australia. *Orangutan* is a Malayan word that means "man of the woods." Most people know about these great apes from their lovable roles on TV and in movies.

The orangutan has coarse, reddish-brown hair covering most of its body. The males also have reddish-blond beards and mustaches. A male is 3 to 5 feet (91 to 150 centimeters) tall and weighs an average of 165 pounds (75 kilograms). The females average about 90 pounds (40 kilograms). Scientists have found fossil remains in China of giant orangutans that lived thousands of years ago. Both males and females have very long arms that reach clear down to their ankles when they stand erect. Males can stretch their arms out to span an average of 7.5 feet (2.3 meters). Compare this to a person 5 feet tall only able to span 5 feet; then you can imagine how long orangutans' arms really are. Since they spend so much time in the trees, their arms are very strong. All four of their "hands" have big toes like our thumbs to hold on very well.

Orangutans live most of their life in groups of two to five high up in the trees. They seldom come down to the ground. They use their long arms to climb and swing from tree to tree to eat fruit, leaves, and a few bird eggs. When they get thirsty they find a hollow spot in a tree that has collected rainwater. They are diurnal creatures, meaning they're active in the daytime. They build a crude nest to sleep in at night about five or six stories above the ground. They feel very safe and comfortable in their lofty habitat.

After a gestation of about nine months, females usually have one baby. Since it will stay with her for three or four years, she may not raise more than four young in her life. Females raise their little babies quietly up in the forest canopy. It sounds very scary for babies to be up so high! A tiny baby clings to its mother's hair as she travels 60 feet up in the rainforest canopy.

The orangutan is such a quiet, peaceful creature that the people of Sumatra and Borneo have a legend that explains how the "man of the woods" can speak, but he chooses not to speak for fear that humans will put him to work.

Orangutans really have no known enemies other than humans. If humans don't stop cutting down the forests, the orangutan won't have any habitat left. It is possible the species could become extinct because so many females are killed in order to capture their babies for zoos. Scientists are trying to raise some orangutans in captivity to star in movies and supply zoos all over the world since people just love to watch these funny great apes perform.

Man of the Woods

Vocabulary Checkup   Write the words from the box on the correct blanks.

ape
canopy
fossil
coarse
erect
gestation
habitat
legend
lofty
diurnal

_____ prints formed by prehistoric life in rocks

_____ standing upright

_____ tailless monkey (orangutan, gorilla, etc.)

_____ overhanging cover forming a shelter

_____ very rough texture; not fine

_____ active in the daytime

_____ story handed down from the past

_____ the period of pregnancy

_____ natural environment of an animal

_____ very high, tall, or towering

Comprehension   You may need to look back at the story to answer the questions correctly.

1. _Orangutan_ means _____ in Malayan.

2. Where in our world do wild oranguatans live? _____
   _____
   _____

3. Where do orangutans usually get a drink of water? _____
   _____
   _____

4. Why are some female orangutans killed by humans? _____
   _____

5. Orangutans eat _____
   _____.

Name _____   Date _____

© 2000 by The Center for Applied Research in Education

Man of the Woods

Thinking About Orangutans Think carefully before answering the questions.

1. What features can you think of that make orangutans great climbers?

   _____

   _____

   _____

2. Do you think the natives' legend about orangutans speaking is true?_____

   Why? _____

   _____

   _____

3. How do you think the orangutan babies are raised so high off the ground safely?

   _____

   _____

   _____

4. What are two examples of opinions that you read in the story?

   _____

   _____

   _____

5. What is the best hope to keep orangutans from extinction?

   _____

   _____

   _____

Check It Out Find out about
   Baboons
   Gorillas
   Chimpanzees
   Macaques
   Celebes black apes

Name _____ Date _____

12. The Biggest Snake in the World

Many people are confused about the world's biggest snake. They aren't sure if the python, boa constrictor, or anaconda is the largest. If you are talking about a long, heavy snake, then the anaconda is the biggest. The boa constrictor gets up to 20 feet long. The anaconda, a member of the boa family, can grow to more than 30 feet (9 meters) long. That is as long as a bus! The python of Asia is about the same length as the anaconda, but 30-foot pythons only weigh 350 pounds. Thirty-foot anacondas weigh in at more than 550 pounds! They are so heavy that they move slowly on land. Those heavy snakes are better off living in the water, where they swim very well. The water helps support their heavy body. The color of the anaconda varies from dark green to olive green to yellowish green with dark spots or rings on it.

Anacondas like to lie in muddy water with just their eyes and nose sticking out. Like all snakes, they flick their tongue out to sniff the air. Their sense of smell seems to be better than their eyesight. Pits by the side of their mouth sense the heat of their prey, too. They use their jaws and teeth to grab animals that come to get a drink, then coil around it with lightning speed, constricting or squeezing so tightly that the prey can't breathe. Often they just drown their prey since anacondas can hold their breath underwater for more than ten minutes.

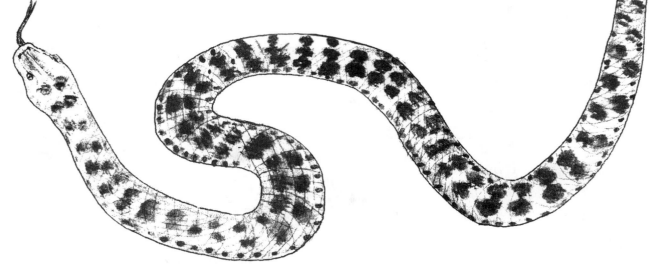

Anacondas stretch their jaws like other boas and pythons do, swallowing their whole meal at one time. They may have to stretch their elastic jaws for more than an hour to swallow the whole animal. They swallow the whole prey even if it is twice as big as their own head. They have even killed and eaten small deer and a whole jaguar! However, the main food eaten by these giant snakes is live birds, rodents, and wild pigs. Anacondas may sleep for a week after a good meal, and they can go for months without eating if necessary.

Most snakes lay eggs, but anaconda babies are born live. Their brood may have forty to sixty babies in it, and the babies are all the same colors. They are about 2 feet long at birth, and they can swim and hunt immediately. They live primarily on water animals like fish and frogs until they grow much larger. These young anacondas have to shed their skin to grow larger just like other snakes do. They will continue to do this their entire life since their old skin wears out, too. They simply split the old skin open at the mouth and crawl out of it. They already have a complete new "suit" of scaly skin underneath that old one.

Even though anacondas have no venom (poison), they can bite to defend themselves. People don't have to worry because these snakes swim away from humans whenever they can. Strangely, humans are their main enemy since they hunt anacondas for their skin and cut down their rainforest habitat.

The Biggest Snake in the World

Vocabulary Checkup Write the words from the box on the correct blanks.

| anaconda | brood | coil | constrict |
| elastic | jaguar | python | venom |

1. A snake as long as the anaconda is the _____.

2. A number of young born or hatched together is a _____.

3. Anything flexible and stretchy is said to be _____.

4. To wind up in spirals or rings is to _____.

5. A large, tropical cat is the _____.

6. To squeeze or make very narrow is to _____.

7. A poisonous fluid from the fangs of some snakes is _____.

8. The world's largest, heaviest snake is the _____.

Comprehension You may need to look back at the story to answer the questions correctly.

1. Anacondas are in the _____ family and live in the jungles on the continent of _____.

2. Anacondas sense their prey using their _____ to smell them and their _____ to feel the heat of their prey.

3. Anacondas grab prey and either _____ it underwater or _____ the prey until it can't breathe.

4. Anacondas are better off in the water than on land since _____.

5. The two main reasons snakes shed their skin are because _____.

Name _____ Date _____

The Biggest Snake in the World

Thinking About Anacondas Think carefully before answering the questions.

1. How can the anaconda possibly swallow a whole deer or jaguar at one time?

   _____

   _____

2. Why do you think humans don't fear the anaconda very much? (Or do you?)

   _____

   _____

3. What is the most important thing anacondas have to do to catch a jaguar?

   _____

   _____

4. What did you think was most amazing about the anacondas?

   _____

   _____

Reading Concepts Circle the letter of the correct answer.

1. The python of Asia is about as long as the anaconda, but it's not so
   (a) smart. (b) heavy. (c) pretty. (d) mean.

2. Anaconda babies are
   (a) born alive. (b) hatched from eggs. (c) cute.

3. Boas, anacondas, and pythons are all
   (a) venomous. (b) clever. (c) constrictors.

4. Anacondas' favorite place to live is
   (a) in trees. (b) in water. (c) in apartments.

5. The world's biggest snake is the
   (a) anaconda. (b) python. (c) boa constrictor.

Check It Out Find out about

Boa constrictors   Jacobson's organ
Indian pythons   Estivation
Snake skin uses

Name _____ Date _____

13. The Ant Bear

One of the funniest-looking noses is on the giant anteater from Central and South America. This most famous member of the anteater family is called an "ant bear" by some people, probably because of its coarse, brownish hair and bear-like walk. The giant anteater can grow over 6 feet (1.8 meters) long from the tip of its tail to the tip of its snout. The tail alone makes up about 2 and a half feet (0.76 meter) of that length. Their snout is more than 2 feet long. Male anteaters weigh up to 90 pounds. The females are a bit smaller at 50 to 60 pounds. Giant anteaters lumber along on all four legs with their 6-inch-long claws on their front feet tucked under while they walk on their knuckles.

Giant anteaters love to eat termites and beetle larvae (grubs), but ants are their favorite food. Anteaters have a sense of smell that is forty times better than ours. They can smell ants over 100 feet away (the length of three classrooms!). They use their long claws to tear open ant nests. Then they use their tongue to pull out (extract) ants. What a tongue! It can be up to 23 inches long. Their 25-inch-long snout helps them probe ant tunnels. Then their sticky tongue reaches deeper to extract more ants. Their tongue has little hooks on it to catch hundreds of ants. Ants seldom get away from that hooked, sticky probe. Most of the water the ant bears need comes from the food they eat. They don't have any teeth, but they eat a little soft fruit for moisture, also. Ant bears are nocturnal animals and hunt for ants mostly at night. They can't see very well, but their keen nose and sharp hearing enable them to find ants and termites and listen for enemies at the same time. Most of their daylight hours are spent sleeping curled up in a hole

they scrape out in the ground. They often sleep with their tail curled up over their nose. They need lots of sleep and a very low body temperature of 35 degrees since their food gives little energy. They are camouflaged well enough that most predators can't see them. Their worst enemies are the big cats, especially the jaguars. Since the giant anteaters have no teeth, their only defense is to roll over on their back and scratch at an attacker with their long claws.

Giant anteaters usually only have one baby every other year. When it is born the baby will look just like the adults. Babies usually climb up onto their mother's back right away to ride and hide. If you looked at the mother shuffling along searching for food, you probably wouldn't even see the baby on her back. The baby anteater will nurse on its mother's milk for six months, and it will stay with her until she is expecting another baby in two years. Finally, the young anteater has to go away to find its own area to hunt for anthills.

Wild giant anteaters have become more and more rare in recent years. It is not so much due to their poor defense ability, however. It is because people have moved into much of their territory and changed the habitat. Some people have even used the anteaters for food at times. Fortunately, there are many zoos that keep giant ant bears. Zookeepers can't possibly get enough ants and termites to feed their giant anteaters. The babies born at the zoo drink their mother's milk, and when they get older they are fed eggs and hamburger. Perhaps the anteaters raised in the zoos will be the only ones left in a few more years.

The Ant Bear

Vocabulary Checkup Write the words from the box on the correct blanks.

| camouflaged | coarse | defense | extract | larva(e) |
| lumber | moisture | nocturnal | probe | rare |

1. To reach into or to check and search is to _____.

2. Anything that is _____ is very rough and uneven.

3. Grub form that beetles and other insects go through is _____.

4. The _____ animals come out at night.

5. Another word for water is _____.

6. To _____ is to pull or draw out of its place.

7. Anything that is scarce or not plentiful is considered _____.

8. _____ means it blends in with the background.

9. A way of protection from harm is called a _____.

10. To _____ is to move clumsily or heavily along.

Comprehension You may need to look back at the story to answer the questions correctly.

1. Giant anteaters are called ant bears because of _____
_____.

2. Giant anteaters can defend themselves from predators by _____
_____.

3. The giant anteater's foods are _____
_____.

4. When the ant bear sticks out its tongue, the snout and tongue together can be about _____ feet long.

Name _____ Date _____

The Ant Bear

5. The big giant anteater can live on little food because _____

_____

_____ .

Thinking About Ant Bears Think carefully before answering the questions.

1. Why do you think giant anteaters are more rare now? _____

_____

_____

2. Why do you think anteaters walk on the back of the knuckles of their front feet,
   curling their claws under?

_____

_____

_____

3. Why do you think ant bears have such a large, bushy tail? _____

_____

_____

_____

4. I think the strangest thing about the giant anteater is its _____

   because _____

_____

_____ .

Check It Out Find out about
   Aardvarks
   Silky anteaters
   Echidnas
   Pangolins
   Collared anteaters

Name _____   Date _____

14. The Sea Bear

It was amazing to see a large bear swimming out in the ocean more than 50 miles from shore! The guide on our tour boat told us that polar bears are often called sea bears. He told us that they can swim 60 miles without stopping to rest and can average about 6 miles per hour. He said they close their nostrils and swim underwater for as long as two or three minutes, too.

I saw that the polar bear swimming beside our boat was long and smooth in the water. It was only paddling with its front legs and seemed to use the back legs for steering. I asked the guide how sea bears could swim so fast, and he said that they have webs between the toes of their front feet. So they have built-in swim fins like ducks. This arctic tour was full of surprises. I could hardly wait until we flew to the polar bear nursery grounds on the other side of Hudson Bay.

The guide told us that polar bears are the largest meat-eaters on land in the world. They feed mostly on seals all winter. They are skilled hunters that will sneak up on a seal. They are hard to see since they are the same color as the snow and ice. A seal that comes up for a breath of air can become a quick snack. In the summer the polar bear will eat arctic ducks, foxes, and whale or walrus remains that wash onto shore. Polar bears have such good noses that they can smell a beached whale as much as 20 miles away! Polar bears even eat a little kelp and other vegetation in the summer.

The next day we flew over to the area called the nursery, where many baby polar bears are born. A large female came right up close to our snowbuggy window. I was amazed to see that her hair looked more like glass as the sunlight hit it just right. The guide said that each hollow hair helps keep her warm. Her skin underneath the hair is almost black to help the sun warm her even more. I couldn't believe white polar bears are really more black than white. The guide told how the bears will cover their black nose and mouth with a white paw to hide better from seals they are stalking.

© 2000 by The Center for Applied Research in Education

(The Sea Bear, *continued*)

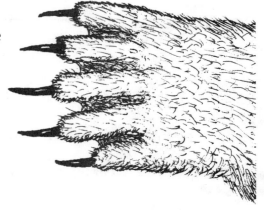

The female bear put her front paw on the window. I could see the webbing between the toes. I saw very thick hair on the bottom of the foot. The guide told me the hair helped the bear walk quietly and kept it from slipping on the ice. It also helps the feet stay warmer. I couldn't miss seeing the long claws. I knew why they said to keep the windows closed as the bear pressed her nose to the window. The guide said the bear has special cells in her nose to warm the freezing arctic air she breathes.

We followed her in our snowbuggy for an hour. She began digging with her long claws in the bank of snow and tundra. The guide explained that she was making a den. Polar bears don't really hibernate, but the females have built these dens to give birth to their young. The mother had gained about 400 pounds in a 5-inch layer of fat to keep her alive for the next four months in the den. Most polar bears will have twins, but many will have triplets. The babies only weigh a pound at birth and have almost no hair. They will gain about 35 pounds before leaving the den in April. The mother will nurse them for two more years before starting all over again with a new litter.

I thanked the guide for the wonderful tour of the Arctic. I learned that the polar bear population was being protected and there were more of them now. I also found out that pollution in the ocean is getting into the polar bears' food chain. This could endanger them if we don't stop polluting the ocean. I hope to come back to see these sea bears again next year.

The Sea Bear

Vocabulary Checkup Write the words from the box on the correct blanks.

arctic	food chain	kelp	nostrils	nursery
	stalking	triplets	tundra	webs

1. The openings or holes in the nose are called _____.

2. An area where babies are kept and raised is a _____.

3. The _____ are the pieces of skin connecting toes together.

4. The cold area near the North Pole is called the _____.

5. _____ is to sneak up on or chase after the prey.

6. A large, brownish-green seaweed is often called _____.

7. The _____ is the cold, treeless ground in the arctic area.

8. Three babies born to the same mother at a birthing are _____.

9. A set of plants and animals where the smaller ones are food for larger and larger

   creatures is called a _____.

Comprehension You may need to look back at the story to answer
the questions correctly.

1. What helps the polar bear swim so fast? _____

   _____

2. Why does a polar bear sometimes cover its nose and mouth with a paw while

   hunting? _____

   _____

3. The hair on the bottom of a polar bear's paw helps in three ways. Explain two ways

   it helps. _____

   _____

Name _____ Date _____

© 2000 by The Center for Applied Research in Education

The Sea Bear

4. Why is it important for mother polar bear to gain 400 pounds before babies arrive?

_____

_____

Thinking About Polar Bears Think carefully before answering the questions.

1. What do you think is most amazing about the polar bear's swimming ability?

_____

_____

_____

2. What do you think is the most important thing polar bears use to help hunt food?

_____

_____

_____

3. How and why do polar bears really have more black on them than they do white?

_____

_____

_____

4. Thousands of people go to the Arctic and see the polar bears each year. Tell why you would like to go on a field trip up there.

_____

_____

_____

Check It Out Find out about
   Kodiak bears
   Brown bears
   Arctic foxes
   Kermodes white bears
   Grizzly bears

Name _____ Date _____

15. Those Old Ducks

Mallard hen

The largest, most abundant, common and beautiful of all our ducks is the mallard. Mallards are found just about everyplace there is water in the Northern Hemisphere. Scientists have estimated that there are over 18 million mallards in North America. Nearly all farm ducks have descended from the mallard. They were domesticated (tamed) and raised by the ancient Egyptians before any other birds.

Wild mallards normally live in groups called flocks, and they prefer the shallow feeding areas in lakes, ponds, rivers, and reservoirs of fresh water. The males are brightly colored and are called drakes. The females are called ducks, but we will call them hens as most people do. The hens have more dull, brown colors, as do most female birds, but they are the ones who can quack. Drakes can only whistle and grunt.

You may want to color the drake, shown below. He has a shiny green head, white collar, reddish-brown breast, and very light gray belly. His brownish-gray back blends into a curly black tail with white feathers on the tip. The bottom of his brown wings has a patch of black and white stripes with glowing blue in the middle. This patch is called the speculum, and it is the only bright color on the hens.

Mallards spend most of their time eating, sleeping, or preening their feathers. It is funny to watch them preen. They shake all over to ruffle the feathers, then run their bill over them to smooth and clean them. They also pick up oil from a gland near the tail and spread it on the feathers, making them waterproof. So preening helps to keep them clean, dry, warm, and beautiful.

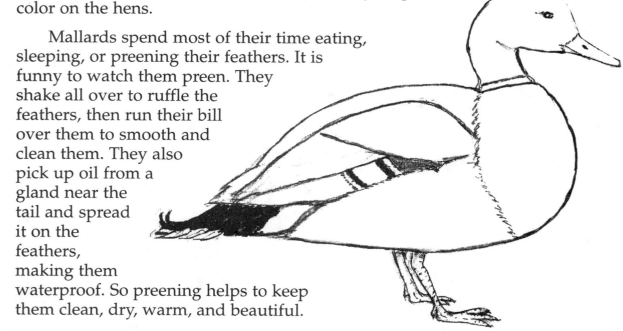

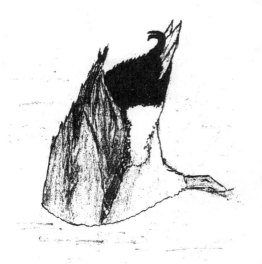

Scientists divide ducks into two groups: dabblers and divers. Mallards are dabblers, feeding by tipping the tail up in the air and sticking the upper body underwater while paddling with the feet. They pick aquatic plants from the shallow waters with their flat bill. The bill has jagged edges to let the water run out the sides. They love the leaves, flowers, seeds, and berries of smartweed, pondweed, and duckweed especially. They also like new plant sprouts and the roots, bulbs, and stems of aquatic plants plucked off the bottom. Only 10 percent of their diet is made up of insects, minnows, tadpoles, worms, and snails. Chicks and their mothers will often eat 10 percent plants and 90 percent animals when they come out of the nest. Mallards do graze on land sometimes and will eat grains from a field when available in the fall.

The hens choose a mate during the winter and begin building a nest in spring. The drake usually helps her choose a nesting spot and watches as she plucks grass and leaves from the spot to both soften the nest and camouflage it. The hen then lays an egg each day and pulls some downy feathers from her chest to keep it warm. She will incubate the clutch of eggs when she has eight to ten. She pulls out more down for the nest to keep the eggs warm. The drake will stay around to protect the nest for a short time, then will go off to eat and be a mallard, which means "wild one." After four weeks, chicks begin cheeping inside the eggs. It may take them a couple of days to peck their way into the world, eyes wide open and covered with brown and yellow natal (baby) down. The hen will keep them near her at the nest for a day or two so they know who she is. This is called imprinting. Then she will lead them to the water for their first swim, often teaching them to eat insects along the way. She will protect them from predators all summer, but many wild creatures love to eat baby ducklings. Large fish, snapping turtles, and cats and dogs even get a few. The hen does well if 50 percent survive all summer and grow flight feathers to join the adults at the staging area. Mallards stage together in November for winter migration before their waters freeze over. If you see or hear large flocks flying in a V formation, you won't forget it. They fly on four main flyways, or migration routes: Atlantic, Mississippi, Central, and Pacific flyways. As they stop to rest on their long migration, they face great danger from duck hunters and predators. Their greatest danger, however, is coming back to their home range in the north in spring to find that more marshes and wetlands have been taken over by people.

Those Old Ducks

Vocabulary Checkup Write the words from the box on the correct blanks.

dabblers	descended	domesticated	down	drake	flyways
imprinting	natal	preening	reservoirs	speculum	staging

1. The soft feathers of birds is called _____.

2. _____ are ducks that stay on top of water to feed.

3. The routes used by migrating ducks are called _____.

4. The _____ is the color spot on a mallard's wings.

5. _____ is to fix an idea firmly in the memory.

6. The male duck is called a _____.

7. _____ are storage ponds for fresh water.

8. Tamed or bred for human use is _____.

9. _____ is when ducks gather in one place to migrate.

10. Anything connected to baby animals' birth is called _____.

11. _____ means to inherit or bring down in a family.

12. _____ is birds smoothing, cleaning, and oiling feathers.

Comprehension You may need to look back at the story to answer the questions correctly.

1. Mallard males are called _____.

2. Female mallards are called _____.

3. Mallards preen to _____

_____.

4. Mallards don't dive, they're _____.

5. Label the flyways on the lines on this map as the Atlantic, Pacific, Central, and Mississippi.

Name _____ Date _____

Those Old Ducks

Thinking About Mallards Think carefully before answering the questions.

1. I think mallards were the first domesticated birds because _____
   _____
   _____.

2. I think mallards like shallow water better because _____
   _____
   _____.

3. I think hens and chicks eat 90 percent animals at first because _____
   _____
   _____.

4. I think the hen's choice of nest materials is clever because _____
   _____
   _____.

5. I think mallards know when to stage for migration by _____
   _____
   _____.

6. I think hens keep their chicks at the nest for a day or two to _____
   _____
   _____.

7. I think seeing and hearing a flock of mallards fly over would be great because
   _____
   _____.

Check It Out Find out about

Pintail ducks   Muscovy ducks

Pekin ducks   Teal ducks

Redhead ducks

Canvasback ducks

Name _____ Date _____

16. Where Has Little Dog Gone?

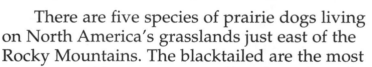

You may step out the door at sunrise to hear what sounds like a dog howling if you visit the Central Plains of the United States. It really isn't a dog at all. You look carefully and decide that the animal looks more like a squirrel or a woodchuck. You find out that these creatures are named prairie dogs since they live on the prairie and make a barking and howling sound like a dog. There were so many of these "dogs" back when America was young that they excavated huge underground cities. The state of Texas estimated in the early 1900s that more than 800 million prairie dogs lived there. But ranchers and farmers had livestock breaking their legs in the burrows, so now there are only about 2 million prairie dogs left there.

There are five species of prairie dogs living on North America's grasslands just east of the Rocky Mountains. The blacktailed are the most common, with a range extending from Canada to Mexico. They're close to a foot long, weigh about 2 or 3 pounds, and have short legs and a 3- to 4-inch tail. Their fur is yellow-tan, with the belly and chest being a lot lighter colored. They're related to ground squirrels, even though they are larger.

Prairie dogs live in burrows they dig as deep as 12 feet underground. They chew off roots, then dig with their strong front claws while throwing dirt behind them with their hind feet. The mound left on top keeps rain from running into the entrance. Their home has a network of burrows over 100 feet long with cozy chambers for sleeping, nursing, hiding, and

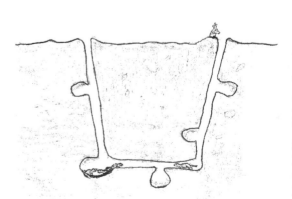

storing extra food. Half of their life is spent down there, where it's cool in summer and warm in winter. Prairie dogs build a colony of burrows called a town which can cover acres of land and have thousands of prairie dogs in it. The town is divided into coteries, which are really families. A coterie usually has an adult male, three or four mothers, and the young ones under a year old. The young in most animal species leave home when they are old enough, but in a prairie dog coterie it is the parents that move out and leave home to build a new home on the edge of the town.

The prairie dog eats the grasses that grow near its burrow. You can tell where a town is by the shorter grasses as well as the mounds the blacktails make. Cutting of tall prairie grass encourages shorter plants to sprout. These grow faster and produce more seeds and food for the town. It also helps the blacktails not to have tall grasses that can hide predators near their burrows. The prairie dogs always have a lookout on a mound ready to bark if he sees a hawk, coyote, fox, or other predator. Acute vision and hearing help prairie dogs detect enemies outside, but they often fall prey to ferrets and badgers at night. Rattlesnakes and burrowing owls also move into the burrows.

Baby prairie dog pups are usually born in late spring. The litter of four or five pups is hairless and blind, and each pup is as tiny as half an ounce at birth. Pups get constant cleaning, nursing, and protection from the mother. By the time they are six weeks old they're able to leave the burrow and eat some grasses. The pups are allowed to leave the coterie area and roam all over town if they mind their manners and don't bother lookouts or adults busy eating. Adults don't have this privilege and must stay within a boundary of their own coterie. They will go to the edge of it, meet neighboring prairie dogs, and touch teeth with each other. This ritual looks like they are kissing, but if they aren't members of the same coterie, a fight may break out. Sometimes those strangers will stand up, throw their head back, and make a yip-n-howl sound. This seems to declare to strangers, "This is my territory! Back off!" Pups can play without worrying about fights, but they do imitate the yip-n-howl.

Cattle ranchers and farmers consider the prairie dogs such pests that they got permission to poison millions of them. Sometimes burrows are filled with poison gasses, but this kills other animals living there, also. Scientists are finding ways for farmers and prairie dogs to get along. Some areas have been saved just for blacktails.

Where Has Little Dog Gone?

Vocabulary Checkup Write the words from the box on the correct blanks.

acute	boundary	coterie	detect	chambers
ferrets	imitate	lookout	privilege	vision

1. A right or benefit enjoyed by an individual is a _____.

2. A group that works and gets along together is a _____.

3. The one left to watch or stand guard is the _____.

4. To discover or notice the presence of is to _____.

5. Something like a line that shows the edge is a _____.

6. _____ means very sharp or sensitive.

7. _____ are little weasel-like animals with black feet.

8. _____ is sight or the ability to see.

9. _____ means to copy, mimic, or to act like.

10. _____ are rooms for certain uses or purposes.

Comprehension You may need to look back at the story to answer the questions correctly.

1. Prairie dogs live in communities called _____ with separate areas
   called _____ for each family-type group. They live on the
   _____ side of the Rocky Mountains.

2. Prairie dogs get their name from _____
   _____.

3. Mounds of dirt by the entrance of a burrow helps prairie dogs in two ways. They
   help _____
   and _____.

Name _____ Date _____

© 2000 by The Center for Applied Research in Education

Where Has Little Dog Gone?

4. Prairie dogs do a yip-n-howl at neighbors to _____

   _____ .

5. The main reason there aren't so many prairie dogs living now is because

   _____

   _____ .

Thinking About Prairie Dogs Think carefully before answering the questions.

1. I think prairie dogs look most like a _____ because

   _____

   _____ .

2. I believe prairie dogs are not safe in their own burrows because

   _____

   _____ .

3. I feel prairie dogs' lives are a lot like humans' lives since

   _____

   _____ .

4. I think the pups have life better than mine because they get

   _____

   _____ .

5. I believe farmers (circle one)   should   should not   kill prairie dogs because

   _____

   _____ .

Check It Out Find out about
   Mexican prairie dogs
   White-tailed prairie dogs
   Utah prairie dogs
   Gunnison's prairie dogs
   Gophers
   Black-footed ferrets

Name _____   Date _____

17. Largest Land Animal in the United States?

When most people try to answer the question of the largest land animal in North America, they think of the moose, grizzly bear, or perhaps the polar bear. Very few will ever think of the bison. Oh, you may call them by their more common name of "buffalo," but the accurate name is American bison since they really aren't related to the buffaloes of Asia or Africa.

Our plains bison is the largest land animal at about 12 feet long, 6 feet tall, and weighing as much as 3,000 pounds. These biggest ones are the males, called bulls, and the cows are a lot smaller. Bulls and cows both have horns, humps over the front shoulders, and shaggy, dark brown hair around the head and shoulders. Most people would very quickly recognize any picture of the bison, but they would probably call it a buffalo, too. The early French explorers on our continent called these huge creatures *boeuf* which means "beef" in French. Plains Indians did use the bison as beef and depended on it for many of their other needs, also. The French *boeuf* was later called buffalo by English-speaking people, and that name became popular.

Most people, when asked to describe the bison, would mention the hump, or the horns, or maybe the big, shaggy head. The horns are quite visible, frightening, and useful. The record horn is over 23 inches long, but most bulls' horns are closer to 18 inches. They are great weapons for defense against predators and in fights between bulls. A bison's hump is mostly muscle, instead of fat like a camel's hump. The shaggy coat of dark brown hair on bisons' front sections can grow to be a foot long in winter. The long hair is shed in the spring, and the bison will rub gobs of loose hair off on trees and rocks. The hair on the rear section is normally only 2 inches long.

Bison have very poor vision. They can see movement, but not very clearly and not far away. They have such a great nose, however, that they can smell predators up to a mile away and can even smell grass through a foot of snow. Since bison hear sounds we can't, Indians used to beat drums to prevent camps from being stampeded.

Bison eat grass most of the time. They graze early in the morning, swallowing their food without chewing it well. When they lie down to rest later, they spit up this cud and chew it better. This is called rumination or chewing the cud, and cattle do the same thing. Bison may

also eat a few buds and leaves of some trees. They don't really migrate in the winter unless they live far north in Alberta, Canada. They can run as fast as 30 miles per hour, but they would use too much energy migrating long distances.

The bison cow will only have a calf every other year. Her gestation period is a little over nine months. She nurses and protects her calf from spring birth to the end of the winter. The calf weighs over 60 pounds at birth. Its eyes are open and it can stand in an hour or so. It looks more like a member of the cattle family since it won't get its hump and horn growth for a few months. If cougars or grizzlies try to get the calves, all of the females make a circle around the calves. Then the males get on the outside of that circle, and only a crazy predator would dare to venture into that circle of horns.

No matter whether you call them buffalo or bison, they have been one of the most significant animals in American history. You may have already learned how Plains Indians used the bison for nearly everything. The bison hunt was so important that it had its own rituals, with dances, songs, and campfire tales. Indians used just about every part of the bison. The hides were their clothing, blankets, bowls, and house (called a wigwam). They used rib bones for frames for round boats covered with hide. The fat of bison was used as a sunscreen, the hoofs for glue, and muscle tendons for string. Even the dried dung or droppings were gathered and burned since wood was scarce on the plains.

You can see how vital the bison was in the life of Indians on the plains east of the Rocky Mountains. Settlers moved west and began killing huge numbers of bison. Railroad builders and pioneers killed some for food, but many bison were killed just for the skin or to get them off land that ranchers and farmers wanted. Rifles were designed for buffalo hunters like the famous "Buffalo Bill" Cody. The slaughter in the 1800s continued until there were only about 500 of the original 50 million bison left. People called conservationists knew they had to save the bison, so they set up parks from the Dakotas to Nebraska where bison were kept. Thanks to the conservationists, we now have over 50,000 bison in the United States and Canada and you can go to Yellowstone, Custer, and other parks to see our largest land animal.

Largest Land Animal in the United States?

Vocabulary Checkup Write the words from the box on the correct blanks.

conservationists	dung	rituals	rumination	significant
slaughter	stampede	sunscreen	tendons	vital

1. Dried bison manure or droppings is also called _____.

2. Things that are necessary or essential to live are _____.

3. To kill in great numbers is to _____.

4. Activities practiced or performed regularly are _____.

5. Very important or having great meaning is _____.

6. People who save or conserve nature are _____.

7. The tough fibers that attach muscles to bones are _____.

8. When groups of animals run out of control, it is a _____.

9. Bringing food up to chew again is called _____.

10. A substance to protect the skin from sun is _____.

Comprehension You may need to look back at the story to answer the questions correctly.

1. Where did the American bison get the name *buffalo*? _____
   _____

2. What are two of the more unusual uses the Plains Indians had for bison?
   _____

3. Bison calves look more like cattle for the first few months because
   _____.

4. About how many American bison lived at the turn of each century?
   1800? _____ 1900? _____ 2000? _____

Name _____ Date _____

© 2000 by The Center for Applied Research in Education

Largest Land Animal in the United States?

Thinking About Bison   Think carefully before answering the questions.

1. Do you think the bison have to worry much about predators? _____

   Why? _____

   _____

2. What do you think the bison's most unusual feature is? _____

   Why? _____

   _____

3. An army general told the government that buffalo hunters were doing more to get Indians onto reservations than his own troops were able to do. What do you think he meant?

   _____

   _____

4. Think of examples using buffalo or bison for each of these categories in America:

   (city) _____ (sports team) _____

   (landform)_____ (other) _____

5. Have you ever heard the expression "buffaloed"? Even if you haven't, what do you think it means?

   _____

   _____

   Are you buffaloed? Try a dictionary.

Survey Questions It might be fun to survey students, teachers, or parents who have not read the American bison story. Here are some ideas, but you can add more. Survey people individually, record answers, and report the results. (Get your teacher's instructions!)

1. What is the biggest land animal in North America?

2. Do you usually call them *buffalo* or *bison*?

3. What do you first see as you picture a bison?

4. How many bison in 1800? 1900? Now?

5. Have you seen a real bison? Where?

Name _____ Date _____

18. Watch Your Fingers!

Tom and I got off our bikes on the bridge to watch two men wading in Alum Creek. It was almost dark, so we couldn't figure out why they were wading in the cold creek waters. We saw one guy set his burlap bag on the bank and reach up under an overhanging bank where roots stuck out. He was feeling around under there for only a few seconds when he shouted, "Hey, I've got one!" He stood up quickly and held his hand straight out toward the other guy. He had a turtle about as big around as a basketball, and we could see its legs flailing as he swung it by its tail. The other guy held a stick in front of the turtle, and it bit the stick. The stick was still in its jaws as they dropped it in the burlap bag. Tom startled them as he yelled, "What kind of turtle is that?" They laughed and told us it was a snapping turtle. I couldn't believe they were grabbing snapping turtles! As they headed on up the creek with their sacks, Tom and I got on our bikes and headed for home before it got dark. We talked loudly all the way home about those two crazy men groping for snapping turtles.

I told my dad about those guys, and he started shaking his head in disbelief. He said they must be fools. He asked me if I remembered that little snapper we caught while fishing last summer. I recalled how he made me stay back from it, telling me it could lunge and strike out like a rattlesnake. And I remember he had me hold a twig in front of it, and it snapped that stick in two easily. I was glad it wasn't my finger! Dad cut his fishing line that day and let the little snapper disappear back into the river. As we continued to fish, he told me about a guy named Charlie at work that was missing the end of his pinkie finger from an encounter with a snapping turtle. He said snapping turtles don't have teeth, but they have a hooked, razor-sharp beak on their powerful jaws. He also told me how Grandma used to make turtle soup back when he was a kid, and how Grandpa had the state record for the biggest snapper caught: a 76 pounder.

It was raining the next day, so Tom and I went to the library to find out more about snapping turtles. We found some great books on reptiles with large sections on turtles. It seemed strange that turtles were grouped with crocodilians, lizards, and snakes. Turtles are the only vertebrates with a backbone that won't bend. The shell or carapace is part of the backbone and ribs. Most turtles also have a bottom shell called a plastron.

Many of them can pull their legs and head inside the shell for protection, but the snapping turtle can't pull inside its shell. Snapping turtles do have tough scales covering their head and legs. Since they can't hide in their shell, biting is their main defense.

It said in the book that there are three kinds of snapping turtles in North America. Common snappers live from Canada down to South America and average 19 inches long and up to 50 pounds. Florida snappers are very similar to common snappers, but the big alligator snapper of the Mississippi Valley averages 24 inches long and 150 pounds. A record alligator snapper weighed in at 403 pounds! Fortunately, they cannot lunge and snap so fast as the common snapper. Instead, they have a worm-like thing on their tongue to wiggle and lure fish and other prey close enough to devour. Snapping turtles eat fish, frogs, salamanders, snakes, baby ducks and other water fowl, insects, and a little plant material. Dead animals found in the water, snails, crawfish, and even a muskrat or other small water mammal are also devoured. Snapping turtles spend a great deal of time hiding in the mud, beneath a log, or under a bank or roots, where they can strike out and catch prey that comes too close.

The books said that in late June or early July snappers make their only trip out of the water to find a soft bank of soil to dig a hole to lay their eggs. They usually lay about twenty-five eggs which they cover with dirt. The eggs may take two or three months to hatch. The baby snappers will head for the water as soon as they hatch. They grow so fast that some will have 6-inch-long shells in their first year unless they hibernate all winter in the mud in areas with harsh winters. Turtles get most of their growth in the first five to ten years of their life despite the fact that many live to be over 100 years old.

Snapping turtles are not an endangered species even though some people, like the two guys we saw, catch them to eat. Many tortoises, box turtles, and sea turtles are endangered, however. Humankind's pollution has been the greatest threat to snappers.

Tom and I did not find the answer to one question we had: How could those guys catch the snapping turtles without getting bitten? We think there is some secret way to catch them. We would like to know their secret, but we don't really want to learn how to do it ourselves. We want to keep all of our fingers.

Watch Your Fingers!

Vocabulary Checkup Write the words from the box on the correct blanks.

burlap	carapace	devour	encounter	flailing
groping	lunge	lure	plastron	vertebrates

1. Beating or swinging through the air is _____.

2. A coarse fabric of hemp or jute used for sacks is _____.

3. Animals with backbones are called _____.

4. To eat hungrily or greedily is to _____.

5. Feeling around uncertainly with the hands is _____.

6. The _____ is the hard top shell of a turtle.

7. The _____ is the belly covering of a turtle.

8. To _____ is to meet or come upon.

9. To _____ is to attract, tempt, or entice something.

10. To _____ is to leap or jump forward suddenly.

Comprehension You may need to look back at the story to answer the questions correctly.

1. What is the snapping turtle's best defense? _____

_____

2. The three kinds of snapping turtles in the United States are _____

_____.

3. How does the alligator snapping turtle catch prey? _____

_____

4. What is the strange thing about the spine of turtles? _____

_____

Name _____ Date _____

Watch Your Fingers!

Thinking About Snappers Think carefully before answering the questions.

1. Why did the father say those men must be fools? _____

_____

_____

2. Why do you think snapping turtles wait until the middle of summer to lay their eggs?

_____

_____

_____

3. Why is it considered fortunate that alligator snappers can't lunge and snap well?

_____

_____

_____

4. What do you think is the secret to groping for snapping turtles without being bitten?

_____

_____

_____

5. If you had to catch a snapping turtle for your job at the zoo, how would you do it?

_____

_____

_____

Check It Out Find out about

Terrapins
Box turtles
Mud turtles
Musk turtles
Wood turtles
Painted turtles
Spotted turtles
Turtle hibernation

Alligator Snapping Turtle

© 2000 by The Center for Applied Research in Education

Name _____ Date _____

19. The Fastest Creature on Earth!

If you have ridden in a car going 70 miles per hour (mph) on the freeway, you know that is pretty fast. Do you know what bird cruises along at 75 miles per hour, then dives at its prey reaching speeds of 217 miles per hour on the radar gun? The swiftest bird is the peregrine (pair′ i grin) falcon, often nicknamed the "duck hawk" in the United States. These birds are listed in the *Guinness Book of World Records* as the world's fastest animals.

Peregrine falcons are 15 to 18 inches long and weigh from 2 to 4 pounds. Females are larger than the males. These birds are nearly the same size as a crow. Adults have dark gray backs, and the white underside has dark stripes of gray or brown in it. They have a white mustache across their beak and dark gray sideburns down the neck. Their eyes are larger than your eyes, and they can see as clearly at a half mile as you can from across your classroom.

Peregrine falcons got their name from a Latin word that means "wanderer" or "foreigner," because they fly over a wide range to hunt and migrate from their Arctic breeding grounds to southern wintering areas in the United States. Their hunting methods in either region are amazing. They climb to 1,000 feet or more above the Earth, spot a pigeon, dove, or other tasty bird, and fold their wings back to go into a steep dive called a stoop. They hit the prey at 180 to 200 miles per hour with both feet in a closed fist. The falcon often will catch the stunned prey in its talons before it ever hits the ground.

The peregrine falcon may be nicknamed the "duck hawk," but it really prefers to eat many smaller birds. In addition to pigeons and doves, the peregrine eats gulls, starlings, robins, and other songbirds. Peregrines do eat some small ducks at times, but this may be done mostly when they are feeding a nest of hungry young falcons. They will catch a rabbit or other small mammal once in a while, too.

Peregrine falcons mate for life just like the bald eagles. A mating pair will seek a nesting site on a remote mountain cliff so it's difficult for other animals to get there. Falcons in city areas have nested on ledges on skyscrapers, however. The female doesn't really build a nest on that chosen high spot called an eyrie. She will lay her three to five eggs in a scraped-out spot of gravel or vegetation on the ledge. The female will incubate the eggs while her mate brings her food. The chicks hatch in a month with a downy covering of white feathers. She protects them from rain and sun while the male continues to bring food to his family for a couple of weeks. The fledglings begin to get their protective feathers, and by the time they are a month old it takes both parents to keep the family fed. Parents begin flying by with chunks of food, teasing the fledglings into catching it in midair. By the time it is migration time in the fall, the young falcons will have become efficient hunters on their own. They are ready to migrate to a falcon winter hunting region.

The peregrine falcons almost became extinct in North America in the 1950s and 1960s. The insect-eating birds the falcons were hunting were being poisoned by pesticides like DDT. The pesticides and other chemicals went through the food chain and caused the falcons' eggshells to be very thin, which resulted in eggs being broken before they were hatched. There were only thirty pairs of adult falcons left in the United States by 1972, when a law was passed banning DDT. A Peregrine Fund began raising chicks, and three to four thousand falcons have been released to the wild. These falcons have made an amazing recovery. We can see them every fall now from Texas to the Brigantine Refuge in New Jersey.

The sport of falconry has been around for centuries. Falconry is the training of birds of prey to be used by humans in hunting. Only a few people in the United States get a license to use the peregrine in this sport. They also help expand peregrine populations and understanding. It looks like peregrines may be forever fastest.

The Fastest Creature on Earth!

Vocabulary Checkup Write the words from the box on the correct blanks.

banning	efficient	eyrie	falconry	fledgling
mustache	nickname	remote	stoop	teasing

1. A name substituted for the proper name is a _____.

2. Pretending to offer to taunt or irritate is _____.

3. Stopping or prohibiting by law is _____.

4. The growth of hair just above the mouth is a _____.

5. A baby bird ready to fly is called a _____.

6. The lofty nest site of a bird of prey is called an _____.

7. The sudden dive of a bird is called a _____.

8. Working effectively with the least waste is _____.

9. Training and hunting with a bird of prey is _____.

10. Far away or distant is _____.

Comprehension You may need to look back at the story to answer the questions correctly.

1. Where does the name *peregrine falcon* come from and what does it mean?

_____

_____

2. What do peregrine falcons like to eat most of the time? _____

_____

3. Why did peregrines almost become extinct in the United States by 1972?

_____

_____

Name _____ Date _____

The Fastest Creature on Earth!

4. What did humans do to bring the peregrine falcon back from near extinction in the United States?

_____

_____

Thinking About Falcons Think carefully before answering the questions.

1. Why do you think the pesticides were so much harder on birds of prey than on the other birds?

_____

_____

2. What did you find was the most amazing thing about the peregrine falcon?

_____

_____

3. Would you want to try falconry? _____ Why? _____

_____

_____

4. Should we be measuring the speed of the peregrine falcon as it flies or dives? _____ Why? _____

_____

Survey Questions You may want to ask your teacher if you can ask these questions to parents at home, students at school, or elsewhere. Then you can tally the data.

1. What is the fastest animal on Earth?
2. How fast do you think peregrine falcons go? (Nearest hundred)
3. Do you know what falconry is?
4. Have you ever seen a falcon? Where?
5. Are peregrine falcons endangered?

Check It Out Find out about

Falconry   Gyrfalcons

Prairie falcons   Merlins

American kestrel

Name _____ Date _____

20. The Beautiful Killer Whale

One of the favorite sights at marine parks is the orca whale, also called the killer whale. Orcas have sharp teeth to catch and tear apart their prey, so scientists group them with the toothed whales. Other zoologists say they belong with the dolphins by the shape of their nose. Orcas are definitely carnivorous mammals, and they are found in all oceans from the equator to the polar seas. You may wonder as you read how the beautiful and intelligent orca can get its reputation as a killer whale.

Killer whales can get as long as most classrooms (about 30 feet long) and weigh as much as 17,000 pounds. They are easy to recognize by their black back and white belly and that large white spot above each eye. Each orca also has a distinct gray-white saddle mark on its back that scientists use to tell individuals apart. The dorsal fin of the males can stand as tall as 6 feet, but the female's fin is usually only 3 feet tall and is bent backward. Powerful tail flukes help killer whales swim up to 34 miles per hour, and they are the fastest-swimming mammals. They also use their tail flukes to slap the water surface at times. It makes such a loud noise that schools of fish can be paralyzed by the sound. The orcas send out sounds from their blowhole as a radar signal. They use their sensitive hearing to hear and feel the echo of the sound to determine what is up ahead and just how far away it is. Scientists discovered that orcas can tell exactly what is in the water even when it is very murky. They call this method of hearing *echolocation.* Scientists are studying other squeaks, whistles, and scream-like sounds made by orcas as communication. They've learned orcas can tell voices of individual members of their own group, or pod, as well as other pods.

The feeding habits of killer whales vary according to location and pod size. If a killer whale is hunting alone, it may echolocate one fish or seal to eat. If the whole pod is hunting, they may herd a school of fish together by surrounding them and closing in. The orcas will attack and eat just about any sea creature, but they feed mostly on fish, squid, seals, walruses, and other dolphins and porpoises. They will attack smaller whales, and they seem to love the tongue of baleen whales. Orcas tear their prey into smaller pieces, but they swallow the chunks without chewing. They are the only ones to eat other marine mammals, but you'll be glad to know they do not attack humans.

A pod of orcas usually has a fertile mother, her calves, an adult male, and his sisters with their calves. There may also be some older females that are infertile but acting as nannies to care for calves. The mothers carry a calf for nearly a year and a half before it is born. The calf is almost 6 feet long and is gently nudged to the surface by some member of the pod so it

can get its first breath of air. Its mother will feed it for two years with her milk by squirting it into the calf's mouth. The milk with 50 percent fat is so rich that the calf will grow quite rapidly. Mother orcas may only have one calf every five or six years. Calves have few enemies and are well cared for by their whole pod.

Orcas are seen more often in coastal waters than some of the other marine mammals. They stand on their tail flukes to look around above the waves at times like dolphins. They romp through the waves sometimes, splashing loudly as they leap from the sea in an act we call breaching. Sea World and other marine parks love to have the orcas as trained performers to attract a large audience. They may be the most feared predator in the ocean, but they are loved in aquatic shows.

Orcas used to be hunted for their meat and oil. A few killer whales are being killed by fishing people in accidents, but the species is not in great danger from hunting. The greatest threats to the orcas is pollution of the seas and loss of food supplies. Scientists are now testing and trying to take care of these problems.

The Beautiful Killer Whale

Vocabulary Checkup Write the words from the box on the correct blanks.

breaching	communication	distinct	echolocation
fertile	individual	nannies	pod
romp	zoologists		

1. A group of whales swims in a bunch called a _____.

2. Able to produce offspring or new organisms is _____.

3. Clearly different in nature or appearance is _____.

4. One single, separate thing or person is an _____.

5. To frolic or play in a lively way is to _____.

6. _____ are scientists who study animals.

7. _____ is whales leaping and splashing down.

8. _____ is species giving and getting messages.

9. _____ are like nursemaids to the young.

10. _____ is using echoes of sounds to find things.

Comprehension You may need to look back at the story to answer the questions correctly.

1. Describe an orca to a person who has never seen one. _____

_____

_____

2. How can zoologists tell which orca they are seeing? _____

_____

3. Explain how echolocation works. _____

_____

_____

Name _____ Date _____

The Beautiful Killer Whale

4. What are the main dangers the orcas face now? _____

_____

_____

Thinking About Orcas Think carefully before answering the questions.

1. Do you think orcas should be grouped with whales or dolphins? _____
   Why? _____

   _____

2. Do you feel orcas have a language and can talk? _____ Why? _____

   _____

   _____

3. Do you believe they deserve the name *killer*? _____ Why? _____

   _____

   _____

4. Do you think the population of orcas will get very large? _____
   Why? _____

   _____

   _____

5. Why do you think people love to watch the orca at the theme parks so much?

   _____

   _____

   _____

Check It Out Find out about
   Narwhals
   Sperm whales
   Beluga whales
   Porpoises
   Whaling industry

Name _____ Date _____

Answer Key for Activity Sheets

Whales *(The Biggest Mammal)*

Vocabulary—mammal, flukes, migrate, plankton, buoyancy, inhale, exhale, baleen, extinct, blubber, species, sleek.

Comprehension—1) They give birth to live young, nurse them with milk, and are warm-blooded. 2) They strain plankton from seawater in mouth. 3) Mom's milk is very rich. 4) Blubber keeps them warmer and they can feed on it when food is scarce. 5) For birth of a calf.

Thinking—1) Water helps support their weight. 2) Fish are coldblooded, have vertical tail fins, and have gills. 3) Answers will vary. 4) Answers will vary. 5) Answers will vary. 6) Answers will vary.

Otters *(Playful River Otters)*

Vocabulary—1) burrow 2) submerge 3) nostrils 4) insulate 5) carnivore 6) frolic 7) expert 8) nocturnal.

Comprehension—1) Otters have webbed feet and they can close ears and nostrils. 2) The young nurse on milk from the mother. 3) Oily fur and a layer of fat. 4) Fish; carp, suckers, bullhead, shellfish, frogs, snails, turtles, snakes.

Thinking—1) Answers will vary. 2) Humans are closer than before. 3) Probably slide or swim. 4) Answers will vary. 5) May mention laws.

Beavers *(The Largest Rodent in North America)*

Vocabulary—1) steer 2) pioneer 3) mature 4) incisors 5) superb 6) forepaws 7) ambitious 8) fossils.

Fact or Opinion—1) O 2) F 3) O 4) F 5) F

Comprehension—1) They slap their tail on the water. 2) Their incisors grow all of their life. 3) Their furs were valued for coats and hats by pioneers. 4) Steering, balance, and warning.

Thinking—1) May say food lacks variety or life is always the same. 2) Answers will vary. 3) Answers will vary. 4) Answers will vary.

Badgers *(Dig Those Badgers)*

Vocabulary—1) hibernate 2) habitat 3) fierce 4) gestation 5) gland 6) omnivore 7) weaned 8) badgering.

Comprehension—1) Strong legs and sharp claws help them dig. 2) When backed into a corner. 3) The badge look on their face. 4) People teased a badger by sending a dog into a barrel for it. 5) Killed by cars and trapped for fur.

Thinking—1) Its short legs on a wide body. 2) Answers will vary, but they fight ferociously. 3) Badgers would be better off in their natural habitat. 4) Answers will vary. 5) To prevent extinction.

Bald Eagles *(The Great American Bird)*

Vocabulary—1) majestic 2) salmon 3) carrion 4) talons 5) osprey 6) prey 7) soar 8) rare
9) pesticides 10) keen.

Comprehension—1) No, because the California condor is larger. 2) Laws protect them from being killed, and deadly pesticides are controlled better. 3) Aerie; sticks, twigs, grass, and leaves. 4) The stronger one eats most food and attacks the other. 5) They have keen eyesight and strong talons.

Thinking—1) Answers will vary, include mention of eagles as symbols of freedom, power, and pride. 2) Fish are their main food source. 3) The white head looks bald from a distance. 4) The salmon were dead or dying anyway! 5) It doesn't have the white head yet.

Electric Eel *(A Real Shocking Story)*

Vocabulary—1) related 2) organs 3) current 4) volts 5) stun 6) fry 7) surface 8) pollution.

Fact or Opinion—1) F 2) O 3) F 4) O 5) O.

Comprehension—1) It's related to carp and catfish. 2) They send out electric pulses like radar to find prey. 3) As much as 650 volts, enough to stun a horse! 4) Loss of habitat and food.

Thinking—1) Scientists haven't been able to follow. 2) Answers will vary. 3) Answers will vary. 4) Drawings will vary.

Armadillo *(A Night in Armor)*

Vocabulary—1) nocturnal 2) armor 3) burrow 4) buoyant 5) defense 6) litter 7) forage 8) flex.

Comprehension—1) Southern areas. 2) It's Spanish for "small armored one." 3) They swallow air and paddle across, or they hold their breath and walk across on the bottom. 4) ants, termites frogs, snakes, worms, and snails. 5) 4, 4. 6) They may eat harmful insects.

Thinking—1) Answers will vary. 2) Hard on equipment. 3) Probably to have one close to escape their enemies. 4) Unusual. 5) Answers will vary.

Hippos *(The River Horses)*

Vocabulary—gestation, emit, seldom, tusks, fluid, consume, herbivorous, aquatic, protruding, moist.

Comprehension—1) River horse. 2) They can close their nostrils and ears and can stay underwater for up to 6 minutes. 3) Farmers don't want crops destroyed and want even more cropland. 4) They lose too much water through their skin.

Thinking—1) They are huge and have tusks. 2) May mention how they sun as Mom swims, or swim at birth, or nursing underwater. 3) They emit reddish-pink fluid to cool skin on land. 4) Answers will vary.

Reading Concepts—(b) It eats plants and nurses its baby with milk.

Octopus *(The Most Intelligent Invertebrate?)*

Vocabulary—invertebrate, octopus, paralyzing, eject, gills, inject, tentacles, siphon, pigment, mantle.

Comprehension—1) Because 8 legs, big eyes, and a sharp beak look scary to them. 2) Eight feet. 3) It jets water out of its siphon after ejecting a cloud of ink. 4) It can grow a new tentacle.

Thinking—1) It has no shell like most mollusks. 2) Experiments where they recognized shapes. 3) Answers will vary. 4) Answers will vary.

Reading Concepts—(b) It has no bones, but its brain is developed.

Black Widow *(Our Most Dangerous Spider)*

Vocabulary—1) widow 2) victim 3) abdomen 4) arachnids 5) distinguish 6) venomous 7) stressed 8) fatal 9) aggressive.

Comprehension—1) Guarding an egg sac or stressed and can't get away. 2) Killing their mate. 3) They prefer to hide in dark corners. 4) Counting their legs 5) Markings.

Thinking—1) They're poisonous. 2) Stay away from it and tell an adult. 3) Observing them in their natural habitat or carefully catching them and providing a good habitat. 4) Answers will vary. 5) Answers will vary.

Orangutan *(Man of the Woods)*

Vocabulary—fossil, erect, ape, canopy, coarse, diurnal, legend, gestation, habitat, lofty

Comprehension—1) "Man of the woods." 2) Forests of Sumatra and Borneo located between India and Australia. 3) From a hollow spot in a tree with rainwater in it. 4) So humans can capture babies for zoos. 5) Fruit, leaves, and eggs.

Thinking—1) Long arms and four thumbs. 2) Answers will vary. 3) Answers will vary. 4) "They feel safe…," "That sounds scary for babies…," and "People love to watch…" 5) We need to stop cutting their forest habitat or raise more in captivity.

Anaconda *(The Biggest Snake in the World)*

Vocabulary—1) python 2) brood 3) elastic 4) coil 5) jaguar 6) constrict 7) venom 8) Anaconda.

Comprehension—1) boa; South America. 2) tongue; pits. 3) drown; squeeze. 4) They are so heavy, and swim so well. 5) They outgrew the old one, and it was worn out, too.

Thinking—1) They dislocate their jaws. 2) Answers will vary. 3) Hide, bite the neck, and squeeze or drown it. 4) May mention the size, eating habits, live babies, etc.

Reading Concepts—1) b 2) a 3) c 4) b 5) a

Anteater *(The Ant Bear)*

Vocabulary—1) probe 2) coarse 3) larva 4) nocturnal 5) moisture 6) extract 7) rare 8) camouflaged 9) defense 10) lumber

Comprehension—1) Their hair and walk. 2) Rolling onto their back and using their long claws. 3) Ants, termites, and beetle larvae. 4) four. 5) It sleeps a lot and lowers its body temperature.

Thinking—1) People have taken their territory. 2) It's comfortable and protects claws. 3) Answers will vary. 4) Answers will vary.

Polar Bear *(The Sea Bear)*

Vocabulary—1) nostrils 2) nursery 3) webs 4) arctic 5) stalking 6) kelp 7) tundra 8) triplets 9) food chain

Comprehension—1) Webs between toes of front feet. 2) To cover the black areas so it can blend in on snow and ice background. 3) Walk quietly, better traction, and warmer. 4) To keep her alive for four months in the den to feed babies.

Thinking—1) May say 60 miles without rest, swimming underwater 2–3 minutes with the nostrils closed, or 60 mph speed. 2) May say nose (sense of smell), camouflaged white, or stealth skills. 3) Should explain how skin under white fur is black to absorb sun's heat. 4) May mention how they would like to see the animals or snow and ice.

Mallards *(Those Old Ducks)*

Vocabulary—1) down 2) dabblers 3) flyways 4) speculum 5) imprinting 6) drake 7) reservoirs 8) domesticated 9) staging 10) natal 11) descended 12) preening

Comprehension—1) drakes. 2) ducks or hens. 3) clean, oil, and smooth feathers. 4) dabblers. 5) From east to west reads: Atlantic, Mississippi, Central, and Pacific

Thinking—1) Maybe because they were pretty or easy to tame or tasty or available. 2) More food is there, plants aren't so deep. 3) They need protein for growth or it's easier to get bugs and worms (or other ideas). 4) It hides or camouflages her better to use materials near the nest and down keeps eggs and ducklings warmer. 5) Watching the weather or using instincts or other signs of nature. 6) Imprint on chicks who their mother is before venturing out, or to gain strength, or to learn communications. 7) Answers can vary, but hopefully they'll mention awesome sight of a V or the volume.

Prairie Dogs *(Where Has Little Dog Gone?)*

Vocabulary—1) privilege 2) coterie 3) lookout 4) detect 5) boundary 6) acute 7) ferrets 8) vision 9) imitate 10) chambers.

Comprehension—1) towns; coteries; east. 2) Their barking sounds like dogs. 3) Keep rain from running in burrows and provide a higher viewpoint for the lookouts. 4) Let them know that it is their territory so stay out. 5) Farmers poisoned them to save livestock.

Thinking—1) Squirrel? Woodchuck? Beaver?; due to body style. 2) There are ferrets, badgers, rattlesnakes, and burrowing owls that get in. 3) Answers will vary, but they may mention towns, families, property boundaries, etc. 4) May say how pups can roam over town and get to keep parents' house. 5) Answers will vary, not endangered yet.

Bison *(Largest Land Animal in the United States?)*

Vocabulary—1) dung 2) vital 3) slaughter 4) rituals 5) significant 6) conservationists 7) tendons 8) stampede 9) rumination 10) sunscreen.

Comprehension—1) French word *boeuf,* meaning "beef," English said as buffalo. 2) Dung for fuel, house, boat, sunscreen, or glue were all unusual. 3) They don't have the hump, horns, or shaggy mane yet. 4) 50 million; 500; 50,000 all approximations.

Thinking—1) No; They are big and strong and gang up on predators. Yes, if predators go after the calves. 2) Answers will vary, but may say the hump or huge head or shaggy hair. 3) They were destroying their way of life, buffalo, forcing them to accept help since they couldn't feed people or supply their own needs. 4) Buffalo, NY; Buffalo Bills, Sabres, Colorado Buffaloes; Buffalo Dam, River, Mtn., etc.; CO and WY flags, nickels, stamps, etc. 5) Students who are buffaloed, puzzled, or baffled should find it in a dictionary.

Snappers *(Watch Your Fingers!)*

Vocabulary—1) flailing 2) burlap 3) vertebrates 4) devour 5) groping 6) carapace 7) plastron 8) encounter 9) lure 10) lunge.

Comprehension—1) Its sharp, powerful jaws are better than its shell. 2) Common; Florida; and Alligator. 3) It has a worm-like thing on its tongue to lure prey close to snap. 4) It is attached to the carapace shell, and it does not bend.

Thinking—1) He knows how a snapper can bite, and men were taking big risks. 2) Probably so the sun can heat the eggs and soil to hatch them. 3) They are huge, and have big jaws. 4) Answers will vary, but I suspect they hope to feel the jagged back of the carapace, grab a tail, and pull the snapper out without getting bitten. 5) A baited wire trap would be an excellent idea.

Falcon *(The Fastest Creature on Earth!)*

Vocabulary—1) nickname 2) teasing 3) banning 4) mustache 5) fledgling 6) eyrie 7) stoop 8) efficient 9) falconry 10) remote.

Comprehension—1) A Latin word meaning wanderer or foreigner. 2) Small birds and sometimes ducks. 3) Pesticides like DDT were passed down from insects to the birds the falcons ate. 4) Humans raised falcons and released them into the wild.

Thinking—1) They must be concentrated doses in the birds the falcons eat. 2) Answers may include their speed, eating birds, gravel nests, skyscraper dwellings, etc. 3) Answers will vary. 4) Flies, since other animals measured that way; dives because it is part of the flight pattern of the falcon.

Orcas *(The Beautiful Killer Whale)*

Vocabulary—1) pod 2) fertile 3) distinct 4) individual 5) romp 6) zoologists 7) breaching 8) communication 9) nannies 10) echolocation.

Comprehension—1) About 30 ft. long, black back with 6-ft. tall fin on it, white belly, a fluke like a whale and a nose more like a dolphin. 2) The gray saddles on the back are each different. 3) Orcas send out sounds that strike objects and bounce back to tell them the shape and distance. 4) Humans' pollution of their waters and the loss of the foods they want to eat.

Thinking—1) Whales due to the flukes and size of them. Dolphins due to the nose and body shape. 2) Answers will vary, but should mention that research done shows there is communication. 3) Yes, they do kill other warm-blooded mammals. No, they don't attack humans and are fine in marine exhibits. 4) Probably not because of the birth interval of 5 to 6 years, food supply. 5) Answers may include the spectacular tricks or the danger/thrill aspect or their beauty.

Enrichment Activities:
Teaching Ideas and Answer Key

1. **Information About** _____: This activity could be used with any lesson for students to summarize the major concepts and statistics about the animal being studied. The first time students do the activity, you may need to tell them how you want it done.

2. **Pretend You Are the**_____: This can be done after any lesson. You can fill in the animal you want featured or have students choose the animal to pretend to be.

3. **Word Search:** This could be done at any time, but students may need some help with what group certain animals belong to if they do this before they've read about it. Answers for blanks are M, M, M, M, B, F, M, M, Mo, A, M, R, M, M, M, M, B, R, B, M. Difficult ones include eel as a fish, octopus as mollusk, black widow as arthropod, and snapping turtle as reptile.

4. **Animal Puzzle:** The mazes are not too difficult and are a fun visual experience to be used with any lessons.

5. **Drawing with Shapes:** You could also choose to do this activity at any point, but students may need to see some illustrations before they could draw them. You could change the shape to fit your own needs, or allow varied shapes to be used. Perhaps they want to develop a scoring system for the guessing game.

6. **Name That Rock Band:** I did not advise students to get your permission before substituting other words in their band's name, as I decided to let you set those rules. You decide what you want to do at the conclusion: hand them in for your perusal, sharing in class, voting on best band name, posting on the bulletin board, etc.

7. **Animal Crossword Puzzle:** *Across:* 1) bison 2) cow 6) carp 8) ate 10) coiled 12) badger 13) area 16) preens 18) black 19) falcon. *Down:* 1) breach 3) whale 4) orca 5) red 7) pod 9) tern 11) iguana 12) bear 14) rebel 15) eel 16) Puff 17) scan.

8. **The Tale of Matching Tails:** Tails' tale from top to bottom reads GLAD CHIRP BY NEST.

9. **Create a Terrific Title:** You may want to encourage students not to overuse animal names.

10. **Mystery Animal Puzzle:** It might be necessary (dependent on student ability) to provide a list of names of animals (see the list given in Reading Level 4). *Puzzle 1:* 1) polar bear 2) mallard 3) armadillo 4) eagles 5) otters 6) orca (secret animal = BADGER). *Puzzle 2:* 1) falcon 2) anaconda 3) electric eel 4) widow 5) hippo 6) turtle 7) bison (secret animal = OCTOPUS).

1. Information About _____

Where on Earth do they live?

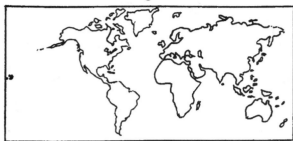

Describe the home or habitat:

Describe the looks:

Colors—

Body covering—

Weight—

Height or length —

Special features—

Babies, Babies, Babies:

Gestation or Incubation time—

Number born—

Birth size—

Born with or without—

Length of time with parents—

Food and Eating Habits:

Favored food—

Also eat—

Obtained by—

Interesting Facts:

Name _____ Date _____

2. Pretend You Are the _____

1. The best feature of my new animal body is the _____

   because _____

   _____.

2. However, I would like to change my _____

   because _____

   _____.

3. One thing I can do now that I couldn't do well before is _____

   _____

   _____.

4. I live on the continent of _____ and my main habitat is in the

   _____

   _____.

5. The food I like that we animals eat is _____,

   but I don't like eating the _____

   _____.

6. My biggest fear as one of these animals is _____

   _____

   _____.

7. The thing I enjoy most about being a member of this species is _____

   _____

   _____.

8. The main thing that makes our kind special is _____

   _____

   _____.

9. The reason I want to go back to being human is because I miss the _____

   _____

   _____.

Name _____ Date _____

3. Word Search

Find the names of the twenty animals listed in the box and circle them in the word search. (Five diagonals and one L-shape make it difficult.) You may also find some other names listed, and those you can write on the lines at the bottom of the search. When you have found all twenty animals listed in the box, print the following letters on the blanks:
M = Mammal, **B** = Bird, **F** = Fish, **R** = Reptile, **A** = Arthropod, and **Mo** = Mollusk. Good luck!

_____ WHALE
_____ OTTER
_____ BEAVER
_____ BADGER
_____ BALD EAGLE
_____ ELECTRIC EEL
_____ ARMADILLO
_____ HIPPOPOTAMUS
_____ OCTOPUS
_____ BLACK WIDOW
_____ ORANGUTAN
_____ ANACONDA
_____ ANTEATER
_____ POLAR BEAR
_____ BISON
_____ PRAIRIE DOG
_____ MALLARD
_____ SNAPPING TURTLE
_____ PEREGRINE FALCON
_____ ORCA

C	S	E	E	L	E	C	T	R	I	C	E	A	N	T
A	N	T	E	A	T	E	R	M	I	T	E	R	O	O
B	A	L	D	E	A	G	L	E	N	D	L	M	A	N
O	P	B	L	A	C	K	W	I	D	O	W	A	P	Y
B	P	I	G	G	U	M	M	I	C	E	A	D	R	B
H	I	P	P	O	P	O	T	A	M	U	S	I	A	O
O	N	S	G	L	O	C	B	N	L	A	W	L	I	R
O	G	O	O	D	L	T	R	A	I	L	H	L	R	A
T	T	O	W	N	A	O	I	C	D	O	A	O	I	N
O	U	T	N	M	R	P	A	O	H	G	L	R	E	G
M	R	H	E	A	B	U	R	N	A	M	E	N	D	U
A	T	C	A	R	E	S	A	D	O	T	E	R	O	T
S	L	A	A	E	A	B	E	A	V	E	R	A	G	A
P	E	R	E	G	R	I	N	E	F	A	L	C	O	N

Other names found: _____

_____

Name _____ Date _____

4. Animal Puzzle

Help these puzzled animals find their way through the maze to the burrow where they will be safe. If they get stuck three times, they are prey.

Name _____ Date _____

5. Drawing with Shapes

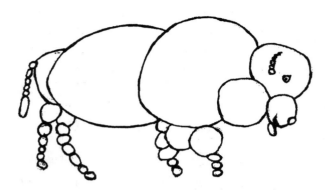

Use various circles, spheres, and ovals to draw a picture to represent some animal you choose. Keep the identity of that animal secret from everyone else. You will need to pair up with another person when both of you are done, and take turns trying to guess what the other has drawn. You want them to guess what you have drawn, so add as much detail as you can.

If they can't guess what you drew in three guesses, give them the following clues:

1. Tell them the country or habitat where it is most likely to be found.

2. Tell them what food(s) it eats most of the time.

3. Give them clues as to its size, like "its about the size of a _____."

4. This animal's name begins with the letter _____.

5. If they haven't gotten it yet, you either made it too hard or it's too unfamiliar.

Name _____ Date _____

6. Name that Rock Band

You may already know some weird names of bands. Did you ever wonder how they got their name? Maybe they used a list like the one below. You get to try your hand at naming your band. Just choose one word from each list and write them down in that order to create an interesting name. You may try out several to find the one you think will attract the biggest audience to make millions.

Fierce	Fatal	Whales
Keen	Polar	Beavers
Sleek	Stunned	Octopuses (Octopi)
Aquatic	Coiled	Turtles
Seldom	Slippery	Orangutans
Flailing	Elastic	Eagles
Ambitious	Lofty	Badgers
Black	Preening	Spiders
Superb	Lunging	Electric Eels
Leaping	Fatal	Bison
Coarse	Carnivorous	Hippos
Rare	Stalking	Otters
Flexible	Flying	Falcons
Crude	Romping	Anacondas
Distinctly	Sly	Vertebrates

1. _____

2. _____

3. _____

4. _____

Decide what instruments will be in your band and who will play them. Use the back of this sheet for your answer.

Name _____ Date _____

7. Animal Crossword Puzzle

Solve this puzzle using the clues listed for across and down.

ACROSS:

1. Instead of buffalo, American _____
2. A female whale
6. Goldfish and koi family
8. Past tense of eat
10. Anaconda's strangling position
12. Fierce burrowing mammal; to nag
13. Extent of surface length X width
16. What birds do to clean and oil feathers
18. Dominant color on black widows
19. The fastest animal in the world

DOWN:

1. A whale jump and splash
3. The largest mammal to ever live
4. Proper name for killer whale
5. Color of hourglass on black widow
7. Name for a group of whales
9. White arctic bird of the gull family
11. Large tropical lizard, often a pet
12. Polar, black, and grizzly are examples
14. Resist control or be defiant
15. Snake-like fish, some shock
16. Name for a "magical dragon"
17. Glance at hastily; look over quickly

© 2000 by The Center for Applied Research in Education

Name _____ Date _____

8. The Tale of Matching Tails

Print the letter beside the drawing of the animal's tail on the blank by its name. If you get stuck on a letter, go to a different tail. Do all of the ones you know first, then maybe the rest will fall into place.

1. _____ Armadillo

2. _____ Prairie dog

3. _____ Orca

4. _____ Badger

5. _____ Beaver

6. _____ Hippopotamus

7. _____ Anaconda

8. _____ Electric eel

9. _____ Peregrine falcon

10. _____ Otter

11. _____ Mallard

12. _____ Bison

13. _____ Eagle

14. _____ Polar bear

15. _____ Snapping turtle

(A)

(B)

(C)

(D)

(E)

(G)

(H)

(I)

(L)

(N)

(P)

(R)

(S)

(Y)

(T)

Name _____ Date _____

9. Create a Terrific Title

The titles for the twenty stories in this section seldom told you the name of the animal. Perhaps you could create (make up) an interesting title with what impressed you about that animal. Write an interesting *new* title beside the name of each animal.

1. Blue whale _____

2. River otter _____

3. Beaver _____

4. Badger _____

5. Bald eagle _____

6. Electric eel _____

7. Armadillo _____

8. Hippo _____

9. Octopus _____

10. Black widow _____

11. Orangutan _____

12. Anaconda _____

13. Giant anteater _____

14. Polar bear _____

15. Mallard _____

16. Prairie dog _____

17. American bison _____

18. Snapping turtle _____

19. Peregrine falcon _____

20. Orca/killer whale _____

Name _____ Date _____

10. Mystery Animal Puzzle

There is a mystery animal hidden in each puzzle below. All you have to do is use the information you learned about the animals to fill in the squares with their names. If you fill all squares correctly, you will find a name in the rows of letters down.

Puzzle 1

1. The biggest bear in the world

2. Origin of all domestic ducks

3. Mammal in armor

4. American freedom symbol

5. Playful river weasels

6. Killer whale's real name

Mystery animal = _____

Puzzle 2

1. Fastest animal in the world

2. Biggest snake in the world

3. Highest voltage animal

4. She devours her mate and is a…

5. The great river horse

6. Hibernating reptile in a shell

7. Largest American land mammal

Mystery animal = _____

Name _____ Date _____

Reading Level 6

Before Reading the Story:
New Vocabulary and Questions to Ask

1. Our Favorite Dolphin

New Vocabulary:

blunt	expanse
bond	intelligent
compete	melon
distinguish	navigate
distress	submerge

Questions to Ask:

How many of you have seen dolphins? Where?
How can we tell a dolphin from a porpoise?
Are dolphins very intelligent?
How do dolphins communicate? Do they talk?
Why are dolphins endangered?

2. Andes Truck

New Vocabulary:

bleat	jerky
bray	minerals
browse	nutrition
domesticated	resemble
endure	tanned

Questions to Ask:

What does a llama look like?
Have any of you seen one?
What family do llamas belong to?
Are there wild llamas? Where did llamas originate?
What are llamas used for in the Andes Mountains?
Are there llamas in the United States?
Are llamas good pets?

3. The Largest Reptiles Are Scary

New Vocabulary:

agile	lifespan
compost	lifestyle
dissolve	olive
encounter	slither
exhibition	tourists

Questions to Ask:

Which are the largest reptiles?
How do we tell alligators from crocodiles?
How big do gators and crocodiles get?
How do gators hatch their eggs?
Why did alligators become endangered?
Are alligators endangered now?

4. The Miniature Dinosaurs

New Vocabulary:

arthropod	molt
camouflage	ootheca
cannibal	pincers
devour	seize
greedy	variegated

Questions to Ask:

What is a mantid?
Why is the European mantid called a praying
   mantis? Where do they live?
Would praying mantises bite us? What do they eat?
Do praying mantises have any enemies?
What defense do praying mantises have?
How do praying mantises reproduce?

5. The Mighty Rhinoceros

New Vocabulary:

dominance	parasites

Questions to Ask:

What was the largest land mammal ever?

gouge	poachers	What do you think of first about the rhino?
joust	sanctuary	Why did rhinos become endangered?
keratin	solitary	Why did people want rhino horns?
nub	tolerate	Why do rhinos let birds sit on their back?
pachyderms		

6. The Powerful, Peaceful Primates

New Vocabulary:

Questions to Ask:

dew	infancy	What is a primate? What group are we in?
elaborate	intruders	Are gorillas the largest primate? Are they mean?
furrow	juveniles	Where do wild gorillas live?
gnash	primates	What do gorillas eat? Where do they sleep?
herbivorous		Why are there so few gorillas left?

7. Where the Wild Geese Fly

New Vocabulary:

Questions to Ask:

alter	invade	Have you seen Canada geese migrating?
foiled	loyal	Do you know about the unique habits of
gander	proclamation	Canada geese?
gorge	reservoir	Why do people dislike geese in public spots?
gosling	rival	Why don't people like geese at reservoirs?
harvest	urban	What caused changes in migration routes?

8. Magnificent Mammal Migration

New Vocabulary:

Questions to Ask:

crustaceans	massive	How can you recognize seals?
depletion	naturalist	There are fur seal rookeries on the Pribilof Islands.
external	pinnipeds	Where are those islands?
flourish	proficient	Cows migrate 5,000 miles a year. Why?
harem	rookery	Why were many fur seals killed in the past?
		Why have the numbers of fur seals increased lately?

9. The Feline with Many Names

New Vocabulary:

Questions to Ask:

carcass	mauled	What are the diifferences among pumas, cougars,
contrary	secluded	and mountain lions?
cunning	stealth	Do you know any other names for mountain lions?
feline	strategies	What makes mountain lions such great hunters?
lean		Why did people kill most of the cougars?
		What is the best way to save these big cats?

10. Some Scary Arachnids

New Vocabulary:

Questions to Ask:

| adhere | hinged | Do you remember what arachnids are? |

adversary	invertebrate	What is the biggest, scariest arachnid?
aggressive	lurk	Have any of you seen a tarantula? Describe one.
arachnids	recluse	What do tarantulas eat? Do they spin webs?
exoskeleton	vulnerable	What's a trapdoor spider? Where do they live?
		Do people have pet tarantulas? Why?

11. World's Largest Venomous Snake

New Vocabulary: *Questions to Ask:*

characteristic	flared	Can you name the world's biggest venomous snake?
dense	lethal	How do people identify cobras easily?
depression	metabolism	Why do cobras have a "face" on their back?
deterrent	receptors	When are king cobras most dangerous?
evacuate		What is a king cobra's main prey?

12. The Fastest Land Mammal

New Vocabulary: *Questions to Ask:*

accelerate	exceeding	What is the fastest land mammal? What is its speed?
accompany	lacrymal	Where do cheetahs live?
capacity	pursuit	Do cheetahs have any distinguishing looks?
essential	sociable	Are they great fighters?
estimate	suffocate	Why were many cheetahs killed?
		Cheetahs are protected now, so why are they still endangered?

13. Second Most Intelligent Mammal

New Vocabulary: *Questions to Ask:*

antics	grooming	What's your favorite zoo animal?
astounding	laboratories	What is the most intelligent mammal?
embrace	remedy	Why are chimps so popular?
experiments	susceptible	What other uses are there for chimps?
gestures		How intelligent do you think chimps are?

14. The Queen and Her Court

New Vocabulary: *Questions to Ask:*

decades	proboscis	What insect makes food we eat?
entomologist	regurgitate	What is the most important job bees do?
fertile	royal	How do bees make honey?
metamorphosis	sterile	What does a queen bee do? A drone?
pollinate		Who's allergic to bee stings?

15. King of the Northwest

New Vocabulary: *Questions to Ask:*

| boughs | lope | What's the scariest animal in Yellowstone? |
| carrion | scavenge | How did they get named "grizzly" bears? |

conjure	spawn	Are grizzlies carnivores, herbivores, or omnivores?
discern	subdue	Why were so many grizzlies killed?
disciplined	wilderness	Are grizzlies endangered? Why?

16. The Only True Vampires

New Vocabulary:　　　　　　*Questions to Ask:*

anticoagulant	lactating	Are there really any vampires?
bloated	rabies	Have any of you ever heard of vampire bats?
coagulation	saliva	Where do they live?
consecutive	sustain	Are they dangerous? How?
docile	twinge	What do you think vampire bats eat?
incisors		Have any of you ever heard of rabies? What is it?

17. The Tough Rulers of Antarctica

New Vocabulary:　　　　　　*Questions to Ask:*

bizarre	frigid	What does a penguin look like?
courtship	hardy	Where do penguins live?
créche	harsh	What is the biggest penguin? How big?
desolate	hordes	How do penguins move around best?
embryo	pinnacle	What would you like to learn about penguins?

18. The Man-eating Fish Tale

New Vocabulary:　　　　　　*Questions to Ask:*

bladder	regenerate	How many of you have seen *Jaws*?
cartilage	sensational	What kind of shark starred in the movie?
denticle	sequel	Do sharks often prey on people?
gruesome	serrated	Why do you think sharks swim constantly?
lateral	womb	How can people surf and swim safely in seas?

19. The Wolf that Cried Boy

New Vocabulary:　　　　　　*Questions to Ask:*

acute	sentinel	Why do wolves have a bad reputation?
converge	siblings	Where do most North American wolves live?
descended	stamina	Can you tell any good things about wolves?
despise	subordinate	Who likes dogs? (All dogs are of wolf stock.)
fables	traits	Are wolves endangered? Why?

20. Are Dragons Only a Myth?

New Vocabulary:　　　　　　*Questions to Ask:*

arboreal	perils	Did dragons ever really exist?
associated	photographer	Have you ever heard of Komodo dragons?
confronted	restrain	Where do these dragons live? How big are they?
elusive	solitary	Are Komodos dangerous? Why?
mythology	terrain	Are Komodos endangered? Are they valuable? Why?

1. Our Favorite Dolphin

Dolphins and porpoises are the most intelligent, playful, and interesting members of the whale family. They can be found in all of the oceans, in most seas, and even in some rivers. They usually live near the coast, but some are found out in the great expanse of the largest oceans, too. Many people have a difficult time distinguishing dolphins from porpoises since both belong to the family of toothed whales. The following pictures and descriptions should help you tell apart the bottlenose dolphin, common dolphin, and porpoise.

Common dolphins grow to about 7 feet, weigh up to 160 pounds, and have about a 6-inch beak. Their back is black, their belly is white, and they have distinctive brown and gray stripes on their sides. They are

Common Dolphin

probably the most playful of the toothed whales, and hundreds of them are often seen leaping around ships at sea. They are the fastest of the smaller toothed whales, achieving speeds up to 27 mph. They do not do well in captivity since they are difficult to tame.

Bottlenose dolphins grow to about 12 feet long and weigh up to 700 pounds. They have about a 4-inch beak and are dark gray on the back fading to a lighter gray belly. They swim about 25 mph in large

Bottlenose Dolphin

pods and are quite playful, also. They are very friendly and easy to tame. Most of the performing dolphins seen in aquariums and marine parks are bottlenoses.

Porpoises grow to about 5 feet long and weigh about 100 pounds. They have a blunt snout with no real beak. Their back is dark gray and their underside is white. Porpoises travel in small schools of two to five and do not frolic so much as dolphins.

Porpoise

All three species communicate and navigate using a system of echolocation. They make sound waves by emitting clicks and high-pitched whistles from an area in their forehead called the melon. When the waves bounce off objects and come back to the melon, the brain of these great creatures translates each signal. Many experiments have been done to determine how well they can "see" with echolocation. Several have shown that they can even distinguish what is inside many objects. They navigate their environment, find their food, and communicate with each other this way. They hear distress calls and come to the aid of any sick or injured dolphin, and stories about them helping human divers or swimmers have been told all over the world.

Dolphins are famous for their leaping ability. Leaps higher than 20 feet have been recorded for bottlenose dolphins. That is twice as high as a basketball hoop! No scientists know for certain, but they think dolphins at sea jump to spot seabirds feeding or to locate schools of fish and splash down to herd the fish together. They may jump to communicate, too, or perhaps they simply "jump for joy" or the fun of it. Bottlenose at marine shows steal the show when dolphins make spectacular leaps for a fishy reward. As carnivores, they also eat octopus, shrimp, squid, and cuttlefish.

Dolphins only have a calf every two or three years. The calf is born tail first after a ten-month gestation. Other females in the school assist the mother with the birth by pulling the baby out and chasing away sharks that may be attracted by blood released during the birth of the baby. The calf can swim well as soon as it gulps a few breaths of air. The bottlenose can remain submerged for about fifteen minutes, but common dolphins must nurse quickly as they can only submerge for three or four minutes. Calves nurse for about sixteen months, so they develop a close bond with the mother. Other females help her teach the calf to hunt for prey using echolocation so the calf can become independent.

The very intelligent dolphins know that sharks and killer whales are enemies. They still trust humans even though they compete with us for food. Nets to catch tuna, salmon, and other food fish often catch and kill many dolphins competing for those fish. More than 100,000 dolphins a year were killed in nets, but laws now protect them better. Make sure canned fish labels say "dolphin safe." Ask people to vote to stop polluting our oceans.

Our Favorite Dolphin

Vocabulary Checkup Write the words from the box on the correct blanks.

blunt	bond	compete	distinguish	distress
expanse	intelligent	melon	navigate	submerge

1. _____ means to see or perceive details clearly.

2. _____ is to sink below the surface of the water.

3. _____ is having a dull, rounded point; not sharp.

4. _____ is to find a way and steer a course or path.

5. _____ is a cry or call for help due to danger or pain.

6. The dolphin's sound chamber in the forehead is called a _____.

7. A broad, unbroken space or area is called an _____.

8. To try hard to outdo an opponent is to _____.

9. Very bright or smart in some way is _____.

10. A close tie that fastens together is called a _____.

Comprehension You may need to look back at the story to answer the questions correctly.

1. What dolphins are used in most marine shows? _____
   Why? _____

2. What are three big differences between common and bottlenose dolphins?

   _____

   _____

   _____

3. How can we tell apart dolphins and porpoises?

   _____

   _____

Name _____ Date _____

Our Favorite Dolphin

4. What can we do to help save the lives of dolphins? _____

_____

Thinking About Dolphins Think carefully before answering the questions.

1. Why do you think dolphins jump so much? _____

_____

_____

2. What evidence can you think of to prove that dolphins have a language and "talk"?

_____

_____

3. Do you think dolphins can "see" by listening to other dolphins' clicks? _____
   What other sounds do you think might help them navigate or find prey?

_____

_____

4. What do you think is most amazing about dolphins, and why?

_____

_____

5. Would you swim with and pet a dolphin if you had the chance?_____
   Why? _____

_____

_____

Check It Out Find out about
    White-sided dolphins
    Risso's dolphins
    Amazon River dolphins
    Striped dolphins
    Spotted dolphins

Name _____ Date _____

2. Andes Truck

The Andes Mountains span the entire west coast of South America and are the longest mountain range above sea level in the world. The natives there have used the llama, a member of the camel family, as their main source of transportation for thousands of years. Llamas give these people the same type of service that horses and mules once gave people in North America. Trucks and cars have replaced the horses as the major transportation in the United States, but the llamas are still the trucks of the Andes.

Llamas look almost as large as many horses, but they are really much smaller. The largest llama is only about 4 feet tall at the shoulders and weighs about 400 pounds. It has a long neck like a camel, which puts its head at about 6 feet. The large eyes and neck and the split upper lip help the llama resemble the camel. Llamas have long ears and no humps, however. Their feet resemble those of a camel since they also have a split hoof that is two-toed with a soft pad. The llama's toenails grow all the time just like yours do, so they need to be cut. Llamas have a thick coat of wool growing in various patterns and in many shades of white, brown, and black.

Llamas were domesticated for use by the natives of the Andes Mountains over 4,000 years ago. Many scientists believe they were developed from breeding with wild guanaco or vicuña, which are also members of the camelid family. The alpaca is also a domesticated camelid living in the Andes. Evidence shows that the much smaller alpacas came from a crossbreeding of the llama and the vicuña. The Inca Indians used hundreds of llamas in caravans to transport goods to market. The Incas used thousands of the llamas to haul gold and silver ore out of their mines. There aren't wild llamas or alpacas, but people of the Andes allow them to roam free to browse for food.

Llamas supply many of the needs of the people of the Andes, who dry the llama meat in strips called *charqui,* which is the origin of what we call *jerky.* The wool is made into rope and warm clothing. The hide is tanned

(Andes Truck, *continued*)

and made into shoes, bags, and tents. The fat is used for candles and cooking, and the droppings are a fuel to burn. The male llamas are usually the pack animals since the females are either busy nursing babies or are pregnant. Good pack llamas can carry 100 pounds and are very surefooted on mountain trails since they walk on those pads behind the toenails.

Llamas are so friendly and easy to raise that they make ideal pets, companions, and small farm animals. They graze on most kinds of grass and browse on leaves of shrubs. You can raise three or four of them on an acre as long as you supply fresh water and a few minerals for nutrition. They can endure freezing cold; however, they do need some shade in hot weather. They usually deposit their droppings in the same spot if they can, so cleanup is pretty easy. People find it's best if they have two or more llamas so they are companions to each other. A 4-foot-high fence is adequate to keep the llamas penned in, but you may want something taller if you want to keep big dogs out. Llamas also need their toenails trimmed and an occasional brushing.

Female llamas can begin having babies at two years of age, but only produce one offspring every other year. They usually have a single baby (called a cria) after an eleven-month gestation. The 20- to 30-pound cria gets up soon after it's born and nurses in about thirty minutes. It is weaned when it's five or six months old and will be ready to train.

Llamas are curious animals and will come right over to people to sniff them. People who raise these remarkable animals learn to tell what mood they are in by reading the position of their ears and listening to the sounds they make. They hum in a purr when they are happy, hum in a whine when they're alarmed, hum with a growl when they're angry or ready to spit, and bleat when they're unhappy at being separated from others. They can bray like a donkey if they're scared or real upset.

There are now more than 16,000 llamas in the United States and Canada, and they cost less than most good horses. Perhaps you know someone in your area who has llamas and you could visit them. If you're interested in getting a pair as unique pets, it may be best to get young ones to grow up with you.

Andes Truck

Vocabulary Checkup Write the words from the box on the correct blanks.

bleat	bray	browse	domesticated	endure
jerky	minerals	nutrition	resemble	tanned

1. To eat or nibble at leaves, seeds, and berries is to _____.

2. *Charqui* in Spanish; or dried strips of meat is _____.

3. When chemicals turn hides into leather, it is _____.

4. Natural substances, not animal or vegetable, are _____.

5. A sound like that of a sheep or goat is a _____.

6. _____ means tamed for people to use.

7. A _____ is a harsh cry like that of a donkey.

8. _____ means to look a lot like another.

9. _____ is the food for proper health and development.

10. _____ means to withstand or last despite hardship.

Comprehension You may need to look back at the story to answer the questions correctly.

1. What other peoples used an animal to meet many needs? _____

_____

2. Why are llamas called the trucks of the Andes? _____

_____

3. What is jerky, and where did we get that word? _____

_____

4. What would you need to take care of a pair of llamas? _____

_____

Name _____   Date _____

Andes Truck

5. What are the negative (bad) parts about having llamas as pets?

_____

_____

Thinking About Llamas Think carefully before answering the questions.

1. What do you think makes llamas look almost as large as horses?

_____

_____

2. What features do you think make llamas resemble camels? _____

_____

_____

3. What reasons can you think of that might make a pack llama refuse to carry a load?

_____

_____

4. Since other animals could carry bigger loads, why do you think Andes people chose the llama?

_____

_____

5. Pretend you want a pair of llamas. What convincing arguments could you use to get them?

_____

_____

Check It Out Find out about
   Alpacas
   Guanacos
   Vicuñas
   Peru
   Inca Empire

Name _____ Date _____

3. The Largest Reptiles Are Scary

Crocodilians are just about the only surviving creatures from the prehistoric age of dinosaurs 100 million years ago. The four members of this family are the crocodiles, found mostly in Africa; the cayman found in Central and South America; the two types of alligators found in China and the United States; and the gavials of India. They look so similar that many people have difficulty telling them apart. The pictures of the heads and descriptions below should help you identify each one easily.

The gavial, or gharial, of India can be 30 feet long. Notice the long, skinny jaws it uses to catch fish.

Gavial

The cayman, or caiman, found in South and Central America, has a black crest between the eyes and is only 5 or 6 feet long.

Cayman

The crocodile is found mostly in Africa, although a few are found at the southern tip of Florida and on islands in the Gulf of Mexico. Some crocodiles are 20 to 25 feet long and are heavy, at 1,500 pounds. They are most easily identified by their lower teeth sticking out over the upper jaw when the mouth is shut.

Crocodile

Alligators are found in China and in the southeastern United States from North Carolina to Texas. They used to be as long as 19 feet, but only 12- to 13-footers are now found. Bull alligators average about 500 pounds, but females are closer to 160 pounds. They have a broader, flatter head than other crocodilians and you can't see their teeth when they close their mouth.

Alligator

The rest of the body of crocodilians looks quite similar to lizards. The Spaniards even called the alligators they saw in America *el lagarto*, which means "the lizard." You probably noticed that all crocodilians have the eyes, ears, and nostrils located on top of the head so they can use them while the rest of the body is underwater. All species have tough, scaly hide of a dull gray to dark olive color. They all have four short legs with four or five toes and a long, strong tail they use to swim or whack prey or a predator.

Now let's concentrate on the American alligator's lifestyle since we are more likely to encounter them than the others. Much of the information about our alligators is true throughout the entire crocodilian family. Like other reptiles, they are cold-blooded, so they have to lie in the sun to warm their body. They also bury themselves in the mud at night or when weather is cool. They can run and slither along on the land, but they are much more agile and quick in the water.

Mature alligators eat fish, snakes, turtles, and most other swamp creatures that swim too close. The alligator lies motionless in the water to ambush unsuspecting prey. Snap! The deadly jaws clamp down on prey and it is swallowed whole. Gators don't chew their food, so powerful juices dissolve it in the stomach. Larger prey like a young deer, pig, calf, or dog are pulled underwater, drowned, and torn into smaller pieces before disappearing down the gator's throat. Unlike the crocodiles, alligators do not usually attack humans, but I certainly wouldn't count on that. There are some people who actually wrestle gators! They avoid the tail while holding the jaws shut. Gators have powerful muscles to close the jaws but weak ones to open them. Some alligator farms in the Southeast have exhibitions like this to attract tourists.

The female alligator builds a 3-foot-high mound of mud and plants as a nest for approximately fifty eggs. She piles more vegetation and mud on top of the eggs. This pile begins to compost or decay, and the heat produced helps the sun keep the eggs warm for the two to three months needed for them to hatch. The female will stay close to protect them so they don't get eaten by predators. If the nest temperature is close to 85 degrees, all females will hatch, but closer to 95 degrees and males will hatch. The 8- to 9-inch babies have an egg tooth like baby birds to break out of the leathery shell. Babies sound a croaking noise if they can't get out, and the mother will help. If water is far away, the babies will crawl into the mother's mouth for a ride to the water's edge. They can swim right away and begin eating insects, worms, snails, tadpoles, minnows, shrimp, and crayfish. They grow at the rate of a foot per year until they are about six, if they survive long enough. Several will be eaten by large birds, fish, and other alligators. If they survive the first year and are good hunters, they have a good chance of a lifespan of fifty to sixty years.

Humans killed many alligators, thinking they were a threat or for the hides to make valuable leather boots and purses. Crocodilians all over the world became endangered. Laws now protect all gators, and they are no longer endangered.

The Largest Reptiles Are Scary

Vocabulary Checkup Write the words from the box on the correct blanks.

agile	compost	dissolve	encounter	exhibition
lifespan	lifestyle	olive	slither	tourists

1. _____ is the time members of a species expect to live.

2. _____ are people who travel to an area to see sights.

3. An _____ is a show or act for people to watch.

4. _____ means to decay, rot, and turn into soil.

5. _____ is to slide and move in a snake-like manner.

6. _____ is to melt, liquefy, or break down a substance.

7. _____ is a species' typical way of living.

8. _____ is to meet or run into unexpectedly.

9. _____ is a brownish-green color.

10. _____ means nimble and moving in a coordinated way.

Comprehension You may need to look back at the story to answer the questions correctly.

1. What are the names of the four main kinds of crocodilians? _____

_____

_____

2. What are the best clues to look for to tell apart alligators and crocodiles?

_____

_____

3. Why do alligators bury themselves in the mud? _____

_____

Name _____ Date _____

The Largest Reptiles Are Scary

4. Why do alligators bury their eggs in rotting vegetation? _____
_____

5. Why did alligators almost become extinct forty years ago? _____
_____

Thinking About Alligators Think carefully before answering the questions.

1. Use the clues in the story to figure out where we get the word *alligator.*
_____
_____

2. Could we tell apart the four crocodilians by just seeing the backs and tails? _____
Why? _____
_____

3. Why do you think people wrestle alligators? _____
_____
_____

4. Do you think people need to be very careful around alligators? _____
Why? _____

5. How do you think the temperature of the hatching eggs determines whether babies are male or female?
_____
_____

6. What did you think was the most interesting thing you learned about crocodilians?
_____
_____

Check It Out Find out about
Gavials   Caymans
Nile crocodiles
Crocodile toothpicks—plovers

Name _____ Date _____

4. The Miniature Dinosaurs

It may look like a prehistoric creature from the dinosaur age, but it's a member of the arthropod (jointed legs) family and is an insect. Scientists call these insects *mantids.* The majority of the mantids live in all tropical regions of the world, but the European mantid can live as far north as Canada. People often call them "praying mantis" because of the way they hold their front legs under their mouth as they wait for prey. They may or may not be praying, but they are preying carnivores.

An adult mantis is anywhere from 2 to 5 inches long. It has six legs and three body sections, so it is classified as an insect. The head is triangular with a pair of feelers or antennae on top and a chewing mouth at the bottom. A pair of large eyes bulge out beside the antennae. The forelegs have many sharp spines along the bottom, while the other four legs resemble grasshopper legs. The body section below the head is long and thin and is called the thorax. The most mature mantids have a pair of wings attached to the thorax and folded back over the abdomen or fatter part at the rear end.

Praying mantises defend themselves mainly by their camouflaged colors. The ones that live primarily in the grass are green. Tree-dwellers are usually variegated shades of brown. There are mantises living in Africa and the Far East that are the color of the nearby flowers. Other insects make the mistake of thinking the mantis is a flower, and they get caught and eaten when they try to get nectar from it. How clever they are; looking like a meal to get a meal!

The greedy praying mantis seems to spend most of its time eating. It sits nearly invisible on a twig and when an insect comes close, the mantis grabs it quickly in those spiny front legs.

© 2000 by The Center for Applied Research in Education

It bites the head off and devours any insect that comes close. The female is a cannibal since she even gobbles up her own mate after they have mated! Then she sits there cleaning her face and spiny legs like a cat.

Some larger praying mantises seize and eat insects as large as grasshoppers or katydids. The big mantids in the tropical rainforests have even seized tree frogs or small birds to eat. Those strong pincers with the hooked spines on them make it difficult for prey to escape.

The female mantis will attach an egg case to a twig, blade of grass, tree trunk, or fence post. A stream of foamy bubbles is forced out of the back of the abdomen to stick on the case with its rows of eggs inside. This will dry and become a tough envelope called the ootheca. That thumb-sized ootheca has to protect the 100 to 400 eggs during all kinds of weather. The eggs may take as long as six months to hatch, although tropical mantids' eggs may hatch in as little as three weeks. The eggs are nearly the same size no matter what size the mantis may be. The babies emerge through tiny holes in the ootheca, but each one is still in a little sac that hangs by a thread from a hole in the egg case. They soon burst out of the sac, and the mosquito-sized baby mantids run for cover.

As they eat and grow, each baby mantis will have to shed its skin (molt) as many as five or six times. The skin is like an outside skeleton and doesn't grow. Their body won't fit into the old skin, but after they molt they will fit into the new one. After the last molting is the time when they get their wings. The females are larger at this time due in part to having an abdomen full of eggs. They also might have just devoured their very unlucky mate!

The main enemies of praying mantises are birds that happen to spot them. The main defense of the mantis is its ability to hide. If mantises remain on sticks or vegetation of the same color as their own body, they are camouflaged very well. If they are seen and attacked by a bird, they will strike out with their spiny pincers. The praying mantis in the United States is not known to bite or pinch humans, however, so you don't really have to fear these fierce, dinosaur-like cannibals. You should respect them and protect them since you now know that they eat many pests, like aphids, mosquitoes, grasshoppers, and other crop-eaters. You may even want to try hatching out an ootheca to watch the babies emerge, eat, molt, eat, and build their own ootheca. They will keep you very busy supplying enough insects to prevent them from gobbling up each other.

The Miniature Dinosaurs

Vocabulary Checkup Write the words from the box on the correct blanks.

arthropod	camouflage	cannibal	devour	greedy
molt	ootheca	pincers	seize	variegated

1. _____ means to shed or cast off the outer layer.

2. _____ is to eat up hungrily.

3. A _____ eats its own species or kind.

4. _____ is to blend with the surroundings to hide.

5. _____ is having great desire for food or wealth.

6. An _____ is an insect with jointed legs.

7. The _____ is the scientific name for the egg case.

8. _____ are the claw-like forelegs on creatures.

9. _____ means to mix in a variety of colors.

10. _____ means to grab or grasp firmly.

Comprehension You may need to look back at the story to answer the questions correctly.

1. Why do people often call mantids "praying mantises"?_____

_____

2. Why is the praying mantis classified as an insect? _____

_____

3. What is the main defense of the praying mantis? _____

_____

4. Why do praying mantises molt? _____

_____

Name _____ Date _____

The Miniature Dinosaurs

5. Why are praying mantises good, valuable insects? _____

_____

Thinking About Praying Mantises Think carefully before answering the questions.

1. Do you think mantids look like mini-dinosaurs? _____

   Why? _____

   _____

2. Do you think the male lets the female gobble him up? _____

   Why? _____

   _____

3. Why do you think any insects ever come close to the mantids? _____

   _____

   _____

4. What reasons can you think of that we aren't overpopulated by praying mantises?

   _____

   _____

5. What do you think is meant by "They may or may not be praying, but they are preying"?

   _____

   _____

6. If you had a terrarium with mantids, how would you get enough food to keep them from being too cannibalistic?

   _____

   _____

Check It Out Find out about
   Cockroaches
   Mantis flies
   Ant-lions
   Stick insects

Name _____ Date _____

5. The Mighty Rhinoceros

Millions of years ago there were more than 100 kinds of rhinoceroses, but now the five surviving species are endangered. The rhinoceros, or rhino, was one of the more common land mammals in North America until 5 million years ago. The largest land mammal known to ever live on Earth was a 40,000-pound rhino. (Dinosaurs were not mammals.) The elephant, hippo, and rhino do belong together as pachyderms, which means "thick-skinned." The rhinoceros gets its name from Greek words that mean "nose horns," and this feature is what most people picture first in rhinos. The five rhinos are pictured and described below.

About 7,000 white rhinos live in South Africa. The tallest are 6 feet tall and weigh 4,500 pounds. The horn by the eyes is close to 16 inches, but an end horn is closer to 5 feet. The mouth and nose are square at the end for these grazers who are dark gray, not white. A Dutch word *wijde* means "wide," and people thought they were saying white.

White Rhino

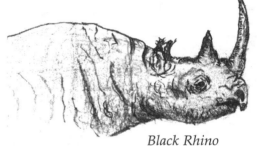

Black Rhino

In 1970 there were about 65,000 black rhinos, but now only 2,500 live in central and southern Africa. They are about 5 feet tall and weigh up to 3,000 pounds. The horn by the eyes is also 16 inches, while the nose horn can be 4 feet long. They have a pointed lip to grasp leaves and twigs as they browse. They are dark gray, not black.

About 2,000 Indian rhinos live in northeast India and Nepal. They are the largest at 6.5 feet and 5,000 pounds. They have large skin folds and bumps that give them an armored look. They have a square lip and one 2-foot horn and are also a gray color.

Indian Rhino

Sumatran Rhino

About 400 Sumatran rhinos live on Borneo and Sumatra Islands in Indonesia. They are the smallest at 4 feet tall and 1,500 pounds, and the only ones with hair all over. Lips are pointed to browse, the skin is gray, and the nose horn is 2 feet while the other horn is only a nub.

About seventy Javan rhinos live on the island of Java. They are 5 feet tall and weigh 2,500 pounds. They have one 10-inch horn and a pointed lip to browse, and their skin looks scaly.

Javan Rhino

The rhino horns are made of keratin, the same substance as your nails and hair. The keratin is like tightly packed strands of hair, and if the rhino breaks off a horn it will grow back, just like your nails. Rhinos sharpen the horns by rubbing them on trees and rocks. The horns are used to gouge, lift, and throw predators. The bulls also use their horns to joust in a rough type of playing. They often use them in fights for dominance of territory. Bulls may tolerate each other in the zoos and in a fenced sanctuary, but they are solitary, territorial beasts in the wild. Cows get along fine with other cows most of the time.

Rhinos spend twelve to fifteen hours a day eating, usually during the cooler times of the evening, night, and early morning. White and Indian rhinos graze on the grass by using their wide lips to grasp it and pull it off. The other three rhinos browse using their pointed, prehensile, upper lips to grab leaves and twigs to eat. Since all of the rhinos live in hot climates, they drink 15 to 25 gallons of water a day. They wallow in mud to cool off and protect themselves against parasites like ticks. Rhinos also let birds, like the mynah bird of India and the oxpecker or African tick bird, sit on their back and eat the bugs. They don't seem to mind the birds picking bugs out of their ears or nostrils, and the birds also sound an alarm when danger is near. The rhinos have very poor eyesight, but they do have good senses of smell and hearing.

The mating of two rhinos can be a violent event as the cow often uses her horn to jab the neck and sides of the bull. The cow will normally only have one calf at a time after a gestation of fifteen or sixteen months. She hides in the brush for the birth and a few days afterward because the bulls often attack newborn calves. The 2-foot-tall, 70- to 130-pound calf has a flat plate where the horn will grow in about five weeks. The calf will gain 4 to 6 pounds per day nursing for the first year. It will weigh over 1,000 pounds by the time it's a year old, but it will stay with the mom for two to three years for protection from hyenas, lions, and tigers. You can see why cows only have a calf every three or four years.

You can tell by the numbers that rhinos are endangered. Thousands were killed to get the horns to make medicines and dagger handles. Fenced parks and sanctuaries protect rhinos, but poachers sneak in and kill them because they can get $45,000 for a horn. Some countries shoot the poachers. Time will tell whether laws, fences, and penalties will save the rhinoceros for the future.

The Mighty Rhinoceros

Vocabulary Checkup Write the words from the box on the correct blanks.

dominance	gouge	joust	keratin	nub	pachyderms
parasites	poachers	sanctuary	solitary	tolerate	

1. _____ are thick-skinned animals.

2. _____ are people who kill animals illegally.

3. A _____ is a safe place of refuge.

4. A _____ is just a knob or lump.

5. _____ means to put up with, permit, or endure.

6. _____ is to dig or poke a hole or groove in a thing.

7. _____ is all alone, by yourself.

8. _____ is a substance that makes up nails and hair.

9. _____ is to play or fight with sharp objects.

10. _____ are organisms that live on other organisms.

11. _____ is ruling or controlling power over another.

Comprehension You may need to look back at the story to answer the questions correctly.

1. All rhinos are some shade of _____, are pachyderms because they have _____ , and have at least one nose _____.

2. Some rhinos are called white because _____ _____.

3. Rhinos wallow in the mud to _____ and _____.

Name _____ Date _____

The Mighty Rhinoceros

4. Thousands of rhinos have been killed to make _____
_____ out of their horns.

Thinking About Rhinoceroses Think carefully before answering the questions.

1. Do you think any rhino species will become extinct? _____
Which species is most likely? _____
Why? _____
_____

2. Why do you think rhinos tolerate birds pecking on them, even in the ears and nose?
_____
_____

3. Why do you think poachers still risk killing rhinos? _____
_____

4. What steps would you suggest next to protect the rhinos? _____
_____
_____

5. What do you think would happen if rhinos roamed freely in the United States today?
_____
_____

Survey Questions   Talk to your teacher about ground rules if you are going to do the survey. Should you survey students, teachers, parents, etc.? How will you record responses? What will you do with the results? Will you add any questions?

1. What do you see first when you picture a rhinoceros?
2. How many of the five species of rhinos can you name?
3. What color are white rhinos? Black rhinos?
4. Why have so many rhinos been killed?
5. Do you think rhinos will ever become extinct?

Name _____   Date _____

6. The Powerful, Peaceful Primates

Despite its amazing strength, the largest members of the primate family are gentle giants. The gorilla's peaceful, easy-going nature hasn't been recognized until recently. People used to live in fear of the gorilla and tell stories of attacks where the huge apes tore trees out of the ground and threw them at intruders. Several scientists know the great apes better now because they've gone to central Africa's rainforests and lived close to them. One of the first people brave enough to live with gorillas was Dian Fossey. She observed their peaceful family life in the wild and wrote a book called *Gorillas in the Mist.*

The male gorilla has broad shoulders, a huge chest, and long arms, but you're probably still looking at the shiny, black face. The ridge of bone above the eyes seems to furrow the brow into an angry frown. The crest of bone above the forehead helps make the gorilla look fierce. The oldest male is called a silverback because of the gray color of some of the hair on his back. He can stand about 6 feet tall and weigh about 500 pounds. Mature females usually weigh about 200 pounds and stand 5 feet tall. Black to brownish hair covers the whole body except for the palms of the hands, soles of the feet, and the face. The family group led by the silverback usually consists of as many as ten adult females with their babies and juveniles, and some younger males called blackbacks, who may be the leader's sons. They all follow the silverback, as he is their protection and makes all of the decisions about where to travel, eat, and sleep.

Gorillas support most of their weight on their feet as they walk on all fours. They use the knuckles on the back of the hands to support some of the upper body weight. They can only walk a few steps without putting the knuckles back on the ground. Look at the sketch of their hands and feet and you can see how similar they are to yours. The gorilla's big toe spreads like a thumb to help the gorilla grab.

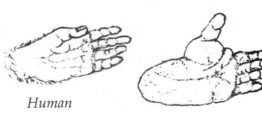

Human

Gorilla

© 2000 by The Center for Applied Research in Education

Gorillas don't spend so much time in trees, as other primates like chimpanzees and orangutans do. The females and young gorillas will build a nest to sleep in a fork of a tree a few feet up, but the larger males build their crude nest on the ground below them. Old silverback will get the family up at sunrise to wander in search of breakfast. Both mountain and lowland gorillas are herbivorous. They love bamboo shoots, but they eat the fruit and leaves of a wide variety of tropical plants. They seem to obtain enough moisture from the dew on the plants they eat, but if they do ever take a drink, they just dip their hand in the water and suck it off the soaked fur. The group moves each day and doesn't spend more than one night in the same location. If they find another group in their feeding area, they visit awhile and seldom ever fight.

Females begin having babies when they are about seven and have a baby about every fourth year. If the mother loses the baby at infancy, she may have another one the next year. Baby gorillas are born after a nine-month gestation, weigh about 4 pounds at birth, and have very little hair. Just like a human baby, it is very dependent on its mother who will cradle the tiny gorilla in her arms and nurse it. In three months the baby can crawl and hang onto the fur on Mom's back as she travels, and at five months it can walk. It will nurse until it's about a year old, and will ride on its mother's back until it's at least three years old.

The reputation for violence probably comes from the silverback's elaborate display used to warn intruders. He will growl and hoot, beat his chest like a drum, and tear up grass and bushes. If this doesn't scare the intruder away, he may charge, gnash his teeth, and wave his arms wildly. He and another silverback may be nose to nose, glaring and growling until one of them usually stomps off into the woods. Leopards won't even attack those big male gorillas; they just wanted a tasty baby one, and they probably saw this big guy snap large limbs like they were twigs. Dian Fossey said she made an ugly face at a charging gorilla, and he stopped and sat looking at her. They aren't mean. They have to behave this way to protect their family.

Gorillas used to be hunted for food and trophies, but thanks to conservationists they are now a protected species. Sanctuaries have been set up in Africa, but people there are so poor they are cutting the forests and making cropland. More than 300 gorillas live in zoos in America. These captive gorillas are having babies and doing very well, but it sure would be great to save the natural habitat for wild gorillas.

The Powerful, Peaceful Primates

Vocabulary Checkup Write the words from the box on the correct blanks.

dew	elaborate	furrow	gnash	herbivorous
infancy	intruders	juveniles	primates	

1. _____ are any who come in without permission.

2. _____ is showy or worked out with great detail.

3. _____ is moisture that condenses onto objects at night.

4. _____ are mammals like apes, monkeys, and us.

5. To grind the teeth together in rage or pain is to _____.

6. The young, not quite mature of a species are _____.

7. Animals that only eat vegetation are _____.

8. To make grooves in or wrinkle up is to _____.

9. The first stage for babies and young tots is _____.

Comprehension You may need to look back at the story to answer the questions correctly.

1. Describe a gorilla to someone who has never even seen so much as a picture.

   _____

   _____

2. What is a silverback? _____

   _____

3. What is a blackback? _____

   _____

4. How are gorilla and human babies similar? _____

   _____

Name _____ Date _____

The Powerful, Peaceful Primates

5. Why have gorillas become an endangered species? _____

_____

Thinking About Gorillas Think carefully before answering the questions.

1. What happens in a typical day for a gorilla family? _____

_____

_____

2. How would you convince people that gorillas are peaceful? _____

_____

_____

_____

3. Why do gorillas move their nest every night? _____

_____

_____

4. Why don't gorillas spend so much time in trees as some other primates?

_____

_____

5. In one word, what would you do if a big gorilla charged you? _____

Why? _____

_____

6. What do you think should be done to save the gorillas' rainforest habitat?

_____

_____

_____

Check It Out Find out about
Gibbons   Drills
Koko the Gorilla   Dian Fossey

Name _____ Date _____

© 2000 by The Center for Applied Research in Education

7. Where the Wild Geese Fly

The common wild goose of North America is the Canada goose. People in the southern United States are familiar with the visit of these birds each winter. People in the northern states recognize the migrating V-shaped flocks as a proclamation of the arrival of either spring or winter weather. The Canada goose traditionally lived only in the wild, but recently many of them have taken up residence in densely populated urban areas. Some of them have taken over golf courses and park ponds and quit migrating. They have become year-round residents and cause problems due to the large numbers of droppings left behind. When they move into reservoirs used for a city's drinking water, that is even more difficult to live with!

The Canada goose gets its name from the huge numbers that nested in the arctic regions of Canada. There are a dozen different types of Canada geese, so the sizes and looks vary considerably. The common, more plentiful Canada goose is about 3 feet long and weighs about 9 pounds. The head and neck is long and black with a chinstrap of white just behind the eyes. All of the species have the black head with the white stripe. They have a grayish-brown back and light gray underbelly. The adults have a wingspan of 4 to 6 feet, and the rival males often use their wings to beat at each other powerfully while holding onto each other's bill during mating season.

The migration habits of the Canada geese also vary quite a bit. As you know, some of them quit migrating and hang around urban areas all year long if food can be found. Most of the "honkers" migrate as far south as Mexico or Florida. Their routes have changed over the years to take advantage of farm crops or wildfowl refuges. The Canada geese are clever to adapt to changing food supplies and safe sites. They seem to alter their course when they find out about any new feeding sites.

Canada geese are herbivores and feed on a wide variety of plants. A marsh may contain eel grass, sedge, bulrush, wigeon grass, or other marsh plants. They move on to lakes, ponds, or reservoirs to eat the roots, leaves,

(Where the Wild Geese Fly, *continued*)

stems, or tubers of some of the aquatic plants. Their long neck can reach the bottom in the shallow area, and a long neck is also an advantage as the geese graze in fields not too far from water. Canada geese often invade farm fields to gorge on wheat, corn, or other grain especially before or during migration. Farmers don't mind them cleaning up spilled grain, but they don't want the geese to get their fill before the harvest time. Hunters are often foiled by honkers feeding in open fields, where there is no place for the hunter to hide. The clever geese always take turns watching for any hunters or predators, so everyone gets their fill. You may be surprised to learn that these geese can still fly up to 30 mph after eating so greedily. Huge V-shaped formations have been seen by pilots at 30,000 feet as they flew over mountain ranges! They have caused serious problems for some planes.

Pairs of Canada geese are very loyal to each other. When they choose to be mates, it is for life. A young male, called a gander, goes through an elaborate display, honking, flapping his wings, and twisting his long neck in strange ways until some hen is impressed enough to mate with him forever. They will be seen together year-round from that day on. Many pairs have stayed together for more than twenty years, and the record is forty-three years. The pair will choose a nesting site where the female piles leaves, twigs, and grass before adding some of the loose down from her breast. She lays five or six eggs and incubates them for a month before the babies, called goslings, hatch. The gander will help her protect and raise the goslings. The goslings learn very quickly to find food, but they will stay with their parents for nearly a whole year. They may migrate once and be two-year-olds before they choose their lifelong mates.

Where the Wild Geese Fly

Vocabulary Checkup Write the words from the box on the correct blanks.

alter	foiled	gander	gorge
gosling	harvest	invade	loyal
proclamation	reservoir	rival	urban

1. A baby goose is called a _____.

2. A pond where water is stored for later is a _____.

3. To change or make different is to _____.

4. An area in or near a city is called _____.

5. To intrude or enter forcefully is to _____.

6. The male goose is called a _____.

7. A person who competes with another is a _____.

8. To eat until stuffed with food is to _____.

9. Being faithful and true to another is being _____.

10. To reap or gather the crops is to _____.

11. Frustrated and prevented from success is _____.

12. An official, formal announcement is a _____.

Comprehension You may need to look back at the story to answer the questions correctly.

1. Why are they called Canada geese? _____

_____

2. Why have Canada geese changed their migration routes? _____

_____

_____

Name _____ Date _____

Where the Wild Geese Fly

3. How do the geese stay safe when eating in farm fields? _____

_____

4. What big problem do geese cause at reservoirs? _____

_____

_____

Thinking About Canada Geese Think carefully before answering the questions.

1. Why don't some people like the geese at parks, golf courses, or reservoirs?

_____

_____

2. What do you think should be done about those geese? _____

_____

3. If you were a goose, how would you choose or get a mate? _____

_____

4. What serious problems could high-flying geese cause for planes? _____

_____

_____

5. How do you think geese select the leader of the V formation? _____

_____

_____

Homophone Selections Circle the correct choice for the homophones below:

1. Canada geese can't altar alter their looks to escape the hunters.
2. Even though they mate for life, Canada geese don't stand at the altar alter.
3. Some geese are permanent residence residents at our local park.
4. That pair of geese have a residence residents at Happy Hollow Golf Course.
5. The roots routes migratory geese take have been changed several times.

Check It Out Find out about

Hawaiian geese ("ne-ne")   Snow geese
White-fronted geese   Barnacle geese
Domestic geese

Name _____ Date _____

8. Magnificent Mammal Migration

The United States bought the territory of Alaska from Russia in 1867 for $7,200,000. It was laughed at by many Americans who thought Secretary of State William Seward was foolish to pay so much for a land they thought was mostly ice and snow. One of the main reasons Seward bought Alaska was to get some tiny islands, called the Pribilof Islands, way out in the Bering Sea. The Pribilof Islands were home to the northern fur seal. The United States sold enough seal fur to pay for Alaska in three years! The species almost got wiped out. Luckily, people discovered many other riches in Alaska thirty years later.

Northern fur seals belong to the group of sea mammals called pinnipeds, which means "wing-footed." Their flippers or fins resemble wings in some ways, and they help them "fly" through the water. Other pinnipeds are the sea lions and walruses. The fur seals use their hind flippers to swim faster than the other pinnipeds. They are such proficient swimmers that the female northern fur seals make an annual migration of more than 5,000 miles to southern California waters. They swim 10 to 100 miles away from the coast, never going ashore. Scientists aren't sure exactly why they make the long journey, and they can only guess that they may use the smell of certain ocean currents to navigate their route in open seas. The bulls stay home in the Bering Sea while the cows make this magnificent mammal migration.

Naturalists first thought that male and female fur seals were different species because the male is five times bigger. This bull can weigh 600 pounds while the cow weighs only 110 pounds. The bull's massive neck has thicker fur, but both have dense underfur that helps keep them warm. That same fur is prized for coats and caused the seals to nearly be hunted to extinction. Blubber as thick as 6 inches helps insulate fur seals from the cold, too. Large eyes help them see well. They have external ears and hear well, but fur seals have a poor sense of smell.

© 2000 by The Center for Applied Research in Education

Seals eat mostly small to medium-sized fish of many kinds. They also eat a few squid and crustaceans when they're hungry. They can dive as deep as 600 feet to feed, but they usually wait until nightfall, when many fish rise closer to the surface. The seals have nerves in their whiskers that can sense the vibrations of fish swimming by. They seize them in their teeth and swallow the smaller ones whole. Larger prey is torn into smaller pieces since the mother seals haven't taught their babies to chew their food well. The fur seals can live off their layer of blubber when food is scarce.

The bulls fight for breeding territory in early summer before the cows return to the rocky breeding grounds, called a rookery. Each bull will have a harem of three to forty cows in his territory. The cows who were bred the previous year usually give birth to one dark-colored pup within a couple of days after arriving at the rookery. That means the gestation was a whole year, ever since last June. After she nurses her new pup for a few days, the mother will join a harem to be bred again. Unfortunately, newborn pups are sometimes trampled by the large bulls. The bull does not help raise his pups at all. The pups are born with black fur, teeth, and the ability to swim right away. If they don't get trampled by the huge bulls, they still have to survive the times when their mother leaves for seven or eight days to find food for herself. When she returns, she searches through hundreds of pups to sniff out her own pup to nurse. Her milk is so rich that the pup will go from 10 pounds at birth to about 35 pounds by the time she weans it in three months and leaves it to fend for itself while she takes off on another migration.

Before electricity was invented, millions of pinnipeds were killed to get the oil from their blubber to burn in oil lamps. Then the fur traders killed seals for the soft fur to make coats. The future looks much better now for the fur seals to flourish. We don't need the oil anymore, and we have warm clothing to use instead of wearing animal skins and furs. Laws have been made to regulate how many fur seals can be killed. Scientists say there are almost as many fur seals now as there were before people started killing them. The greatest dangers they face now are oil spills in the ocean and depletion of food fish. We're trying to keep either danger from threatening the seals.

Magnificent Mammal Migration

Vocabulary Checkup Write the words from the box on the correct blanks.

crustaceans	depletion	external	flourish	harem
massive	naturalist	pinnipeds	proficient	rookery

1. The breeding place where large numbers gather is a _____.

2. Seals, walruses, and sea lions are called _____.

3. A person who studies natural history is a _____.

4. Aquatic arthropods typically having shells are _____.

5. Things that are large and prominent are _____.

6. _____ means being on or coming from the outside.

7. A _____ is a group of females living with one male.

8. _____ means using all of the supply of something.

9. To _____ is to prosper, thrive, and be successful.

10. _____ is skilled or very good at some task.

Comprehension You may need to look back at the story to answer the questions correctly.

1. What mammal group are seals placed into? _____
   What other animals are in that group? _____

2. Why did naturalists think male and female seals were two different species at first?

   _____

3. What are the greatest dangers seal pups face the first three months of life?

   _____

4. Why were so many pinnipeds killed in the last 200 years?

   _____

Name _____ Date _____

Magnificent Mammal Migration

Thinking About Fur Seals Think carefully before answering the questions.

1. Why do you think the female fur seals make that 5,000-mile-long migration?

   _____

   _____

   _____

2. What ways other than smell can you think of that seals could navigate that far out in the open waters?

   _____

   _____

   _____

3. Do you think seal pups have a hard life? _____

   Why? _____

   _____

   _____

4. Fur seals don't "bark" but sea lions do. So why do people think seals bark?

   _____

   _____

   _____

5. If people are competing with sea creatures for food from the oceans, what do you feel should be done if food supplies are depleted?

   _____

   _____

   _____

Check It Out Find out about

   Harp seals
   Weddell seals
   Leopard seals
   Elephant seals
   Sea lions

Name _____ Date _____

9. The Feline with Many Names

The mountain lion may be the champion of all animals when it comes to having many nicknames. People in Florida call them panthers, but if you travel to northeast regions of the United States or Canada they are called catamounts. As you travel west you will hear mountain lions called cougars. Some people call them the puma, especially if you head south. In Central and South America they call them *el leon* in Spanish, meaning "the lion." In other places they are nicknamed painters, big cats, cunning cats, or just mountain lions. Scientists classify them as the *felis concolor* and tell us that they are the largest wild members of the feline, or cat, family in the United States.

Mountain lions don't always live in the mountains. Some are found in desert regions or Brazilian rainforests where there are no mountains. They prefer habitat like forests, where there is some cover for them to hide, and they don't like to live too close to humans. The larger cougars live in colder regions. Most of the surviving cougar population in the United States and Canada lives west of the Rocky Mountains.

The male cougar is about 6 feet long with another 30 inches of tail. He can weigh as much as 230 pounds, but the average is closer to 150 pounds. Females are smaller, averaging about 90 pounds. The colors vary from tawny to reddish brown in the summer to a grayish brown in the winter. The few remaining Florida panthers have more chocolate brown in their coats, while the mountain lion of the most southern part of South America is silver gray to reddish-gray. Most cougars have a white throat and belly, but hunters have shot mountain lions that were totally black, also.

Cougars have a lean, feline body, but their legs are quite thick and powerful. They can pounce 25 feet in a single leap, and leaps of more than 40 feet were seen and reported. They can leap from the ground as high as the top of a basketball backboard and can drop 65 feet to the ground without hurting themselves!

The cougar is one of the most cunning predators in North America. Cougars' favorite prey is deer, and they average eating a deer per week all year

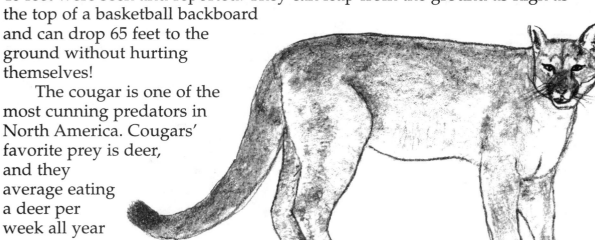

© 2000 by The Center for Applied Research in Education

long. They hunt mostly sick and younger deer, but they are proficient hunters strong enough to kill a bear or a bison, too. They will eat small mammals when deer are scarce. They stalk their prey stealthily, pouncing on it from ambush. Some people think they jump out of trees, but that isn't true. They usually kill their prey quickly by jumping onto the back of the prey and biting the back of the neck or throat. They will drag the carcass to a secluded spot, eat some, and cover the rest with leaves, sticks, or pine needles. They will remain in the vicinity for a few days to eat on the carcass as long as the meat doesn't get spoiled. Contrary to what many people believe, most cougars don't attack livestock unless they can't find wild game. They fear people, but there have been some instances where a cougar has mauled or killed somebody. Many hikers and hunters never see a cougar in the wild unless one gets chased up a tree by dogs. Some people have found they were "tracked" by a cougar, but they only saw its tracks as they returned on a trail.

The only time cougars get together is during mating season. The female and her mate may even hunt together for a couple of weeks. The gestation period is about three months, and the male is long gone by the time the three or four kittens are born. The mother has to guard them from the male cougars, who will sometimes kill kittens. Kittens are born in a cave or hollow log and are blind and quite helpless. Their fur is spotted, with black spots that disappear by the time they are six months old. They nurse until they're six weeks old, when the mother starts bringing them pieces of meat. They wrestle, play, and pounce just like domestic kittens. They begin leaving the den when they're eight to ten weeks old to hunt with their mother. They stay with her to learn hunting strategies until they are nearly two years old and she is ready to mate again.

Cougars were plentiful in the eastern United States until people settled there and killed them. Humans have invaded so much of their territory that cougars are often forced to hunt near where people live. Since people don't trust cougars, they try to eradicate them from the area. Biologists say this is really the wrong approach because cougars help maintain a balance in nature by killing weak and sick animals. Perhaps the National Forests and Parks will become the final refuge for these cats with so many names.

The Feline with Many Names

Vocabulary Checkup Write the words from the box on the correct blanks.

carcass	contrary	cunning	feline	lean
mauled	secluded	stealth	strategies	

1. Private, shut off, or away from others is _____.

2. Showing craftiness and slyness is _____.

3. Members of the cat family are called _____.

4. The dead body of an animal is a _____.

5. Plans and methods for achieving a goal are _____.

6. _____ means not too fleshy or fat.

7. _____ is opposite or counter to what is believed.

8. _____ is a secret, sneaky way of approaching.

9. _____ means handled roughly and injured by it.

Comprehension You may need to look back at the story to answer the questions correctly.

1. What other names were given for mountain lions? _____
_____

2. What are two examples of the power cougars have? _____
_____
_____

3. In what part of the United States and Canada do most cougars live? _____
_____

Why? _____
_____

Name _____ Date _____

© 2000 by The Center for Applied Research in Education

The Feline with Many Names

4. What is a belief that people have about cougars that isn't necessarily correct?

_____

Thinking About Cougars Think carefully before answering the questions.

1. Why do you think those big cats have so many different names? _____

_____

_____

2. What name do you think is best? _____

   Why? _____

_____

3. What would you think if you were hiking and found out a cougar was following

   you? _____

_____

_____

4. Why do you think people are afraid and don't trust having cougars around?

_____

_____

_____

5. Do you think cougars living near people is a problem? _____

   What do you think should be done about it? _____

_____

_____

_____

Check It Out Find out about
   Jaguars
   Leopards
   Bobcats
   Lynx
   Balance of nature

Name _____ Date _____

10. Some Scary Arachnids

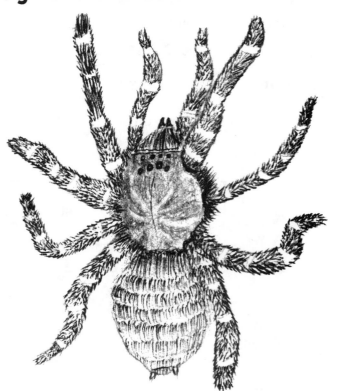

Mites, scorpions, spiders, and ticks belong to a group of animals scientists call arachnids. The arachnids have two major body parts and eight legs. Many people find that the spiders are the scariest arachnids, and most feel the tarantula is the scariest of all the spiders. There are more than 700 different kinds of hairy-legged tarantulas in the world. About forty kinds live in the United States, primarily in the desert regions of southern California, Arizona, New Mexico, and Texas. A large, hairy tarantula frightens many people, but this arachnid is actually a shy recluse, preferring to spend its days hiding. We'll examine a few of these tarantulas to learn more about them, and perhaps you will learn to fear them less.

The two main body parts of a tarantula are the abdomen and the prosoma, or head. The eyes, the fangs, and the jaws are on the front of the prosoma. The skinny waist, called a pedicel, connects the head to the abdomen. The heart and lungs are in the abdomen, and spinnerets for spinning silk threads are found at the rear of the abdomen. Two pedipalps used for feeling and holding prey are beside the fangs. Hairs help the tarantula feel the vibrations of prey moving nearby. The hairs on the ends of the legs adhere (stick) to slick surfaces to help it walk.

Arachnids are invertebrates, so the tarantula has no bones. It has a rigid skin outside, and this is called an exoskeleton. Since the exoskeleton doesn't grow, the tarantula has to molt, shedding its old skeleton that it has outgrown. This takes a few hours, and the tarantula is very vulnerable to attack as it waits for the new exoskeleton to harden so it can walk. Tarantulas normally have several types of defense. Some of them can spray their adversary with a stinky substance. Many can scratch fine hairs off the top of their abdomen that sting or blind the adversary. All tarantulas can lean back on their rear legs and show that their fangs are ready to strike with poisonous venom.

All of the tarantulas prey on insects, beetles, grasshoppers, and other spiders. Some jungle species prey on small birds, snakes, frogs, and rodents. Nearly all hunt by feeling vibrations and dashing out to grab prey with the pedipalps and sink their fangs into the prey to paralyze or kill it. They inject juices that dissolve the insides of the prey, which they then suck up. Just the exoskeleton of the prey is left behind. Tarantulas get much of their moisture this way in deserts, but most only eat once a week, so they need to drink dew that collects at night on surfaces.

Female tarantulas make a golf-ball-sized silk bag to deposit from 300 to 3,000 eggs in their burrows. The eggs hatch in three to fifteen weeks, but the spiderlings look more like white eggs with legs. They have to molt several times the first year as they grow. It takes many tarantulas up to twelve years to grow up. Males only live a couple years after that, but females may live to be more than thirty years old. Let's take a closer look at some specific types of tarantulas.

One type of tarantula, the trapdoor spider, lives all across the United States and on all the warmer continents. It lives in a burrow it digs in the ground. It gets its name from the hinged lid, or trapdoor, that covers the entrance to the silk-lined burrow. Trapdoor spiders may stretch trip webs out from their burrow where they lurk waiting for prey to trip on the web so they can dart out to eat them. The wolf spider is one type of trapdoor tarantula. The trapdoors' main enemy is a wasp that opens the trapdoor to sting the spider and lay an egg on it. When the egg hatches, the wasp grub eats the trapdoor spider.

The Goliath bird-eating spider lives in the tropical rainforests of South America, and is the biggest spider in the world. Its body is as big as the palm of your hand, and its legs would reach out past the edges of this sheet of paper! These spiders hunt mice, frogs, snakes, and baby birds to suck their juices out. Their venom is not deadly to humans, but most people are frightened by their size.

How would you like a pet tarantula? Even though it has a wicked appearance and a bad reputation as a vicious predator, some people think it really makes a nice pet. They say it is only aggressive when it feels threatened. Some colorful tarantulas are kept as pets by people. The Mexican red knee, the South American pink toe, the Chilean yellow rump, and Peruvian pamphobetus are a few examples. Some of these tarantulas are endangered because so many have been collected to sell as pets. You probably know of many other animals that would make better pets. Tarantulas have been around for millions of years and will very likely survive the pet collectors, too.

Some Scary Arachnids

Vocabulary Checkup Write the words from the box on the correct blanks.

adhere	adversary	aggressive	arachnids	exoskeleton
hinged	invertebrate	lurk	recluse	vulnerable

1. Attacking with forceful, daring methods is _____.

2. An enemy or opponent is called an _____.

3. Defenseless or susceptible to harm is _____.

4. An animal without a backbone is an _____.

5. To stick or cling to is to _____.

6. Ticks, mites, scorpions, and spiders are all _____.

7. A skeleton-like covering is called an _____.

8. Fastened at one edge so it can swing is _____.

9. To hide in waiting to attack by ambush is to _____.

10. One who lives alone or in seclusion is a _____.

Comprehension You may need to look back at the story to answer the questions correctly.

1. Four different tarantulas are _____

_____.

2. Label the parts of this tarantula by using the terms in the correct blanks:

abdomen
pedicel
eyes
fangs
pedipalps
spinnerets
prosoma

1) _____

2) _____

3) _____

4) _____

5) _____

6) _____

7) _____

Name _____ Date _____

Some Scary Arachnids

3. Why is a tarantula so vulnerable to predators during and after molting?

_____

_____

4. How do many trapdoor tarantulas know when prey is near? _____

_____

_____

Thinking About Tarantulas Think carefully before answering the questions.

1. Do you think spiders in general and tarantulas in particular are scary? _____
   Why? _____

   _____

2. What did you learn the hair is for on tarantulas? _____

   _____

   What did you think it was for prior to reading this?_____

   _____

3. What would you do to protect yourself during molting if you were a tarantula?

   _____

   _____

4. Would you want a pet tarantula? _____
   Why? _____

   What do you think your family would say? _____

   _____

Check It Out Find out about
   European purse-web spiders
   Funnel-web spiders
   Mexican red-kneed tarantulas
   Trapdoor spiders
   Pepsis, or tarantula hawks

Name _____ Date _____

11. World's Largest Venomous Snake

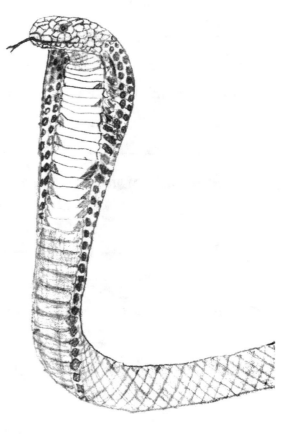

One of the most feared snakes in the world is the king cobra. Other poisonous snakes as well as people live in fear of this most deadly snake. A king cobra's bite is a lethal injection and can kill a full-grown person in fifteen minutes. King cobras are shy and will not attack people unless threatened. They will attack pythons as big as themselves and other poisonous snakes, including cobras. Their name means "snake-eater," or "hooded snake." People recognize the cobra's hood as the identifying characteristic of these snakes. Before you read a single word, did you recognize this drawing as a cobra?

The king cobra averages 13 feet long, but many 16- to 18-footers have been discovered. Their average weight is about 15 pounds, unless they have just eaten. Their skin is olive to tannish-green with faded yellow bands down the sides. The belly you can see as it rears up is a pale yellow color. The flared hood, which is characteristic when a king cobra feels threatened, has an eyespot pattern that scientists believe is to scare predators away. Birds of prey swoop in silently from behind to hit the back of the cobra's head, so that eyespot may be a deterrent. Most other predators are deterred by the hissing sound, the widespread hood, and knowledge of the lethal bite. Fangs a half inch long are connected to venom glands located behind the eyes. The cobra's eyes, like other snakes' eyes, are open and seem to be staring at you all the time because they

have no eyelids. Cobras cannot blink or close their eyes, even when they're asleep. They have no outer ears, so they can't really hear that snake-charmer's music.

The king cobra is found mostly in the forests of southeast Asia in countries from India and southern China across to the Philippines and down into Indonesia. Despite being active both day and night, the king cobra is seldom seen because it tries to avoid people by slithering into deep underbrush or escaping into the water. People of India will actually evacuate a village if a cobra's nest of eggs is found too close.

Snakes and lizards know the king cobra as a dangerous adversary. It detects and tracks them by flicking its tongue out to pick up their scent. The tongue passes by an organ in the roof of the mouth called the Jacobson's organ, which has receptors that pick up and identify scents in the air particles the tongue gets. The king cobra tracks the prey it smells. When it gets close enough, it strikes quickly. The massive dose of venom doesn't kill a snake so quickly as it would a person because of the slower rate of circulation in reptiles. So the cobra eats that paralyzed snake while it still struggles. Cobras can dislocate their jaws like other snakes do in order to swallow large snakes and lizards. It may take several hours for a cobra to swallow a larger prey. This big meal will satisfy the cobra's appetite for several weeks, and it can live for a few months without eating because of its slow metabolism, or time for turning food into energy in its body.

When the female molts and sheds her skin, she releases a scent that attracts her mate. Scientists think cobra pairs mate for life, which is not common for snakes. A male even helps find the nest site, often in a bamboo thicket, where a depression is hollowed out in the ground. The female lays twenty to fifty white eggs in the depression and stays with them for about ten weeks until they hatch. Cobras are the only snakes

who build a nest and incubate their eggs. You don't want to stumble upon a nest, because this is a time when cobras are very aggressive. Both male and female become defensive and will chase off any intruder. The hatchlings are shiny black with pale yellow stripes, poisonous, 2 feet long, and able to hunt for food right away. The juvenile has venom as strong as that of its parents, but it doesn't have much of it yet. The mother leaves the hatchlings to fend for themselves.

The king cobras remain in dense growth much of the time, so they don't need to watch out for birds of prey too often. They do have to watch out for the mongoose, an animal the size of a housecat. It is so lightning fast that it can dodge a striking cobra, kill it, and eat it. The mongoose can stand a bite from a cobra that would kill eight animals its size. The other threat to the king cobra are humans, of course. People are so afraid of cobras that they kill them out of fear even though they know cobras seldom ever attack. As land is developed for a growing population in southeast Asia, cobras and people are forced to live closer together, and you can be certain that isn't going to work.

World's Largest Venomous Snake

Vocabulary Checkup Write the words from the box on the correct blanks.

characteristic	dense	depression	deterrent	evacuate
flared	lethal	metabolism	receptors	

1. A hole or area lower than surrounding surface is a _____.

2. The chemical processing rate in an organism where food is turned into energy is called _____.

3. To leave a place is to _____.

4. Typical feature or quality of a thing is a _____.

5. Nerves or sense organs that detect stimuli are _____.

6. Spread gradually outward is _____.

7. Very thick with parts crowded together is _____.

8. Anything deadly or fatal is _____.

9. A thing that discourages or stops by fear is a _____.

Comprehension You may need to look back at the story to answer the questions correctly.

1. What are distinguishing features or characteristics of king cobras? _____
_____
_____

2. Why do king cobras and other snakes always seem to be staring? _____
_____
_____

3. How do king cobras catch their food? _____
_____
_____

Name _____   Date _____

World's Largest Venomous Snake

4. What are some things king cobras do that other snakes also do? _____

_____

_____

5. What are two things king cobras do that other snakes don't? _____

_____

_____

Thinking About King Cobras Think carefully before answering the questions.

1. What do you think makes king cobras so feared if they seldom attack humans?

_____

_____

2. If cobras can't hear, why do snake charmers play music for them? _____

_____

_____

3. Would you evacuate your village or home if you found a cobra's nest? _____

   Why? _____

_____

4. What do you feel is the most unique or interesting thing about king cobras?

_____

_____

5. If you were surveying people about king cobras, what are three good questions to ask?

_____

_____

_____

Check It Out Find out about
   Indian cobra, Naja naja
   African black mamba
   Australian death adder
   Snake charming

Name _____ Date _____

12. The Fastest Land Mammal

The cheetah is famous for being the fastest animal on land at speeds exceeding 60 mph for a quarter of a mile. Some cheetahs have been timed on radar guns doing 70 mph in short bursts of speed. That is the open freeway speed limit in most states! Since cheetahs don't roam free in the United States, you won't see one getting a ticket, but this freeway speed comparison may help you realize how fast these magnificent cats are. About 10,000 cheetahs have survived to live on the savannah grasslands south of the Sahara Desert in Africa. About fifty Asian cheetahs have survived and live in Iran.

The slender, graceful body of the cheetah is one of the reasons it is so fast. It is 4 to 5 feet long with another 2.5 feet of tail, but it only weighs 80 to 130 pounds. Those long, slender legs are very powerful and allow the cheetah to take long strides. When it's in pursuit of prey at full speed, its strides can be 33 feet long! The cheetah is the only member of the cat family that can't retract its claws. This actually provides greater traction as the cheetah accelerates on the dry savannah grasslands to 50 mph in three seconds. Some invisible features that contribute to its speed are the great lung capacity and a large heart. Cheetahs can run fast for only a few seconds, so speed is essential for them to catch prey on the open grasslands where there are few hiding places.

The cheetah is one cat you can count on to always have dark spots on its tawny coat. The golden yellow-brown fur with the black spots helps camouflage the cheetah on the savannah. You may have also noticed the smaller head or the distinctive black stripes that run from the corners of the eyes down under the chin. The black line is called the lacrymal, or tear stripe. That beautiful fur coat almost caused cheetahs to be hunted into extinction, but it is now illegal to hunt them and sell cheetah furs.

The cheetahs depend on their sharp eyesight in early morning or late afternoon to spot prey. They may stalk the prey or they may just walk right toward a herd of animals until they run. The cheetah singles out the oldest, youngest, sickest, or slowest herd member to chase. A favorite technique is to trip an antelope or gazelle running at top speed. Male cheetahs can kill larger prey by clamping onto its throat to suffocate it. Female cheetahs usually hunt smaller prey like birds, hares, rodents, or young impala. Hyenas, leopards, and lions often steal the meal before the cheetah has a chance to catch its breath and eat it. The cheetah's main defenses are its camouflage and speed to outrun its enemies, so you can guess what it does when challenged over its kill.

The female cheetahs usually only approach males when they are ready to mate (in heat). The female is left alone to raise the cubs by herself. After a gestation of three months, the litter of three or four tiny, gray furballs are born. As soon as the cubs open their eyes, the mother will move the den every few days to protect her cubs from predators. She is also very careful to make sure she isn't seen returning to her cubs. Scientists estimate that only 5 or 6 out of every 100 cubs survive and become adults. Many cubs are killed while the mother hunts, and others starve because the mother wasn't able to feed them. Females often bring prey back alive when the cubs are a little older so they can do some homework. They will be about eight months old before they accompany her to learn to hunt. They will be on their own when they are yearlings. Male cheetahs, usually brothers, may join together to stake out their territory for hunting. If a male intruder is found in their territory, there may be a fight to the death. It seems that cheetahs are not very sociable except during mating season or with their littermates.

It has been very difficult for zoos and game parks to breed captive cheetahs with much success. African game reserves have a hard time keeping them because the cheetahs can't compete with lions for food. Hunting them for their beautiful fur has been banned, but farmers in Africa are allowed to kill cheetahs they think are after their livestock. The cheetahs' food supply and habitat are gradually disappearing. It is very difficult to count how many of these shy cats are still surviving, but people are trying hard to save the species.

359

The Fastest Land Mammal

Vocabulary Checkup Write the words from the box on the correct blanks.

accelerate	accompany	capacity	essential	estimate
exceeding	lacrymal	pursuit	sociable	suffocate

1. To make an approximate guess or calculation is to _____.

2. Near the glands that secrete tears is the _____.

3. To speed up or go faster is to _____.

4. To smother or cut off the air supply is to _____.

5. The amount a thing can hold or contain is its _____.

6. To go along with or travel with is to _____.

7. The chase or act of following to capture is the _____.

8. Going beyond the bounds or limits is _____.

9. Anything absolutely necessary is _____.

10. Friendly or enjoying the company of others is _____.

Comprehension You may need to look back at the story to answer the questions correctly.

1. Where do most wild cheetahs live? _____
   _____

2. What are three features that help cheetahs run fast? _____
   _____
   _____

3. Why were cheetahs almost hunted to extinction? _____
   _____
   _____

Name _____ Date _____

The Fastest Land Mammal

4. What do female cheetahs have to do to protect their cubs? _____

_____

5. Why do cheetahs give up prey they caught to a lion, leopard, or hyena?

_____

_____

Thinking About Cheetahs Think carefully before answering the questions.

1. Why do you think the cheetah is so well known and respected by people?

_____

_____

2. What reasons can you think of for female cheetahs to hunt smaller prey?

_____

_____

3. What do you think is meant by the cubs "can do some homework"?

_____

_____

4. Why is it so hard to save the species by raising cheetahs in zoos or refuges?

_____

_____

5. Do you think cheetahs will become endangered again? _____

   Why do you think that way? _____

_____

Check It Out Find out about
   Leopards
   Hyenas
   Asian cheetahs (Iran)
   African savannah
   Cheetah communications

Name _____ Date _____

13. Second Most Intelligent Mammal

People are the most intelligent mammals. Many scientists now believe that the second most intelligent mammals are those cute, lovable chimpanzees. You have probably observed their antics at a zoo, circus, or in a performance. They learn tricks more quickly and easily than any other animal (except you). They don't have to perform tricks to entertain us. People enjoy watching the chimps' general behavior and changing facial expressions. We all agree that chimps resemble humans more closely than any other creature does, but you should not insult anyone by comparing them to a chimp or monkey. Remember, humans are more intelligent and deserve more respect.

Many chimpanzees have been used in medical lab experiments because the chimp's body is so similar in many ways to a human body. The adult height ranges from 50 to 66 inches, and the weight from 90 to 170 pounds. The males are closer to the top of that range while females are in the lower part. Chimps have dark brown or black hair over most of their body, but both males and females commonly get bald on top with age. Like the other apes (gibbons, gorillas, and orangutans), they have no tail. The chimp's hands and feet are much like yours, except their big toes turn out to help them grasp limbs to climb better. Their eyes, ears, nose, and other sense organs work much the same as yours. They often walk using the knuckles on the back of their hands to support their upper body weight. However, they can walk and run just like we do when they are carrying things or get excited and want to see further. Their ability to change facial expressions to show feelings resembles humans, too. They are the only other animals that can recognize themselves and make faces in a mirror. The chimps are susceptible to many of the same diseases we are, so scientists often test new medicines on them to find a remedy or cure for us. Many people object to using these lovable chimps to do medical experiments, but others believe it is essential to do this.

(Second Most Intelligent Mammal, *continued*)

Chimpanzees roam the African forests in groups called troops and spend more than half of their time in trees. The troop has several females with their young, and a few males with a dominant male leader. They roam the tropical forest searching for food like fruit, leaves, seeds, honey, insects, and eggs. Scientists discovered the chimps also hunt for small mammals to eat. They eat two main meals: breakfast and dinner. The supply of food in the area may determine whether they sleep in the same nest several nights or move on to build new ones. Nests are built a minimum of 15 feet off the ground using twigs, leaves, and branches.

The communication skills of chimpanzees have also been studied a great deal. They talk in grunts, barks, and other sounds that many people love to imitate. Chimps also communicate with the look on their face or by making gestures with their hands. They embrace and touch each other when they meet. They also spend about an hour a day in a social activity called grooming, where they pick dirt, bugs, and burrs out of each other's hair. They appear to take care of others, knowing that they will also be cared for. They don't seem to fight within the troop, so they must understand each other very well. Scientists haven't been able to teach captive chimps to speak our words, but several have learned sign language for the deaf and can use it very well.

Female chimps usually have their first baby when they are about eleven or twelve years old. Their gestation lasts for seven or eight months, and they usually only have a single baby at a time, although twins are born occasionally. The female has sole responsibility for raising the infant, which she will seldom allow out of her arms. The baby will ride in a cradled position as the mother travels until it is about five months old; then will ride piggyback for several more months. It will then get to scamper about in the trees with other young chimps but will remain with its mother until it is about six.

Large numbers of chimps have been trapped to be sold to zoos, circuses, pet stores, and laboratories. Chimps bred in captivity have reduced the need to trap wild ones. Many educational experiments have been done with young chimps in captivity. You already read about chimps taught to speak with sign language, but did you know some have been taught to communicate with special computers? Their problem-solving ability is second only to yours. They can imitate our behavior so perfectly sometimes that it's astounding.

Second Most Intelligent Mammal

Vocabulary Checkup Write the words from the box on the correct blanks.

antics	astounding	embrace	experiments	gestures
grooming	laboratories	remedy	susceptible	

1. Cleaning, brushing, and making neat and tidy is _____.

2. Liable or capable of being affected is _____.

3. Movements of the hands, arms, or body parts are _____.

4. To clasp in the arms or hug is to _____.

5. Playful pranks or silly, funny acts are _____.

6. Tests to check ideas or theories are called _____.

7. Overwhelming with amazement is _____.

8. Places equipped to do science experiments are _____.

9. A cure or relief for a problem or disease is a _____.

Comprehension You may need to look back at the story to answer the questions correctly.

1. Give some examples of how chimpanzees get along well together. _____
_____
_____

2. Explain how chimps groom. _____
_____
_____

3. Compare chimps and humans. How are they alike? _____
_____

How are they different? _____
_____

Name _____ Date _____

Second Most Intelligent Mammal

4. What are three ways chimps can communicate? _____
_____
_____

Thinking About Chimpanzees Think carefully before answering the questions.

1. What example do you think best shows the chimps' intelligence?
_____
_____

2. In what way would you think people should behave more like chimps?
_____
_____

3. Why do you think chimps fascinate people so much? _____
_____
_____

4. Do you think laboratories should test new medical advances on chimps? _____
Why? _____
_____

5. Explain an experiment you would design to test some problem-solving skills of the chimps.
_____
_____
_____

Check It Out Find out about
Jane Goodall
Chimps in medical labs
Pygmy chimpanzees
Chimpanzee skeleton
Yerkes Primate Research Center

Name _____ Date _____

14. The Queen and Her Court

One insect, the Apis mellifera, has been producing a food that people have eaten for more than 80,000,000 years. Apis mellifera is Latin for "honey bearer," so you probably call these insects "honeybees." Entomologists who study insects find the honeybee is one of the most astounding insects. They live in a group called a colony with as many as 50,000 or 60,000 bees in each hive. The social structure of the colony has fascinated entomologists for decades. We can take a closer look at some of what they have learned about the home and life of a honeybee, and we won't risk getting stung.

The colony of honeybees has an amazing social structure where every bee has a special job to do. It all begins with just one queen bee, who is the largest, most essential bee in the colony. Her only job is to lay eggs so the colony never runs out of honeybees. She is the only one that is fertile, capable of producing offspring, and does she ever produce. She can lay 2,000 eggs a day and as many as 200,000 eggs a year! She lives for three to seven years whereas the other bees only live a couple of months except when they huddle together to survive the winter. Without a queen, the colony would soon die.

There are usually about 100 drones, or male bees, in the colony. They are smaller than the queen but larger than the rest of the bees. Their job is to fertilize the eggs by mating with the queen. That is all they do! Entomologists aren't sure why the drones are kept around so long, because they discovered that after just one mating a queen can lay eggs for the rest of her life.

The rest of the bees are all females and are called workers. All of the working females are sterile, incapable of laying eggs to produce offspring. They are very appropriately named, too, since they do all of the work even though they're smallest.

The eggs the queen deposits in the cells are about the size of the dot on the "i." Each egg hatches in just three days into a larva. The workers' first job is as a nurse to these larvae. They feed them royal jelly, a substance produced in glands in the heads of workers. Then they feed them beebread, a mixture of pollen and honey. The nurse workers seal the larvae back in cells with beeswax after three days of feeding. Each larva

Worker

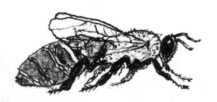
Drone

Queen

(The Queen and Her Court, *continued*)

spins a silky cocoon around itself and becomes a pupa. It undergoes metamorphosis, a change where it transforms from a worm-like pupa to an adult in two weeks. The young adult chews its way out to be a house bee with a job of cleaning and shining the cells for three days before it can become a nurse for 10 more days. Then she is a wax-maker or a court bee. She either makes wax to build or repair the cells or grooms and feeds the queen. At three weeks of age, she finally gets to leave the hive and work as a guard. She chases away any intruders and emits a scent to warn everyone of danger. If she has to sting a wasp, hornet, or other enemy, she will die because her stinger is hooked to parts in her abdomen that will be torn up as the barbed stinger is left in the victim. It is obvious that the worker leads a hard life compared to a queen or her drones.

The workers who survive guard duty now get promoted to foragers. This is the job you may be most familiar with, as foragers are the ones you see buzzing flowers. They use their long mouth, called a proboscis, to suck out the sweet nectar, which is put into a separate stomach called a honey stomach. While she is in the flower, a dust we call pollen is picked up on her hairy legs. Some pollen is left in other flowers and pollinates them, enabling them to produce seeds or fruit. She somehow finds her way back to the hive to then regurgitate, or spit up, the nectar after adding some juices from those glands in her head that help nectar turn to honey. She can visit over 10,000 flowers in a day, but all of the nectar she collects in her two-month lifespan will only produce one teaspoon of honey. Think about that as you eat honey.

Some people are very allergic to bee stings and must be careful. They don't usually die from a sting, but the worker bee always dies after stinging an enemy. Bees don't sting unless they are in great danger or being hurt.

You need to imagine what would happen to much of the world's food supply if we lost our most useful insects, the honeybees. Many insecticides intended to kill harmful insects often kill bees as well. Birds eat a few honeybees, but wasps, hornets, and wax moth caterpillars destroy more. Tiny parasitic mites living on the bees have destroyed whole colonies recently. Entomologists are working hard to save our bees, and we should all help now that we know they are extremely valuable.

Forewing
Hind wing
Abdomen
Stinger has barbs
Thorax
Simple eyes
Compound eye
Antenna
Proboscis

The Queen and Her Court

Vocabulary Checkup Write the words from the box on the correct blanks.

| decades | entomologist | fertile | metamorphosis |
| pollinate | proboscis | regurgitate | royal | sterile |

1. A scientist who studies insects is an _____.

2. A sucking tube tongue of a bee is its _____.

3. A complete change of form or shape is _____.

4. Anything related to a king or queen is _____.

5. To transfer pollen to fertilize plants is to _____.

6. To vomit or spit up is to _____.

7. Capable of producing offspring is _____.

8. Incapable of producing offspring is _____.

9. Periods of ten years are called _____.

Comprehension You may need to look back at the story to answer the questions correctly.

1. Match the letters beside the bee names with their jobs. Use each letter only once.

    N) Nurse   _____ Protects the hive from intruders, even stinging and dying

    H) House bee _____ Fertilizes the queen's eggs

    W) Wax maker _____ Feeds larva and seals it in cell to change to a pupa and adult

    C) Court bee _____ Lays eggs to ensure the hive never runs out of bees

    G) Guard _____ Spends three days cleaning and polishing the honeycomb

    F) Forager _____ Takes care of the queen's needs

    Q) Queen _____ Makes beeswax for the building and repair of the honeycomb

    D) Drone _____ Goes out and collects nectar and pollen to make honey

2. Female worker bees do all of the work for the hive except _____

_____.

Name _____ Date _____

The Queen and Her Court

3. Two important things bees do for people are to _____

    _____.

4. The four stages in the life of a bee are _____

    _____.

5. Honeybees die after they sting a victim because _____

    _____.

Thinking About Honeybees Think carefully before answering the questions.

1. Did it bother you that bees regurgitate the honey to put it into the cells? _____

    Why? _____

    _____

2. What do you think happens when another queen is born in a colony?

    _____

    _____

3. What does the author say we should think about as we eat a teaspoon of honey?

    _____

    _____

4. What would happen if all honeybees in the United States died? _____

    _____

    _____

5. What are two reasons people may get stung by a honeybee? _____

    _____

    _____

Check It Out Find out about
  Carpenter and leafcutting bees
  Mining and Mason bees
  Swarming of bees
  Different flavors of honey
  Remedy for bee stings

Name _____   Date _____

15. King of the Northwest

People who have encountered the "King of the Great Northwest Wilderness" will never forget it. Their mind will conjure up claws over 4 inches long and gleaming fangs 3 inches long. They will forever envision a massive, hairy brute that stands 10 feet tall with a bulky hump on its back. The mighty grizzly bear is the most memorable beast you could ever meet. Perhaps we are fortunate that it remains a recluse in the northwestern wilderness from Alaska down to Glacier and Yellowstone National Parks in Montana and Wyoming. These great brown bears used to live all over the western United States, but they were either killed off or chose to move to wilderness regions away from humankind.

Grizzlies are so named because of the grizzled appearance of their dark brown or reddish-brown, shaggy fur. Ragged fur tipped with grayish-white increases a grizzly bear's grizzled looks. The grizzly bear could bite a basketball hoop as it rears up on its hind legs, and it weighs 800 pounds. Grizzlies should never be confused with a black bear, which may be a similar color but is smaller, has no shoulder hump, and has short hair. Grizzly bears can subdue a black bear with one swat of a mighty paw.

Many scientists refer to grizzlies as brown bears and agree that there are two kinds in North America. One is the immense Kodiak bear which lives only on Kodiak Island off the coast of Alaska. It's even bigger than the grizzly bear, which lives from Alaska's mainland down to Montana. Grizzlies lope along on all four feet most of the time, but rear up, throw their head back, and sniff the air and look around. Despite their immense size, they can run 35 mph for 100 yards. That's faster than a racehorse!

The grizzly, with its keen sense of smell, is able to discern food or foe from great distances. Even though it is a fierce carnivore, the bulk of its diet is plants. Yes, it's an omnivore that dines on roots, leaves, grass, berries, and nuts much of the time. It also tears chipmunks out of their burrows, rips ants out of logs, and eats young mammals. It devours honey from hives while bees try to sting through that dense fur. Grizzlies will steal prey from cougars, wolves, and other predators, who won't dare to fight them. The grizzly scavenges for carrion, too. The Pacific Coastal region has many salmon streams, and the grizzly knows just when each species of salmon spawns. It feasts on spawning salmon at just the right time to fatten up before going into hibernation.

When cold weather arrives, the grizzly finds a sheltered spot like a cave and makes a bed of grass and boughs. It may stay there for up to six months living off its fat layer, which might have grown to 10 inches thick. It isn't in total hibernation, but lowers its body temperature by 10 degrees and slows its heart from fifty down to eight beats per minute. Pregnant females deliver twins in January or February in that hibernation den. Cubs only weigh a pound at birth and have some light, fuzzy hair. They nurse on the mother's rich milk for three months and weigh about 7 pounds by springtime. Every two hours the mother has to stop scavenging for food to nurse the twins. She will defend her cubs ferociously, so this is the most dangerous time to get near a grizzly. People have been killed trying to feed or just admire those cute little cubs. Strangely, she will not readily share her prey with the twins. They have to risk being disciplined with a growl, slap, or nip on the ear just to snatch a bit of her food. They learn to dig roots, eat leaves, and find other food quickly. Many get killed by predators, disease, weather, or male grizzlies. Scientists think only half of the cubs survive this first year. These cubs sleep in Mom's den for two winters before they are weaned and sent off together. The twins often remain together for a couple more years, then split to find a mate.

Thousands of grizzlies lived in California before the gold rush in 1849. People killed many out of fear or belief that grizzlies would eat livestock. In seventy-five years, every grizzly in the state was gone, but Californians put the grizzly's image on the state seal and flag anyway. Poachers and hunters aren't a big threat to a grizzly now. Wild habitat is hard for the King of the Wilderness to find. Perhaps our national forests and parks will be their last refuge.

King of the Northwest

Vocabulary Checkup Write the words from the box on the correct blanks.

boughs	carrion	conjure	discern	disciplined
lope	scavenge	spawn	subdue	wilderness

1. To overpower or conquer is to _____.

2. To take or gather from waste material is to _____.

3. Dead or rotting flesh from carcasses is called _____.

4. To run with long, easy strides is to _____.

5. Punished to get to follow rules is _____.

6. Limbs or whole branches from trees are _____.

7. An undeveloped, uninhabited, wild region is _____.

8. To distinguish by seeing and thinking is to _____.

9. The depositing of eggs in streams by fish is to _____.

10. To bring to mind as if by a spell or magic is to _____.

Comprehension You may need to look back at the story to answer the questions correctly.

1. Write one example you read in the story that must be the author's opinion.

   _____

   _____

2. Why are these brown bears called grizzly bears? _____

   _____

3. Most of the grizzly bear's diet is _____ , but it eats

   animals like _____ and _____ ,

   too. Since it eats plants and animals, it is an _____.

Name _____ Date _____

King of the Northwest

4. What does the grizzly do to survive the winter when food is scarce?

_____

_____

5. Why were many grizzlies killed in the past? _____

_____

Thinking About Grizzlies Think carefully before answering the questions.

1. What characteristics of the grizzly did you find most frightening? _____

_____

_____

2. What did you think was quite strange about the grizzlies' eating habits? _____

_____

_____

3. Why do you think the twins stay together for a time after leaving home? _____

_____

_____

4. When would it be most dangerous to meet a grizzly? _____

_____

Why? _____

_____

5. What do you consider the greatest danger for survival of the remaining grizzlies?

_____

_____

Check It Out Find out about

Kodiak bears   Grizzly fishing methods

Native American grizzly lore

Record grizzly sizes

Glacier Park, Montana

California grizzly history

Name _____ Date _____

16. The Only True Vampires

Vampires have been made famous by horror movies like *Dracula.* Those vampire stories and movies about humans sucking blood from people are fictional. The only mammal that lives on other animals' blood is the vampire bat. A long time ago vampire bats lived in the United States. Before you get nervous, you must know that now they only live in the tropical areas of Central and South America. Also, they prefer the blood of cattle and seldom attack people. Now, don't you feel better? The bats in Canada and the United States are quite beneficial mammals because they eat a lot of insects. So please don't kill these flying mammals. Vampire bats don't deserve the same appreciation and respect, however.

The common vampire bat of Latin America is no bigger than a mouse. It's about 3 inches long, and it would take fifteen or sixteen of them to weigh a pound. Their body has a soft, gray-brown fur covering it. The skin on their wings is thin and stretched between their fingers. There is a thumb with a claw on the front of the wing. The hind legs of these vampire bats launch them into the air powerfully before they spread their wings to fly. Other species of bats open their wings and flap them as they launch. The ears of a vampire bat are not so large as many other bat species. The vampire bat does not rely on echolocation so much as the

insect-eating bats, but it does use the echo of sound to navigate since it is also nocturnal. It flies low to the ground in search of prey.

The mouth of the vampire bat is also one of its distinguishing characteristics. The incisors at the front are sharp like a razor blade and at an angle to slice a bit of flesh from prey. The tongue and lower lip have grooves for the flow of blood since the vampire bats don't suck it out, like people think.

© 2000 by The Center for Applied Research in Education

Vampire bats used to feed on wild animals like deer, monkeys, and smaller mammals. Then domesticated cattle, horses, and pigs were brought to the New World and became their favorite prey. The docile cows and their calves are the easiest prey. When a vampire bat locates prey, it usually lands nearby and sneaks close on the ground to find a spot with blood vessels near the skin surface. Yes, the neck is one spot they like to feed. They also bite the ear, nose, lip, or feet of cattle and horses. Animals who are lactating are often bitten on the nipples, which causes problems for nursing babies, who may get infections. The prey may feel just a twinge of pain, shake a little, and go right back to sleep. The hole scooped out is less than 1/4 inch wide and deep. Blood flows out and the bat begins lapping it up. The vampire bat's saliva has a chemical in it to prevent coagulation or clotting of the blood. Several bats may drink from the same wound for about twenty minutes. Each bat will consume three to five teaspoons of blood per night. Sometimes a bat is too heavy to fly if its stomach is bloated with blood, so it has to walk and hop a while first. The blood keeps flowing from a wound and dries on the animal. Since the wound is tiny, the dried blood is what people find the next day. If a lot of bats bite a calf, it can get weak, but that isn't the main concern. The greatest worry is that vampire bats carry rabies disease. This virus is a deadly killer, and many thousands of animals die from it every year.

Vampire bats live in colonies in a dark cave or hollow tree. They hang upside down all day like other bats. They groom themselves and others in the social colony. The females help each other through the birth of a baby, and will even adopt it if the mother should die. They bring blood back to the new mother for a few days while she nurses her pup. The pup hangs onto her for the first week and nurses for two months. It will then receive blood she regurgitates for it until it can accompany her to find a prey. They forage nearby until the pup can fly well. If they go without blood two consecutive nights, they may die. Other females in the colony will sustain them by sharing some of their food, again regurgitating it into their mouth.

Latin Americans are trying to control vampire bat populations by injecting cows with anticoagulants, drugs that keep blood from clotting. These drugs don't harm the cattle, but bats that drink their blood will die by bleeding to death internally. How odd that a bat that lives on the blood of others winds up bleeding to death! This may seem cruel, but it is the only way humans have found to control the rabies epidemic. The vampire bats are not an endangered species. It's important that you not only know more about these creatures, but now you know they are the only true vampires in the world.

The Only True Vampires

Vocabulary Checkup Write the words from the box on the correct blanks.

anticoagulant	bloated	coagulation	consecutive
docile	incisors	lactating	rabies
saliva	sustain	twinge	

1. A secretion in the mouth often called spit is _____.

2. Animals' front teeth used for cutting are called _____.

3. The clotting of blood is called _____.

4. A sudden, sharp pain is sometimes called a _____.

5. To expand or become swollen due to overfilling is _____.

6. Very tame and easily handled is called _____.

7. A chemical to prevent blood clotting is_____.

8. To keep alive and going is to _____.

9. Following in order with no break is _____.

10. Secreting milk as in a nursing mammal is _____.

11. A fatal virus caused by bites from infected animals is _____.

Comprehension You may need to look back at the story to answer the questions correctly.

1. How are most bats beneficial to us? _____

   _____

2. How do bats navigate and locate prey? _____

   _____

3. What features help vampire bats get blood from their prey? _____

   _____

Name _____ Date _____

The Only True Vampires

4. What is the greatest concern about vampire bats? _____

_____

5. How do vampire bats show they are good colony members? _____

_____

Thinking About Vampire Bats Think carefully before answering the questions.

1. Why do you think vampire stories have lasted for so long? _____

_____

2. Why don't vampire bats need echolocation so much as other species of bats?

_____

_____

3. Why do you think vampire bats switched from wild to domestic animal blood?

_____

_____

4. What are two things you feel are "gross" about vampire bats? _____

_____

5. Vampire bats should not all be killed off. Why? _____

_____

6. What plan can you think of to control vampire bat numbers besides anticoagulants?

_____

_____

Check It Out Find out about

Flying Fox bats   Kitti's Hog-nosed bats

Mouse-tailed bats   Big-eared bats

Hairless Bulldog bats

Spotted bats

The rabies virus

Name _____   Date _____

17. The Tough Rulers of Antarctica

The temperatures are 40 to 75 degrees below zero and the wind is howling at 100 mph a few hundred miles from the South Pole. There are no other rookeries more remote or desolate in the whole world. The area has been abandoned by all other wildlife. Only the emperor penguins, largest of all the penguins, remain in this desolate, frigid land. They are here to meet a mate and raise their chick right in the middle of a blizzard. They must be the most bizarre birds in the world! Scientists are still trying to understand why the emperor of Antartica raises chicks here on top of 15 to 20 feet of ice and 50 miles from the ocean in a howling blizzard.

Emperor penguins have special features that enable them to survive in such harsh weather. They are 3 to 4 feet tall, but they store so much fat on

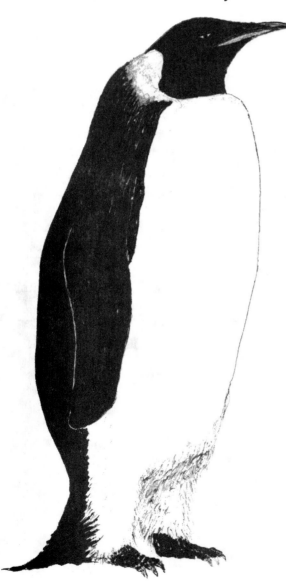

their bodies that they can weigh up to 90 pounds They have from twenty to eighty feathers per square inch, the most dense plumage of any of the seventeen species of penguins. The front is white, the back is black, and they have orange plumage on the neck. The waterproof feathers overlap like roof shingles to trap body heat in and shed frigid winds. Of course, penguins are one of the birds that lost the ability to fly long ago. You probably noticed that their wings have turned into flippers, and they use them to swim well underwater. The beak and the rest of the body is very streamlined for swimming fast enough to catch squid and fish, their usual diet. Their legs are very short, so they waddle when they walk on the ice. The best way for them to move quickly across ice is to lie on their belly and dig their claws into the ice and push with their flippers. They skid along on the belly like they were sledding.

Emperor penguins have a strange courtship, where the females compete for a mate, then spend two months making sure he's a loyal, loving male that can be trusted to help raise the chick. They also make up special songs for each other so they can tell by voices who their mate is. During the two months of dating, neither of them leaves the rookery to eat. The female will lay an egg as big as a grapefruit, then give it to the male to balance on top of his feet under a fold of fat called a brood pouch. She takes off for the water to get something to eat while he stands there incubating their egg during the worst part of Antarctica's winter. She won't be back for two months, so he must go two more months not getting anything to eat in a blustery blizzard, standing on a huge block of ice trying to keep that egg warm. That must be the pinnacle of true love. He does have company, however, since there are from 500 to 30,000 other males in his colony all doing the same thing. They crowd together in a mass of male penguins, huddling to stay warmer. They even have a way of rotating the group so they take turns being in the warmer middle of the huddle or on the coldest side where the wind blows most.

The male keeps turning the egg so the embryo inside will develop correctly, and in two months the chick hatches. The male may somehow produce a milk-like food in a portion of his throat and spit it into the beak of the chick. The mother may be back in time to incubate the egg for the last few days on her feet. Scientists say the male sings at the top of his lungs when he hears his mate returning. He has lost about 25 to 30 pounds, and badly needs relief. The mother can regurgitate a really good meal into the chick's mouth. Now Father gets to "sled" to the sea to get a well-deserved meal while Mother warms the chick in her brood pouch (it would freeze to death in two minutes in such weather). The male returns in three weeks to feed the chick and take it into his pouch again. They take turns doing this until the chick is too large for their pouches. The chicks are left behind in what is called a créche, which is like a daycare nursery. The parents come back from hunting food and sing to all créches until their chick runs out to greet them and receive a meal. Scientists have noted that a chick only gets about fourteen meals in the first five months before it molts to get adult plumage. Hordes of hungry chicks leave without their parents to dive into the sea and eat. About half will live to return in four years to the rookery to find a mate, and continue this whole bizarre cycle.

The Tough Rulers of Antarctica

Vocabulary Checkup Write the words from the box on the correct blanks.

bizarre	courtship	créche	desolate	embryo
frigid	hardy	harsh	hordes	pinnacle

1. _____ is freezing cold temperatures.

2. _____ is barren, deserted, uninhabited wasteland.

3. An _____ is the early stage of a developing organism

4. A _____ is like a daycare nursery for penguin chicks.

5. _____ are huge numbers, like a large crowd.

6. _____ means very strange or odd; peculiar.

7. _____ means sturdy, strong, or courageous.

8. A _____ is the dating time before becoming mates.

9. The _____ is the top, peak, or highest point.

10. _____ means cruel, difficult, or unpleasant.

Comprehension You may need to look back at the story to answer the questions correctly.

1. Emperor penguins live on or near the continent of _____.

2. Two features that keep emperor penguins warm are _____
_____.

3. Describe how an emperor penguin can move fastest on the ice. _____
_____

4. What is the total length of time the male goes without any food? _____
How can he survive that long? _____
_____

Name _____ Date _____

The Tough Rulers of Antarctica

5. How do the males stay warm in such frigid wind chills? _____

_____

Thinking About Emperor Penguins Think carefully before answering the questions.

1. Why do you think the emperor penguins' rookeries are in such desolate regions?

_____

_____

2. If you were a scientist sent to study emperor penguins' rookeries, what equipment would you need to take?

_____

_____

3. What do you think is meant by "pinnacle of true love"? _____

_____

4. Why do you think the chicks don't return to the rookeries for four years?

_____

_____

5. Why do you think emperor penguins have to make up courtship songs to sing?

_____

_____

6. What did you think was most fascinating in the life of emperor penguins?

_____

_____

Check It Out Find out about
    Macaroni penguins
    Chinstrap penguins
    Rockhopper penguins
    King penguins
    Adélie penguins
    Tropical species of penguins

Name _____ Date _____

18. The Man-eating Fish Tale

Their yacht had sunk, so the two men and a woman were trying to make it to shore on their rubber life raft. They panicked as they saw the dorsal fin cutting through the water toward them. As they paddled frantically, the shark broadsided them, flipped the raft, and swallowed one of the men in one gulp. Was it satisfied? As the other guy and the woman struggled to get back in the raft, the shark returned and seized her flailing legs. She vanished! The lucky survivor got to the beach in time and told this gruesome story. Of course, this story could be the source of a scary movie. Maybe we could call it *Giant Jaws* and call the sequel *Man-Eater*. The truth is that the people were ten times more likely to drown than to be attacked by a shark. Sharks have this bad reputation as man-eaters due to sensational tales and movies. There are fewer than 100 reported cases a year in the world of sharks attacking people. Scientists say that it is usually due to sharks mistaking people for seals, penguins, or some prey.

Sharks are members of the fish family even though they are different in several ways. The whale shark is the largest, at 40 to 60 feet and 25,000 to 30,000 pounds, but it eats plankton. The tiger shark is the most likely man-eater in the story of the rubber raft. The blood-thirsty tiger sharks have attacked humans more than any of the other 375 species of sharks. The great white shark of *Jaws* fame is the largest predatory shark at 25 feet long. It can weigh up to 7,000 pounds. Since the great white shark shown below was the species chosen for the movie roles, let's concentrate on it.

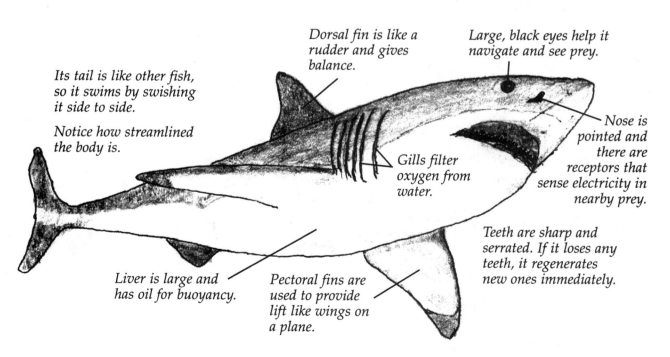

Dorsal fin is like a rudder and gives balance.

Large, black eyes help it navigate and see prey.

Its tail is like other fish, so it swims by swishing it side to side.

Notice how streamlined the body is.

Gills filter oxygen from water.

Nose is pointed and there are receptors that sense electricity in nearby prey.

Liver is large and has oil for buoyancy.

Pectoral fins are used to provide lift like wings on a plane.

Teeth are sharp and serrated. If it loses any teeth, it regenerates new ones immediately.

Sharks are different from other fish in several ways. Their skeleton is made of a tough, gristly, cartilage instead of brittle bones like most fish. Sharks only have slits for gills, whereas other fish have a gill cover. Most bony fish have scales, but sharks have tough, tooth-like pieces called denticles. The denticle is made of the same substance their teeth are, and both the denticles and teeth are replaced as the shark grows. Sharks don't have a float bladder to help them swim like those bony fish. They have a thick oil in their liver that gives some buoyancy, but sharks sink fast if they stop swimming.

All sharks are carnivores and like to dine on fish, including other sharks, so their only enemies are larger sharks and humans. Great whites like to prey on warm-blooded mammals like seals, sea lions, and dolphins, but they also eat bony fish and carrion. The California coast has seals and sea lions, and many great whites. All of the senses we use are also used by great white sharks. They often smell prey before they see it. They may even feel it first. They have lateral lines running on their sides like most fish and can feel vibrations like we hear sound vibrations. Sharks also have a sixth sense on their snout in the form of sensory pores that detect prey's electric signals. This also may explain why metal is found in dead sharks' stomachs and why they attack metal cages. They cruise around at less than 2 mph since they have to keep a flow of oxygenated water going into their mouth and out the gill slits. Great whites can attack at 15 mph, but it has to rely on stealth to sneak up and catch faster prey like dolphins. They either bite off and swallow chunks or eat smaller prey whole. Their metabolism will allow them to wait up to three months after a good meal before they must eat again.

Most fish spawn and place eggs in their environment to be fertilized by males. A few sharks lay fertilized eggs that hatch out on the sea floor. Great whites and most female sharks have their eggs fertilized inside them. The eggs hatch inside the womb, and after the embryo is fully developed, females give birth to live babies called pups. The female travels to a shallow place to have one or two pups where they won't be eaten by other sharks. Since they're well developed, she leaves them to get food and grow up alone.

There are twenty-five species of sharks that will sometimes attack humans, so people destroy many sharks out of fear. Remember, drowning causes more deaths than shark attacks. Most sharks reproduce slowly, so if too many are killed, they may become extinct before we learn to understand them fully.

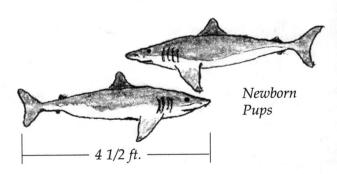

Newborn Pups

4 1/2 ft.

The Man-eating Fish Tale

Vocabulary Checkup Write the words from the box on the correct blanks.

bladder	cartilage	denticle	gruesome	lateral
regenerate	sensational	sequel	serrated	womb

1. _____ is the gristle-like, elastic tissue in shark skeleton.

2. _____ is from or to the side.

3. _____ means startling to the senses, spectacular.

4. _____ is with notched or saw-toothed edges.

5. _____ is so gross as to cause horror and disgust.

6. The tough covering on sharks' skin and teeth is _____.

7. A sac-like organ for liquids or gasses is a _____.

8. A literary or film work that continues a theme is a _____.

9. The female organ where a baby develops is the _____.

10. To restore or make over new tissue is to _____.

Comprehension You may need to look back at the story to answer the questions correctly.

1. The biggest predatory sharks are the _____, but plankton-eating _____ are the largest sharks of all.

2. Scientists say sharks usually only attack humans because _____
_____.

3. Two reasons why sharks have to swim constantly are because _____
_____.

4. The senses sharks use most to locate and catch prey are _____
_____.

Name _____ Date _____

The Man-eating Fish Tale

5. Sharks don't worry about losing, breaking, or outgrowing their teeth because they constantly _____

_____.

Thinking About Sharks Think carefully before answering the questions.

1. Why do you think the tiger shark attacked people in that rubber raft? _____

_____

2. Why do you feel *Jaws* was such a popular movie? _____

_____

3. I think great whites need to use stealth and sneak up to catch a dolphin because

_____

_____.

4. Scientists say sharks probably don't like the taste of humans. Do you agree? _____
   Why? _____

_____

5. Order the statements from most important (1) to least important (5) for safety.

_____ Never swim at night when you can't see what is in the water very well.
_____ Leave the water immediately if a shark is sighted, and don't thrash too much.
_____ Always swim, surf, or dive with others, never alone.
_____ Never hurt or grab any shark, even a young or harmless looking one.
_____ Since blood attracts sharks, you shouldn't go into the sea when bleeding.
   (Please remember, sharks seldom attack people, but it's better to be safe than sorry.)

Check It Out Find out about
   Nurse sharks
   Mako sharks
   Hammerhead sharks
   Basking sharks
   Bull sharks
   Commercial uses of sharks

Name _____ Date _____

19. The Wolf that Cried Boy

There was a young wolf whose job it was to watch for intruders for his wolfpack. He was a lonely sentinel one night and decided to howl "Boy." When the other wolves ran to hide, he thought it was exciting and great fun. He howled "Booooyyy!" again the next night to scare them more. When he did it again the third night, the suspicious old leader of the pack saw there was no boy and punished the young wolf by making him stand out under the moon every night for the rest of his days howling, "Truth! Truuuth!"

The truth of this fable is that wolves are misunderstood creatures that people don't know enough about. Thousands of wolves were killed in the past due to their reputation as the "big, bad, wolf" that was a threat to three little pigs, grandma, or other humans. There is not even one factual case of a healthy wolf ever attacking a person in this country. Fables, folk tales, and farmers have given the wolf its bad reputation, causing it to become endangered in most places.

Wolves belong in the *canidae* family with the coyotes, dingos, and dogs. The various breeds of dogs in the world all descended from wolves that were domesticated thousands of years ago. Traits like loyalty, intelligence, and friendliness cause people to love dogs. Those traits came from the wolf, but people despise them. A German shepherd at 75 pounds even looks a lot like a smaller version of a wolf. The wolf can weigh as much as 175 pounds, stand 30 inches tall at the shoulders, and have bigger feet and a bushier tail than the German shepherd.

Nearly all wolves belong to the family of gray wolves called *canis lupus,* which is divided into two groups: timber wolves and tundra wolves. A tundra wolf is often called an arctic wolf since it lives in arctic regions. Timber wolves live in forested areas, of course. There are a few red wolves, *canis rufus,* left in Texas and Louisiana. Wolves lived all over North America several hundred years ago. As settlers moved west they killed many, and the remaining wolves moved farther away from humans. Wolves are listed as endangered everywhere any are left except Alaska. The gray wolves in Minnesota are a threatened species.

(The Wolf that Cried Boy, *continued*)

Most wolves live in a family group called a pack, but there will occasionally be a lone wolf. An average pack has six to ten wolves that bond together and care for each other. The pack has a social order with a dominant male leader with his mate, and the subordinate wolves that are usually related. Dominant leaders have often won that position, and subordinates know he is the strongest and will tuck their tail or roll onto their back if he growls at them. Every pack member has a role, so there is less fighting than you might think. Instead, they work, eat, howl, and play together, sharing food and even babysitting each other's pups. Each pack has its own territory well marked, and other packs will respect those boundaries to avoid a bloody territorial battle.

Wolves have terrific vision and a sense of smell so acute that they can smell a deer over a mile away. Like most dogs, their hearing is so good that they can hunt small prey like mice just by hearing the squeaks under the snow and converging on the spot of the sound. A wolf will hunt any small mammal or birds alone, but when wolves go after larger prey like deer, elk, moose, or sheep, they cooperate as a whole pack. They will chase large prey great distances since wolves have superb stamina. Then they try to surround the animal and move in for the kill. When a large prey is killed, all members of the pack get to eat their fill, which can be as much as 20 pounds They can go two weeks without eating after a meal like that. Only 2 out of 10 chases end successfully, so the wolves generally pick on old, sick, or injured animals. This actually helps herds of strong, healthy animals to live better.

Pregnant females usually deliver a litter of three to seven pups in the spring in a den like a cave, large burrow, or hollow log. The pups weigh about one pound and are deaf, blind, and helpless at birth. They nurse for about three weeks while the father and other pack members provide food for their mother. Then she and the others will regurgitate some meat, which the pups eat from the adult's mouth. The pups play tag and hide-and-seek like kids in a preschool. An order of dominance is established in the group of siblings. By midsummer the pups lose much of their fuzzy hair and begin looking more like the adults. They are strong enough to join the hunt in the fall but will remain with their pack until they are two-year-olds. Some decide to stay forever, but others go off to form new packs. Hopefully, we will continue to preserve enough wilderness for wolves to howl on Earth forever.

The Wolf that Cried Boy

Vocabulary Checkup Write the words from the box on the correct blanks.

acute	converge	descended	despise	fables
subordinate	traits	sentinel	siblings	stamina

1. _____ means extremely sensitive or sharp.

2. A _____ is one that stands watch or guards.

3. _____ is endurance or strength to keep going.

4. _____ are short stories not based on facts.

5. _____ is lower in rank and under authority of others.

6. To dislike with contempt or scorn is to _____.

7. Distinguishing characteristics or qualities are _____.

8. Inherited or passed down from is _____.

9. Brothers and sisters are _____.

10. To come together at a point is to _____.

Comprehension You may need to look back at the story to answer the questions correctly.

1. How are wolves and dogs alike?_____
   _____

2. How are wolves different from dogs? _____
   _____

3. The two types of gray wolves are _____
   and _____.

4. Why don't wolves in a pack fight much? _____
   _____

Name _____ Date _____

The Wolf that Cried Boy

5. How do wolves hunt down large animals like elk and moose? _____
_____

Thinking About Wolves Think carefully before answering the questions.

1. What do you think is the meaning behind the fable "The Wolf that Cried Boy"?
_____
_____

2. What do you think has hurt the wolf's reputation most? _____
_____
_____

3. How do wolves help by killing some herd animals? _____
_____
_____

4. Why do you think wolves howl so much? _____
_____
_____

5. Compare and contrast a wolf pack and a human family. _____
_____
_____

6. Do you think wolves should be set free in Yellowstone Park? _____
Why? _____
_____

Check It Out Find out about
    Red wolves   Minnesota wolves
    Timberwolf features
    Arctic wolf's life
    Teeth of a wolf
    Wolf fables or legends
    Sayings with *wolf* in them

Name _____ Date _____

20. Are Dragons Only a Myth?

The dragon was an imaginary animal in ancient mythology of many countries. It was shown with a scaly, reptilian body, a lion or eagle head, wings, and clawed feet. Most dragons were said to breathe fire, and many heroes had to slay a dragon to succeed. Those mythical dragons often were associated with gods, and dragons in China were symbols of the emperors.

All dragons are imaginary and exist only in myths except for one, the Komodo dragon, the largest true lizard that has ever lived. Even though it is 10 feet long and weighs up to 300 pounds, the Komodo dragon wasn't discovered by scientists until 1912. This is not a beast of fables! It's the largest member of the monitor lizards and lives on small uninhabited islands of Indonesia just northwest of Australia. Explorers named it after the island of Komodo, and then added the dragon tag since it was so big, had long claws, and was one of the meanest predators around. It does not breathe fire or have wings, but it will flick a 12-inch-long yellow tongue out and hiss through its teeth when confronted. Its head looks like that of other lizards except much larger. It has gray to greenish-brown, tough scales covering its body. It has 1-inch-long, razor-sharp teeth, serrated like a steak knife, and hidden in its huge jaws.

Komodo dragons can drag their long tail and sprint fast enough that you can't outrun them. They are so strong that it takes five or six adults to restrain one to make tests. Komodos use their long, snake-like tail to swim well, and the young ones are agile and use their claws to climb trees very well. Adults are too heavy to climb trees, however. They live solitary lives, hiding in thick brush or holes they dig until the sun warms their blood so they can hunt for breakfast.

The Komodo dragon flicks its tongue to detect the scent of prey as it waits in ambush. It's a carnivore that eats every kind of meat it can get. Monkeys, bush pigs, and deer are favorites. The Komodo's tongue can tell if there is

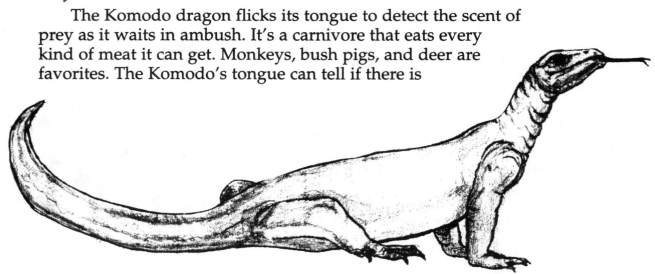

carrion within 2 miles. Komodos also eat eggs and other dragons. Now we know why they live a solitary life; they are cannibalistic! Their long claws can rip open the abdomen of a deer, and the serrated teeth slice and tear chunks off. When the Komodo is done with a deer, the only thing left is the skull and antlers. A photographer who went to Komodo Island to photograph the dragons got separated from his crew. They only found his camera, glasses, and some blood an hour later. He would have died even if he had climbed a tree since scientists tested saliva from the Komodo dragon and found out that they have more than fifty kinds of toxic bacteria living in their mouth. Wounded prey that escapes usually dies from infection within three days and gets eaten as carrion.

Scientists aren't sure how cannibalistic Komodo dragons mate, but they do. A male allows females into his territory in early summer, but he will attack and devour other males that venture into it. A month after mating, the female finds a moist, sandy spot to bury her eggs. The heat from the sun will incubate them for nearly eight months if no dragons or other predators discover them. When the 8-inch-long baby dragons hatch, they are in grave danger of being eaten by other dragons, birds of prey, and large snakes. The lucky ones that survive all of these perils better grow up fast if they want to live for thirty years like some adults. They are arboreal (living in trees) much of the time just to escape larger Komodos that are too heavy to climb trees.

Scientists estimated that 1,500 to 3,000 Komodos are on the islands. Because of rugged terrain and the dragon's elusiveness, it's hard to be certain how many remain, so the species is protected now. Blood tests have shown that the dragons have an antibiotic that kills many germs, including all of those in their own saliva. Scientists are checking that antibiotic for use on human infections. Indonesians on nearby islands are worried because Komodos are swimming over and eating their livestock

and stalking children now. The islanders don't see any reasons to preserve the Komodo dragons. They cannot see the potential to develop new medicines, or the need to save the only real dragons in the world. Can you?

Are Dragons Only a Myth?

Vocabulary Checkup Write the words from the box on the correct blanks.

arboreal	associated	confronted	elusive	mythology
perils	photographer	restrain	solitary	terrain

1. A _____ is a person who takes pictures with a camera.

2. _____ is to hold back or control something.

3. _____ means hard to find and catch.

4. _____ are dangers or grave risks to life.

5. _____ means faced or came in front of hostility.

6. Lots of legends with gods and heroes are _____.

7. Things connected or tied together are _____.

8. Secluded or avoiding company of others is _____.

9. Living in or having to do with trees is _____.

10. Land with its natural features is called _____.

Comprehension You may need to look back at the story to answer the questions correctly.

1. Where do Komodo dragons live? _____

2. What features do dragons in myths have that Komodo dragons don't have?

_____

_____

3. Why are Komodos solitary rather than social creatures? _____

_____

4. What makes survival difficult for baby Komodos? _____

_____

Name _____ Date _____

Are Dragons Only a Myth?

5. Why don't Komodo dragons die from infections from their own saliva?

_____

_____

Thinking About Komodo Dragons Think carefully before answering the questions.

1. What do you feel is most impressive about Komodo dragons? _____

_____

_____

2. Why do you think it took so long to discover Komodos? _____

_____

_____

3. Why do you feel people would not want a Komodo as a pet? _____

_____

_____

4. What do you believe is the greatest danger for these dragons? _____

_____

_____

5. How would you get pictures of them if you were a photographer for a magazine?

_____

_____

6. What do you feel are the best reasons to preserve Komodo dragons? _____

_____

_____

Check It Out Find out about

Komodo Island   Gila monsters
Water monitor lizards   Flores Island
Australian short-tailed monitor
Iguanas

Name _____   Date _____

Answer Key for Activity Sheets

Dolphins *(Our Favorite Dolphin)*

Vocabulary—1) distinguish 2) submerge 3) blunt 4) navigate 5) distress 6) melon 7) expanse 8) compete 9) intelligent 10) bond.

Comprehension—1) Bottlenose; they're friendly and easy to tame. 2) Bottlenose are bigger, have no stripes, more easily tamed, have a shorter beak, and do well in captivity. 3) Porpoises have a blunt nose and don't travel in large schools. 4) Buy dolphin-safe tuna and get votes to stop ocean pollution.

Thinking—1) Answers may include "joy," spots prey, etc. 2) Assist distressed comrades and variety of sounds made. 3) Probably; they likely hear waves and other creatures' sounds, too. 4) Answers will vary. 5) Answers will vary.

Llama *(Andes Truck)*

Vocabulary—1) browse 2) jerky 3) tanned 4) minerals 5) bleat 6) domesticated 7) bray 8) resemble 9) nutrition 10) endure.

Comprehension—1) Indians and settlers used horses and mules. 2) They haul goods like trucks. 3) Dried strips of meat; word comes from Spanish *charqui*. 4) Pasture grass or hay, water trough, minerals, shade/shelter, 4-ft-high fence. 5) Have to have a pair, toenail trimming, brushing, cleaning up manure, and spitting.

Thinking—1) Probably their long, bushy neck and hairy body. 2) Long neck, facial features, feet, and long legs. 3) Perhaps too heavy, pinching, sick, tired, etc. 4) Maybe it was adaptable or available. 5) Answers will vary; could include ease of care, inexpensive.

Alligators *(The Largest Reptiles Are Scary)*

Vocabulary—1) lifespan 2) tourists 3) exhibition 4) compost 5) slither 6) dissolve 7) lifestyle 8) encounter 9) olive 10) agile.

Comprehension—1) gavials, cayman, crocodile, and alligator. 2) Crocodile's lower teeth stick out, and alligators have a broader, flatter head. 3) To stay warmer/keep in body heat. 4) To use heat from decomposition to incubate eggs. 5) They were hunted for their hides too much.

Thinking—1) Spanish word *el lagarto* translates to alligator. 2) No; only great experts could tell just by look at bumps and scales. 3) Maybe it's the challenge, the thrill, or the money from the show. 4) Probably; they are carnivores and who knows when or why they might attack. 5) Answers will vary. 6) Answers will vary.

Praying Mantises *(The Miniature Dinosaurs)*

Vocabulary—1) molt 2) devour 3) cannibal 4) camouflage 5) greedy 6) arthropod 7) ootheca 8) pincers 9) variegated 10) seize.

Comprehension—1) They hold their forelegs under the chin in a praying position. 2) It has six legs and three body sections. 3) Its camouflage is first line. 4) They outgrow their skin and need room to grow. 5) They eat many harmful insects that eat crops.

Thinking—1) Yes; erect position, pincers. No; too small, six legs. 2) Answers will vary. 3) They probably don't see them. 4) Birds eat some, there's plenty of food, insecticides. 5) You can't tell if they're praying, but they are predators that prey. 6) Answers will vary.

Rhinoceroses *(The Mighty Rhinoceros)*

Vocabulary—1) pachyderms 2) poachers 3) sanctuary 4) nub 5) tolerate 6) gouge 7) solitary 8) keratin 9) joust 10) parasites 11) dominance.

Comprehension—1) Gray; thick skin; horn. 2) Dutch had a word, *wijde,* that means "wide," and people thought they said white. 3) Cool off and prevent parasites from biting. 4) Medicines and dagger handles.

Thinking—1) Probably yes; Javans because only 70 are left and loss of island habitat. 2) They want to get rid of parasites that bite. 3) Probably the money involved in poor countries. 4) Answers may include more protection, harsher penalties, or more raised in zoos. 5) Answers should be interesting!

Gorillas *(The Powerful, Peaceful Primates)*

Vocabulary—1) intruders 2) elaborate 3) dew 4) primates 5) gnash 6) juveniles 7) herbivorous 8) furrow 9) infancy.

Comprehension—1) It has dark brown hair all over, furrowed brow, jaw sticks out, long arms, broad chest and shoulders, fingers like people, and walks hunched over on front knuckles. 2) Older male leader that has silver-gray hair on his back. 3) A young male that is likely a son of the silverback leader. 4) Carried for 9 months, similar weight at birth, nursed, crawl before they walk, and dependent on mother. 5) They have lost too much habitat to farms.

Thinking—1) Eat breakfast when silverback gets them up, roam looking for more food and new nest site, visit and play. 2) Answers will vary. 3) Maybe to be safer, or to be near new food. 4) Their weight, or don't need safety of trees due to size. 5) Best answer is to stand still if you can; gorillas bite fleeing critters, but they stop short if you're passive. 6) Answers will vary, maybe financial aid.

Canada Geese *(Where the Wild Geese Fly)*

Vocabulary—1) gosling 2) reservoir 3) alter 4) urban 5) invade 6) gander 7) rival 8) gorge 9) loyal 10) harvest 11) foiled 12) proclamation.

Comprehension—1) Most of them used to nest in northern Canada. 2) Food supply and safe refuges available. 3) They always have guards or sentries watching and it's open so there's no hiding spots for predators. 4) They deposit droppings that can contaminate drinking water.

Thinking—1) Probably due to all those droppings to get through, or into. 2) Students may suggest relocating them. 3) Answers will vary. 4) They have fouled jet intakes and broken windows before. 5) Look for good ideas, but you would not want the fastest or the slowest flyer. Maybe experience is a factor.

Fur Seals *(Magnificent Mammal Migration)*

Vocabulary—1) rookery 2) pinnipeds 3) naturalist 4) crustaceans 5) massive 6) external 7) harem 8) depletion 9) flourish 10) proficient.

Comprehension—1) Pinnipeds; walruses and sea lions. 2) The males are so much larger than females. 3) Being trampled, left alone while mother seeks food. 4) Their fur was valuable and their blubber was used in oil lamps.

Thinking—1) Maybe to get more food, or tradition, or vacation. 2) Maybe a built-in compass, or going with current, or using stars. 3) Yes, I do. They are trampled and not cared about by bulls, then their mother takes off for days at a time leaving them on the rocks. 4) They hear the sea lions barking and doing tricks in shows and think they are seals. 5) Answers will vary.

Mountain Lions *(The Feline with Many Names)*

Vocabulary—1) secluded 2) cunning 3) feline 4) carcass 5) strategies 6) lean 7) contrary 8) stealth 9) mauled.

Comprehension—1) cougar, catamount, puma, painter, big cat, cunning cat, panthers, *el leon*, and *felis concolor.* 2) Jumps of 25 to 40+ feet, leap up on basketball backboard, and dragging down large prey. 3) West of the Rockies; because people killed nearly all of them in the east. 4) They jump out of trees on prey, or they kill lots of livestock, or hunt for humans (all are seldom true).

Thinking—1) Maybe due to so many different areas lived in, or translations from different languages. 2) Answers will vary. 3) May feel scared and cautious. (You may advise them to stand tall and make lots of noise rather than running like a prey.) 4) Tales of cougar attacks on humans and some factual accounts create doubts and mistrust. 5) Yes; trap them and take them far away to parks or on game farms. (Several western communities are having "cougar trouble.")

Tarantulas *(Some Scary Arachnids)*

Vocabulary—1) aggressive 2) adversary 3) vulnerable 4) invertebrate 5) adhere 6) arachnids 7) exoskeleton 8) hinged 9) lurk 10) recluse.

Comprehension—1) Trapdoor or wolf spider, Goliath bird-eater, Mexican red knee, S. Am. pink toe, Chilean yellow rump, Peru Pamphobetus. 2) Top to bottom–pedipalps, eyes, fangs, prosoma, pedicel, abdomen, spinnerets. 3) It has no exoskeleton and can't walk or move. 4) They put trip webs out.

Thinking—1) Yes; sizes, hairy, fangs. No; I guess macho bravado! 2) To feel prey vibrations near and to adhere to surface to walk. 3) Answers will vary, but may say they'd hide. 4) Yes; for unique pet? No; hard to feed, scary? Most families would say no way!

King Cobras *(World's Largest Venomous Snake)*

Vocabulary—1) depression 2) metabolism 3) evacuate 4) characteristic 5) receptors 6) flared 7) dense 8) lethal 9) deterrent.

Comprehension—1) The flared hood, olive to tannish-green color with eyespot on the back of hood. 2) They can't close their eyes or blink. 3) Detects by smelling with its tongue, gets close and bites it with venomous fangs. 4) Slithers, eyes open, runs away from us when they can, sheds skin, eats seldom, dislocates jaws, and eats meat. 5) Builds nests and defends them, and mates for life.

Thinking—1) Reputation as it does defend a nest or the stories of lethal bites. 2) Probably part of the show, but they do mystify the cobra by swaying movements. 3) Yes; it's dangerous when nesting. No; may choose to move the nest somehow. 4) Answers will vary. 5) Check/share questions.

Cheetahs *(The Fastest Land Mammal)*

Vocabulary—1) estimate 2) lacrymal 3) accelerate 4) suffocate 5) capacity 6) accompany 7) pursuit 8) exceeding 9) essential 10) sociable.

Comprehension—1) In Africa on the savannah. 2) Claws grip, long legs, slender and graceful body, great lungs, and a large heart. 3) For their beautiful fur. 4) Hide them in new dens and sneak back undetected. 5) It can't fight well enough to defeat them.

Thinking—1) Probably its speed and its beauty and grace. 2) They aren't so big as males, and it's more plentiful to feed cubs. 3) They get to chase the live prey she brought home for them to practice. 4) They breed poorly in captivity, and they can't compete with other cats in refuges. 5) Yes; likely loss of habitat and food.

Chimpanzees *(Second Most Intelligent Mammal)*

Vocabulary—1) grooming 2) susceptible 3) gestures 4) embrace 5) antics 6) experiments 7) astounding 8) laboratories 9) remedy.

Comprehension—1) Groom each other, seldom fight, live in large troops, eat and sleep together, and embrace. 2) They sit and pick dirt, bugs, and burrs from each other's hair. 3) Bodies are very similar, families, make facial expressions, gesture, see self in mirror, and body chemistry. Different by more hair, longer arms, can't speak language, walk on knuckles, and sleep in trees. 4) Facial expressions, gestures, and sounds made.

Thinking—1) Perhaps signing or problem-solving ability. 2) Answers will vary. 3) Maybe it's their resemblance or the antics they perform. 4) Yes; it's better than testing first on us. No; they have a right to be treated humanely. 5) Answers will vary.

Honeybees *(The Queen and Her Court)*

Vocabulary—1) entomologist 2) proboscis 3) metamorphosis 4) royal 5) pollinate 6) regurgitate 7) fertile 8) sterile 9) decades.

Comprehension—1) G, D, N, Q, H, C, W, F. 2) Fertilizing and laying the eggs. 3) Make honey and pollinate plants for fruit and seed production. 4) Egg, larva, pupa, adult. 5) Their stinger is barbed and pulls out innards.

Thinking—1) Yes; it does mean vomit. No because it came from a honey stomach, which is separate. 2) She has to go off with a few bees to start a new colony. 3) It took one bee its whole lifetime to collect that much. 4) Crops would fail to the level where many people would go hungry, and so would other animals. 5) They hurt the bee somehow, or they made it believe their queen and hive were in danger.

Grizzly Bears *(King of the Northwest)*

Vocabulary—1) subdue 2) scavenge 3) carrion 4) lope 5) disciplined 6) boughs 7) wilderness 8) discern 9) spawn 10) conjure.

Comprehension—1) The mighty grizzly bear is the most memorable beast you could ever meet (a couple more in paragraph one). 2) The hair has gray tips giving them a shaggy, "grizzled" appearance. 3) Plants; ants, chipmunks, young mammals, salmon, and more; omnivore. 4) Semi-hibernates on a bed of boughs after fattening up. 5) Fear mostly, of livestock killed or human encounters.

Thinking—1) May say those long claws, teeth, size, power, etc. 2) May say bulk of diet being plants, or insects eaten, or carrion, etc. 3) Maybe for protection or companionship.

4) Probably either as they were eating or when protecting cubs. 5) Probably loss of wilderness areas and fear.

Vampire Bats *(The Only True Vampires)*

Vocabulary—1) saliva 2) incisors 3) coagulation 4) twinge 5) bloated 6) docile 7) anticoagulant 8) sustain 9) consecutive 10) lactating 11) rabies.

Comprehension—1) They eat lots of insects. 2) They use echolocation, sending out sound waves and checking bounce back. 3) Sharp incisors, grooved lip and tongue, and anticoagulant saliva. 4) They carry rabies, a fatal virus, and transfer it by eating. 5) They groom, nurse, and feed fellow members.

Thinking—1) May say sensational or due to fear or Halloween. 2) Their prey is larger (cows vs. insects) and they fly less and lower. 3) Probably easier access due to fencing, or maybe their blood is richer. 4) Answers will vary. 5) They may have some useful chemical or value unknown yet. 6) I wonder if every source of blood could be "sheltered" for three nights in a row, would most vampire bats die?

Emperor Penguins *(The Tough Rulers of Antarctica)*

Vocabulary—1) frigid 2) desolate 3) embryo 4) créche 5) hordes 6) bizarre 7) hardy 8) courtship 9) pinnacle 10) harsh.

Comprehension—1) Antarctica 2) Their dense layers of feathers and layers of fat. 3) Lying on its belly, pushing with its claws and flippers, and sliding. 4) Four months; He lives on his store of fat. 5) They huddle together and rotate from cold to warm spots.

Thinking—1) Maybe safety from predators, tradition, etc. 2) Warm clothes, shelter, food, water, fuel, camera, writing material, cell phone, etc. 3) The male sacrifices so much. 4) Probably not sexually mature. 5) They all look alike. 6) Answers will vary.

Great White Sharks *(The Man-eating Fish Tale)*

Vocabulary—1) cartilage 2) lateral 3) sensational 4) serrated 5) gruesome 6) denticle 7) bladder 8) sequel 9) womb 10) regenerate.

Comprehension—1) Great whites; whale sharks. 2) They mistake them for seals or other prey as they move. 3) They will sink and they need to keep oxygenated water flowing through the mouth to the gills. 4) Smell, feeling (hear) vibes, electrical, and sight. 5) Regenerate new replacement teeth.

Thinking—1) They thrashed in panic and it thought they were prey probably. 2) Scary, sensational, suspenseful, etc. 3) Dolphins swim twice as fast as sharks. 4) They may, but probably makes me apprehensive. 5) Order will vary, and it may be a good place to debate or discuss such concepts.

Wolves *(The Wolf that Cried Boy)*

Vocabulary—1) acute 2) sentinel 3) stamina 4) fables 5) subordinate 6) despise 7) traits 8) descended 9) siblings 10) converge.

Comprehension—1) Loyalty, intelligence, friendliness, similar builds, pups, senses. 2) Wildlife, endangered, heavier, bigger feet, diet. 3) Timber wolves and tundra wolves. 4) Each one knows who is stronger or dominant. 5) Chase weak ones as a pack.

Thinking—1) Twist on fable to show people misunderstand wolf and persecute it. 2) Fables, stories, food deprivation, misunderstood. 3) Kill young and sickly, etc. 4) Answers will vary. 5) Sharing and caring in both, family endangered, etc. 6) Controversy rages.

Komodo Dragons *(Are Dragons Only a Myth?)*

Vocabulary—1) photographer 2) restrain 3) elusive 4) perils 5) confronted 6) mythology 7) associated 8) solitary 9) arboreal 10) terrain.

Comprehension—1) Indonesian Isles, NW of Australia. 2) Wings, lion or eagle head, and fire breathing. 3) They are vicious cannibals. 4) They are prey to many predators, including bigger Komodos. 5) Their body produces antibiotics that protect them.

Thinking—1) Size, teeth, cannibals, bacteria, etc. 2) Hidden in forests on an island with no real attractions besides them. 3) Hard to keep fed, bite is infectious, big, etc. 4) Loss of food source, cannibalism, humans taking land. 5) Maybe a cage or a crane or a helicopter, etc. 6) Antibiotics, learn more, balance of nature, and only dragon interesting.

Enrichment Activities:
Teaching Ideas and Answer Key

1. **Information About _____:** You could use this activity during any lesson for students to take notes on the major concepts and statistics about that animal. You may need to give some guidance on what belongs in each section for some students.

2. **Animal Profiled:** This could be used with any lesson to profile the animal you list or the one students choose. They might need to review the information on an animal.

3. **Word Search:** Students should be familiar with word searches and should know what mammals, arthropods (jointed legs), reptiles, birds, and fish are. Blank order is M, R, M, A, M, B, M, A, M, M, R, M, A, M, M, M, F, M, B, R. The tricky ones to watch out for are Mantis, Tarantula, and Honeybee (Arthropods), the Vampire Bat (Mammal) and the Penguins (Birds).

```
R  V  A  M  P  I  R  E  B  A  T  P  O  N  G
E  A  T  A  R  A  N  T  U  L  A  H  U  A  R
M  C  O  U  G  A  R  T  H  C  F  O  T  M  E
P  O  C  H  I  D  O  L  P  H  I  N  A  L  A
E  G  R  I  Z  Z  L  Y  C  E  S  E  L  I  T
R  C  A  T  O  K  U  D  O  E  H  Y  L  O  W
O  H  B  L  O  O  D  H  T  S  B  I  N  H  I
R  K  I  T  T  E  N  C  L  A  E  E  G  R  T
P  E  T  N  O  T  O  U  C  H  E  E  A  N  E
E  S  C  R  O  W  N  B  U  L  L  Y  T  L  S
N  H  K  O  M  O  D  O  D  R  A  G  O  N  S
G  O  R  I  L  L  A  M  A  L  L  A  R  D  H
U  P  E  Z  Z  F  K  I  N  G  C  O  B  R  A
I  P  R  A  Y  I  N  G  M  A  N  T  I  S  R
N  Y  C  A  N  A  D  A  G  O  O  S  E  E  K
```

4. **Crossword Puzzle:** *Across:* 3) bug 6) gorillas 9) seal 10) bull 11) ants 12) elude 13) dig 14) bee 15) cobra 19) eat 20) gator 22) slither 23) rot 25) arm 27) llama 28) prey. *Down:* 1) bulb 2) molt 3) bi 4) glued 5) sea 6) gander 7) alligator 8) slug 16) bear 17) rat 18) cat 20) germ 21) roar 24) tree 26) my.

5. **Create Your Own Title:** All animals studied in Reading Level 6 are listed for students to create a title for those creatures. Since students need to know something about the animal first, it probably would be best to wait until they studied all of them. You may need to reiterate that you are looking for good original titles, not to copy the ones already used. You might want to have them share appropriate titles (or preview them first).

6. **Baby Announcements:** This is a good lesson to teach (or review) news-writing skills. You may like to have students look for the 5 W's in a newspaper article first, and the lessons on grizzlies, Canada geese, and penguins should be read beforehand. You also could use this

same concept of a news article without this sheet, using the idea of the blank picture (choice) on any animal story being studied.

7. **Writing Your Own Animal Article:** This activity could be used at any point for students to learn to organize information for an animal report. You might like to provide a list of animals, or allow free choice. My students always liked to pair up to do such reports.

8. **Creating Crazy Captions:** Captions can be fun, but you might want to caution students to only use appropriate ones and to be respectful of others (even the animals depicted).

9. **Endangered or Extinct?:** This follow-up activity may require research, especially on moa and dodo. *Answers:* Dino is X because of natural disaster or ? (Easy beginning). Blue Whale is E due to overhunting. Sea Turtle is E due to being hunted, loss of nesting sites, and babies eaten. Rhino is E due to hunting. Gorilla is E due to loss of habitat. Dodo is X due to humans eating and animals destroying eggs. Wolf is E due to loss of habitat and hunting. Dolphin is E due to fishing nets. Koala and Panda are E due to loss of food. Moa is X as Polynesians ate them. Puma is E mostly in Eastern United States due to hunting. Passenger Pigeon is X due to overhunting by humans. Whooping Crane is E due to pesticides and habitat loss.

10. **Your Amazing "AQ" Test:** Since this test covers all animals, it could be a pretest and posttest. It could be used as a discussion tool as well as a fact evaluation tool. *Answers:* 1) Blue whale 2) Peregrine falcon 3) Cheetah 4) Crocodiles 5) Siberian tiger 6) Vampire bats 7) Giraffe 8) Anaconda 9) Honeybee 10) Komodo dragons 11) Ostrich 12) Polar bear 13) Bee hummingbird 14) African elephant 15) Orca (killer whale) 16) King cobra 17) Bison (hope they don't say buffalo) 18) Elephant 19) Whale shark 20) Us (could name themselves or their teacher).

1. Information About _____

Where on Earth do they live?

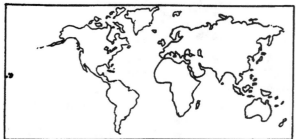

Describe the home or habitat.

Describe the looks:

Colors—

Body covering—

Weight—

Height or length —

Special features—

Babies, Babies, Babies:

Gestation or Incubation time—

Number born—

Birth size—

Born with or without—

Length of time with parents—

Food and Eating Habits:

Favored food—

Also eat—

Obtained by—

Interesting Facts:

Name _____ Date _____

2. Animal Profiled:_____

1. This animal lives on the continent of _____ , and its main habitat is in
   _____.

2. I wouldn't mind being this animal because _____
   _____

3. The one thing this animal can do better than most is _____
   _____.

4. The best feature about the body of this animal is _____
   because_____
   _____.

5. The body would be better if we changed the _____
   because _____.

6. This animal eats lots of _____,
   but it does not eat _____.

7. The main predators they fear are _____,
   and if they see one they _____.

8. The main thing that makes this species special is _____
   _____
   _____.

9. (Circle the correct choice.) Their babies are hatched born after ____ days of
   incubation   gestation. They commonly have about ____ babies at one time,
   and the parents do don't raise them.

10. This animal is isn't endangered because _____
    _____
    _____.

Name _____ Date _____

3. Word Search

Find the names of the twenty animals listed here and circle them in the word search. There are only three diagonally, and the rest are horizontal or vertical. When you find each animal, print the correct letters on the blank beside it to identify its class. Good luck!

M = Mammal   **B** = Bird   **F** = Fish   **R** = Reptile   **A** = Arthropod

_____ DOLPHIN

_____ ALLIGATOR

_____ LLAMA

_____ PRAYING MANTIS

_____ RHINO

_____ CANADA GOOSE

_____ GORILLA

_____ TARANTULA

_____ PUMA and COUGAR

_____ SEALS

_____ KING COBRA

_____ CHEETAH

_____ HONEYBEE

_____ VAMPIRE BAT

_____ GRIZZLY

_____ GREAT WHITE SHARK

_____ WOLF

_____ EMPEROR PENGUIN

_____ KOMODO DRAGON

R	V	A	M	P	I	R	E	B	A	T	P	O	N	G
E	A	T	A	R	A	N	T	U	L	A	H	U	A	R
M	C	O	U	G	A	R	T	H	C	F	O	T	M	E
P	O	C	H	I	D	O	L	P	H	I	N	A	L	A
E	G	R	I	Z	Z	L	Y	C	E	S	E	L	I	T
R	C	A	T	O	K	U	D	O	E	H	Y	L	O	W
O	H	B	L	O	O	O	D	H	T	S	B	I	N	H
R	K	I	T	T	E	N	C	L	A	E	E	G	R	I
P	E	T	N	O	T	O	U	C	H	E	E	A	N	T
E	S	C	R	O	W	N	B	U	L	L	Y	T	L	E
N	H	K	O	M	O	D	O	D	R	A	G	O	N	S
G	O	R	I	L	L	A	M	A	L	L	A	R	D	H
U	P	E	Z	Z	F	K	I	N	G	C	O	B	R	A
I	P	R	A	Y	I	N	G	M	A	N	T	I	S	R
N	Y	C	A	N	A	D	A	G	O	O	S	E	E	K

© 2000 by The Center for Applied Research in Education

Name _____   Date _____

404

4. Crossword Puzzle

Solve this puzzle using the clues for across and down.

ACROSS:

3. Nickname for insects
6. The largest primates
9. Pinniped migrates 5,000 miles
10. Term for male rhino
11. Aardvark's favorite food
12. Escape by evading
13. How animals burrow
14. World's best pollinator
15. Largest venomous reptile
19. Bears do this to get fat
20. Nickname for alligator
22. How snakes move
23. To decay
25. Primate's forelimb
27. Andes Mountain truck
28. What predators seek

DOWN:

1. Globe-shaped root
2. Tarantula does this to grow
3. Prefix standing for "two"
4. Adhered or stuck together
5. Where sharks live
6. Term for male goose
7. Family of largest reptiles
8. Snail-like mollusk with no shell
16. Polar, brown, or black _____
17. Rodent a bit larger than mouse
18. Common name for felines
20. Common term for bacteria
21. Male lion's warning sound
24. Where a chimp sleeps
26. Personal possessive pronoun

Name _____ Date _____

5. Create Your Own Title

Perhaps you thought some animal stories you read had strange titles. Now it's your turn to make up a title. Create appropriate titles of your own for each animal listed below. Think hard, and have fun!

1. Dolphins _____

2. Llamas _____

3. Alligators and Crocodiles _____

4. Praying Mantis _____

5. Rhinoceros _____

6. Gorillas (Ape) _____

7. Canada Goose _____

8. Fur Seals _____

9. Mountain Lions (Cougar or Puma)_____

10. Tarantulas _____

11. King Cobra _____

12. Cheetahs _____

13. Chimpanzees _____

14. Honeybees _____

15. Grizzly Bears _____

16. Vampire Bats _____

17. Emperor Penguins _____

18. Great White Sharks _____

19. Gray Wolves _____

20. Komodo Dragons _____

Name _____ Date _____

6. Baby Announcements

Every animal must reproduce young to continue the species. The pictures show a variety of animals about to deliver their young. As a reporter for your newspaper, it's your job to write a brief news article to announce the birth. Choose an animal (or two) to write about. Reporters always try to tell the "Who, What, When, Where, and Why" in an interesting writing style. (The blank box is just in case your favorite is missing.)

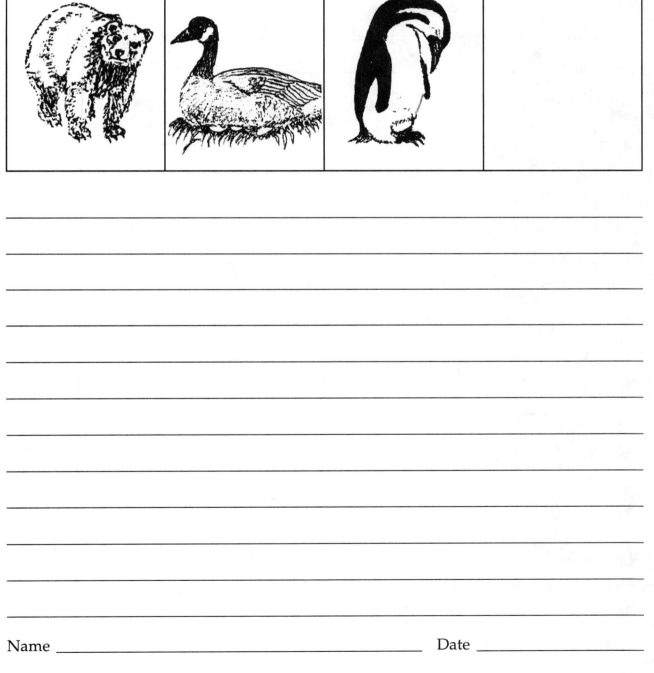

Name _____   Date _____

7. Writing Your Own Animal Article

I'm sorry if an animal you wanted to read about was left out of the stories. You can write about that animal now. Research the animal, take brief notes below, write a first draft, revise it, and write the final draft. Use interesting adjectives to write your animal article. A thesaurus is a handy tool to discover more picturesque words. Try hard to write *brief* notes in each section, *not* sentences. Please make your article interesting by adding illustrations and using descriptive adjectives. You might enjoy sharing, too.

Species: _____ Family: _____

Looks: _____

Weight = (M)_____ (F)_____ Length = (M)_____ (F)_____ Lifespan = _____

Habits: _____

_____

Habitat: _____

_____

Food and Feeding: _____

_____

_____

Producing Young: _____

_____

_____

Interesting Facts: _____

_____

_____

_____

_____

_____

Name _____ Date _____

8. Creating Crazy Captions

A caption is an explanation for a picture or illustration. Study each illustration below and think of an appropriate caption to write below it. The caption might tell what the animal is thinking, feeling, seeing, hearing, or doing at the moment.

Name _____ Date _____

9. Endangered or Extinct?

I am sad to report that there are some animals that we will never get to study up close and first hand. We only know about them by bones, fossils, or other records of their remains. Scientists do a good job of reconstructing those creatures for us. Some animals became extinct due to natural disasters, but humans have killed too many of some species for the 4 F's: Food, Fur, Fun, or Fear. Others are endangered because of loss of habitat or from poisons like insecticides, pesticides, or other chemicals or pollutants.

Check these animals and put an **X** by extinct ones and an **E** by endangered ones. Then tell how you think it became extinct or endangered. You may need to look in the library or an encyclopedia for some species if you don't know its status. There is room at the bottom to add three more unfortunate animals to the list.

© 2000 by The Center for Applied Research in Education

Animal Species:	E = Endangered X = Extinct	How it got that way:
Dinosaurs	_____	_____
Blue Whales	_____	_____
Sea Turtles	_____	_____
Rhinoceros	_____	_____
Gorillas	_____	_____
Dodo Bird	_____	_____
Wolf	_____	_____
Dolphin	_____	_____
Koala	_____	_____
Giant Panda	_____	_____
Moa	_____	_____
Eastern Cougar	_____	_____
Passenger Pigeon	_____	_____
Whooping Crane	_____	_____
_____	_____	_____
_____	_____	_____
_____	_____	_____

Name _____ Date _____

10. Your Amazing "AQ" Test

IQ means Intelligence Quotient and is obtained by your score on an IQ test. You are taking an Animal Quotient (AQ) test of your knowledge of the amazing animals you studied. Write the names of the amazing animals you think fit the descriptions.

1. The _____ is the largest animal that ever lived.

2. The fastest animal in the world at 200+ mph is the _____.

3. A _____ is the fastest mammal on land at 70+ mph.

4. The largest reptiles in the world, at 1,500 pounds, are _____.

5. The _____ is the largest living cat.

6. The only true vampires that ever lived are the _____.

7. The _____ is the tallest land mammal.

8. The longest snake is the python, but the heaviest snake in the world, at almost 500 pounds, is the _____.

9. The _____ is the best plant pollinator in the world.

10. The only dragons that ever lived are the _____
_____.

11. The _____ is the fastest two-legged animal on land since this big bird can run over 40 mph.

12. The largest living land carnivore is the _____.

13. The _____ is the smallest bird, at 0.056 ounces.

14. The largest living land mammal is the _____, and it is also the most powerful.

15. The fastest marine mammal, at 34.5 mph, is _____.

16. The _____ is the largest venomous snake.

17. The largest land mammal in North America's wild is a _____.

18. The longest gestation period (two years) is for the _____.

19. The _____ is the largest fish in the world.

20. The most intelligent mammal we know of is _____.

Name _____ Date _____